D1624483

WITHDRAWN

WITHDRAWN

WOUNDED WARRIOR

THE RISE
AND FALL
OF MICHIGAN
GOVERNOR
JOHN SWAINSON

WOUNDED
WARRIOR

LAWRENCE
M. GLAZER

Michigan State University Press • East Lansing

☉ The paper used in this publication meets the minimum requirements of
ANSI/NISO Z39.48-1992 (R 1997) (Permanence of Paper).

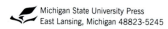 Michigan State University Press
East Lansing, Michigan 48823-5245

Printed and bound in the United States of America.

16 15 14 13 12 11 10   1 2 3 4 5 6 7 8 9 10

LIBRARY OF CONGRESS CATALOGING-IN-PUBLICATION DATA
Glazer, Lawrence M.
Wounded warrior : the rise and fall of Michigan Governor John Swainson /
Lawrence M. Glazer.
p. cm.
Includes bibliographical references and index.
ISBN 978-0-87013-971-0 (cloth : alk. paper) 1. Swainson, John B. (John
Burley), 1925–1994. 2. Governors—Michigan—Biography. 3. Michigan—
Politics and government—1951– I. Title.
F570.25.S93G55 2010
977.4'043092—dc22
[B]
2010003510

Cover and book design by Charlie Sharp, Sharp Des!gns, Lansing, Michigan
Cover art is John Swainson's high school senior picture, 1943. Photo
courtesy of Bentley Historical Library, University of Michigan.

ᵍ green Michigan State University Press is a member of the Green Press
press Initiative and is committed to developing and encouraging
ᴵᴺᴵᵀᴵᴬᵀᴵᵛᴱ
ecologically responsible publishing practices. For more information about the
Green Press Initiative and the use of recycled paper in book publishing, please
visit www.greenpressinitiative.org.

───────────────

Visit Michigan State University Press on the World Wide Web at
www.msupress.msu.edu

No good deed goes unpunished.
　　　　　　　　—CLARE BOOTH LUCE

For PK

CONTENTS

PREFACE

In the state of Michigan, where he once reigned, he is nearly forgotten today. The people of Michigan elected him to the very top of two branches of government—governor and justice of the state Supreme Court, yet his name never appears in the major newspapers. Three decades after he left office, even politicians of his own party rarely invoke him in their speeches. The little memorial room for him, folded into the historical society in his adopted hometown, closed a few years ago, for lack of visitors.

In 1984, nine years after he was forced to leave the public career he loved, the justices of the Michigan Supreme Court invited John Swainson back to the Capitol for the formal presentation of his portrait, a tradition for all retired justices. They saw no reason he should be an exception.

After hearing laudatory speeches by his old friends and supporters, he made a gracious response, assuring them that he was content with his life, and grateful at their having remembered him. He ended by saying, "I will let history, of which I have become quite fond, be the judge of my public career."

And so, this book.

PART 1

THE RISE

CHAPTER ONE

Goad

THE AUTUMN RITUALS OF HIGH SCHOOL FOOTBALL HAVE CHANGED LITTLE OVER THE decades, and on the surface would have appeared, on a chilly Michigan afternoon in October 1942, much like those we see today. But the players' parents, huddled in the wooden bleachers, must have entertained mixed feelings as they watched their sons in the bloom of youth. Soon most of them would be going off to war.

The two teams represented the largest public high schools in their respective towns, Port Huron and Mt. Clemens, which hugged the east coast of Michigan's Thumb, about forty miles apart. They were playing before a crowd of about a thousand, renewing an annual rivalry that went back eighteen years and involved possession of a trophy known as the Little Brown Keg. The visiting contingent of Port Huron supporters was smaller than usual because of wartime travel restrictions.[1]

The trouble began near the end of the first half when a large group of hometown fans invaded the visitor's side of the stadium. About one hundred of the Port Huronites mustered to repel the invaders, but the police got between them and broke it up, and the game continued. At the gun ending the first half, the host Mt. Clemens Bathers were leading the visiting Port Huron Big Reds 13-0.

Halftime commenced. After the Port Huron marching band had finished its performance, the Mt. Clemens band took the field. According to the *Port Huron Times-Herald,* "The Mt. Clemens Band, after a stirring march put on childish horse-play, making Port Huron the goats. This display of poor sportsmanship led to many near-fights and some exchanges of blows."[2]

Once again order was restored, and the third quarter began. After an exchange of punts, Port Huron started on its own 20-yard-line. Quarterback Harvey Henry handed off to end Clarence Hodge, who executed a "beautiful run" to the Big Reds' 49-yard-line. Coach Frank Secory decided to give starting fullback Al Tuoma a breather and sent senior Johnnie Swainson into the huddle. Henry handed off to Swainson, who plunged into the line for a three-yard gain. As Swainson got up to go back to the huddle, a "near-riot" broke out on the Mt. Clemens sideline, and the officials halted the game.

The Mt. Clemens band director had the presence of mind to order his musicians to stand and play "The Star-Spangled Banner," which caused everyone not already engaged in the fighting to stand at attention, while the police waded in and broke up the brawl.

When play resumed, Swainson stayed in. Two halfback plunges gained successive first downs. Then Swainson got the ball again, taking it to the Mt. Clemens 11-yard-line, and the third quarter ended.

The teams marched to the opposite end of the field as the police nervously watched the crowd. The referee blew the whistle to resume play, and quarterback Henry handed off to Swainson, who broke free and ran into the end zone, for the first and only touchdown of his varsity football career.

The Big Reds' extra point attempt went wide, and the score stood at 13-6. In the fourth quarter Port Huron clearly outplayed Mt. Clemens, holding them scoreless, and adding a touchdown, but once again failed on the extra point attempt. Mt. Clemens won, 13-12.[3]

By today's standards the players were not large. Port Huron's heaviest starter was a right guard weighing 196 pounds. No other starter weighed more than 182. The starting fullback, Tuoma, weighed 165.[4] Swainson probably weighed in at about 165 or 170.

No one from Johnnie Swainson's family saw the game, or any game he played in high school. His parents were Canadian, with no experience of American football.

The Swainsons were descendents of a clan that lived in the Lancaster region of eighteenth-century England.[5] Swainson family legend had it that a male ancestor emigrated to Canada as a "remittance man," sent abroad to earn the higher wages of the New World and remit a portion back to his family in the old country.[6]

By 1904, when Carl Swainson, John's father, was born, the family had established a branch in Sarnia, Ontario. Carl attended local schools, taking business courses. He fell in love with a classmate, Edna Mae Burley, and after graduation they became engaged. In 1923 they married. Both were nineteen years of age.

Seeking work, Carl moved his bride to Windsor, Ontario (across the Detroit River from Detroit). There their first child, Carrol, was born in 1924. The next year saw the birth of their first son, John Goad Burley Swainson, on July 31, 1925. Seventeen years later he would score the touchdown against Mt. Clemens.

Carl got a job selling for the R.J. Reynolds Tobacco Company. Ironically, his religion prohibited smoking; he was a member of the Reorganized Church of Jesus Christ of Latter Day Saints, an offshoot of the Mormon Church. He did not own a car, and commuted by ferry across the river to Detroit every day.

After a few years in Detroit the Reynolds Company sent Carl Swainson to Port Huron, Michigan, across the St. Clair River from Sarnia, Ontario. It was in Port Huron that the Swainsons' third child, Thomas, was born in 1928. Soon thereafter Carl was promoted, and the family moved again, to Detroit.

They lived in the city until 1937, when the company once again assigned Carl to Port Huron. The family rented a large two-story frame house at 1219 Ninth Street, a mile from downtown. John was then twelve, yet he would always regard this as the home where he grew up.

In the extended Swainson clan it had long been the custom to give one son the first name "John." As a result, each individual family had fathers, sons, uncles, and cousins named John Swainson.[7] To avoid confusion, the custom had evolved of addressing each John Swainson by a "family" name. Thus, John Goad Burley Swainson, called "Johnnie" by his friends, was known within the family as "Goad."

Goad's childhood appears to have been normal and happy. According to his niece, Gail Main, "He made his first public appearance in a piano recital at age five, playing duets with his sister Carrol, and enjoyed being in the limelight from that time on. His great ambition showed early when he sold newspapers every morning before school, darting in and out of traffic to service his customers with his ever-present smile. He played the bugle with the Boy Scouts and marched in the parade dedicating the Bluewater Bridge.[8] He later became an eagle scout."[9]

The family did not own a car. The children walked to school, and each

Sunday they walked to Sunday School. Their father was often absent, on the road, selling.[10]

In high school, Goad was active in the Dramatics and World Affairs Clubs,[11] and joined a social fraternity. He seemed to be a natural leader, according to his sister, who laughingly remembered that as far as grades were concerned, "[he] did all right, but he didn't break his neck studying."[12] He and a group of friends managed to buy an old Model A Ford, which they worked on in the Swainsons' driveway. They drove it in parades and football rallies, and Goad used it as transportation. By his senior year he was steadily dating a pretty blonde Port Huron High student, Ann Ludlow.[13]

In the summer of 1943 Goad graduated. To accumulate a little money, he went to work at the Grand Trunk railroad yards, as an "icer," hauling ice up the side ladders of freight cars and dumping it in through hatches, to refrigerate the interiors and preserve perishable cargos.

This was a temporary job. With his eighteenth birthday rapidly approaching, Goad knew that he must soon decide whether to await the draft or enlist. He decided to apply for flight training in the U.S. Army Air Forces, and was disappointed to learn that only officers could be pilots and only U.S. citizens could be officers. Swainson was, of course, Canadian.

However, he soon learned that if he volunteered for the army, he would qualify for immediate U.S. citizenship once he completed training. In the fall of 1943 he went to the local recruiting office and enlisted.

He was sent initially to Fort Custer in Battle Creek, where he lost a name. As he later related it, when he signed his name an army bureaucrat told him, "They only allow one middle name," so he had to choose one. At that moment he became John Burley Swainson.[14]

Lighter by one name, he was shipped to Fort Benning, Georgia, for basic training. At the end of ninety days he was qualified for U.S. citizenship, and took the oath at Fort Benning.[15]

Now legally eligible to become an officer, he volunteered and was accepted into a special officer training program conducted at the University of Pennsylvania. There he spent the first three months of 1944.

But then there was a change of plans. On D-Day, June 6, 1944, the Allies launched the largest amphibious invasion in history. It was a huge gamble, and it succeeded. The Allies controlled the beachheads on the Normandy coast. The Germans began to retreat across France, fighting all the way.

Concerned that the Germans might bog them down, the Allied generals called for more troops, as fast as possible, wherever they could be found. The men at the special officer school were needed, needed *now,* and the generals grabbed them. They could always train more officers later. Swainson's entire class was transferred to Indian Gap, Pennsylvania, for infantry maneuvers. Then John Swainson, still a private, was sent east to await a troop transport to Europe.[16]

CHAPTER TWO

Amputee

TEN DAYS AFTER D-DAY THE GERMANS HAD BEEN PUSHED FAR AWAY FROM THE COAST, and the Normandy shore had evolved from a battlefield to a port. A *New York Times* correspondent described it as "a crowded beach where tanks, munitions and men were being unloaded in a steady stream." Britain's King George VI was escorted ashore the same day. He performed an open-air investiture, decorating seven British officers and men. He then walked about for a few minutes, returning the salutes of those who recognized him, and sailed back to England.[1]

John Swainson would not have that option. He was infantry.

Specifically, Swainson was C Company, 378th Regiment, Ninety-fifth Infantry Division. The Ninety-fifth did not participate in the D-Day invasion; it was not until July that Swainson's troop transport landed at Omaha Beach on the Normandy coast.[2]

Although the Allies had secured and expanded the Normandy beachhead, their attempts to break out into the countryside were resisted by the Germans, aided by natural and man-made obstacles. The weather, which had blessed the June 6 landings, turned nasty. The Normandy countryside was divided by hedgerows—shrubbery-topped earthen mounds built and maintained by generations of farmers. The Allied air superiority and tank production would have made it possible to launch a blitzkrieg-like attack against the retreating Germans in open country, but it was impossible while they were still among the hedgerows. The Germans, too, knew the advantages of defensive fighting in such a landscape, and they dug in their heels to keep the Allies from breaking out into the open areas favorable to the Allied air and mobile armor.

It therefore fell mainly to the foot soldiers—the infantry—to capture enough territory to get beyond the hedgerow country. It was a long, hard slog, and for a time the commanders feared that their invasion would bog down into the same stationary trench warfare in France that World War I had seen.

In late July the Americans broke out at St. Lo, and the Germans began to retreat. At this point, George S. Patton arrived to take over the U.S. Third Army. Patton had earned an unparalleled reputation as an aggressive mobile warfare commander in Sicily and Africa. When he saw an opportunity, he moved quickly to exploit it. And now that the Allies were out in open country, Patton saw many opportunities. He just needed more soldiers.

They were on the way.

According to the official *95th Division Institutional Training History,*

In the first week of September the men of the 95th Infantry Division began packing their belongings and preparing to embark. Beginning September 8 a massive convoy of trucks moved from their training grounds to the storied port of Southampton on the English Channel. There they saw "silvery barrage balloons swinging high on cables around the harbor. Signs of the blitz were still here, though sufficient time had elapsed to allow nearly fully repair of the dock area. The Division, with all its vehicles, boarded Liberty ships and converted British commercial vessels. Passage across the English channel was delayed two and three days for most units as following embarkation, it was necessary to lay both in and outside the harbor pending availability of debarkation facilities at the landing point. . . ."

By September 14, however, the last of the boats had gotten underway—in convoy, the Division's first travel in a train of ships. Late that afternoon the tail ends of the convoy arrived off the Normandy coast, sailed past Cherbourg and anchored with the predecessors near Omaha Beach to await debarkation the next morning.[3]

By September 15 John Swainson was in France, a member of a machine gun unit in C Company. He dashed off a "V-mail" to his mother, telling her, "That Channel is the roughest water I ever saw."

The Ninety-fifth then began a four-week bivouac in the Normandy apple orchards. Its men began to integrate into the Third Army, and saw their first combat October 20 when they were sent to defend a bridgehead over the Moselle River.[4]

After the breakout from the Normandy beachhead, Patton's expanded Third Army had begun a dash across France, using U.S. air superiority and, where possible, mobile armor to drive the Germans before them. The Germans resisted at times, but mostly they continued to retreat. Patton's forces advanced so rapidly that they finally outraced their own supply lines and had to halt when they literally ran out of gas.

By the middle of November, elements of Patton's army had advanced to within two miles of the ancient fortress city of Metz, thirty miles from the German border in the province of Lorraine. The Ninety-fifth Infantry Division, which included Swainson's five-man machine gun squad, was advancing from the north and west, having established a bridgehead across the Moselle near the village of Thionville and successfully resisted German counterattacks.[5]

War was not new to the province of Lorraine.

In the Franco-Prussian War of 1870 the French had surrendered a major army to the Germans at Metz, and they were forced to cede the entire province to Germany in the treaty that ended the war. Prussia, and then Germany, built numerous forts in the province and encouraged its nationals to emigrate there. In 1914 the French army suffered a disastrous defeat near Metz, and the French only regained the province when World War I ended in 1919. By that point, after nearly a half-century of German suzerainty, nearly half the population was German-speaking (the "Alsatian" dialect of German is spoken in Lorraine to this day).[6] It was for this reason that the Resistance movement, which was of great assistance to the Allies nearly everywhere in occupied France, was far less so in Lorraine.

By autumn of 1944 the German LXXXII Corps assigned to defend Lorraine had run out of tanks. The corps commander, General Hermann Balck, had to find other means of slowing the American advance toward the German border. According to the official U.S. Army history of the campaign, Balck decided to fall back to a defensible position behind the Moselle River, "supplementing the river obstacle with a series of huge mine fields. Balck recognized the importance of such a defense and divided most of the antipersonnel and antitank mines in his depots between the LXXXII Corps, for use behind Thionville, and the LXXXV Corps, defending the Belfort Gap. The 19th VG Division alone planted some 40,000 mines along its front. The total number used to impede the progress of the American divisions in the attack north of Metz must have been tremendous."[7]

As the *Infantry Journal* put it in a contemporary training manual, German mines were a grave danger, and antimine engineers did not always find them in time:

> It is no longer a job just for engineer troops. The Germans plant mines on the shoulders of roads and seemingly unused roads, tracks and trails. Any terrain suitable for vehicles and tanks are apt to be mined. Road craters and the approaches to by-passes around blown bridges are generally heavily mined. The German likes to mine soft and sandy fords, scattering metal fragments around them to throw off the detectors. Long stretches of road will have a few mines buried far apart—just enough to cause "mine fever." Watch your step—and watch where you drive.[8]

On the night of November 15 C Company came to rest in the recently captured village of Thionville.[9] The weather had been alternating between snow and rain, and mud was everywhere.[10]

Swainson, then three and a half months past his nineteenth birthday, later recalled:

> The first thing we did was search all the houses to make sure there were no German stragglers. In one there was a beautiful little kitchen that had a stove with porcelain tiles. We had just received our C-rations—wieners and beans. My squad and I planned to use that stove. I went to collect wood to build the fire. As I returned a Colonel from the battalion said he wanted volunteers to take some ammunition and rations to the men who had been cut off during the day. Everybody else in my unit had their uniforms and boots off. I was still dressed. Everybody looked at me. I agreed to go, figuring I would get out of guard duty that night if I did this. I thought it would not take more than an hour.[11]

The five members of the patrol loaded a jeep with rations and ammunition and set out. With recent German resistance in mind, they thought it prudent to conduct this supply mission as they would a regular patrol. A Sergeant Deanie drove the heavily loaded jeep. Swainson and a Sergeant Bruso walked about one hundred yards ahead, and Pfc. Ralph Thomas and Pfc. Bill Shurtlift walked alongside the jeep, off the road to the left and right respectively.

The men had been told that army engineers had cleared the route of mines but had found a fallen tree blocking the road.

Swainson and Bruso came upon the fallen tree, and found it too heavy for their combined strength to move, so they backtracked to the advancing jeep. Swainson recalled,

"I went back where Deanie was in the jeep and said, 'When they [Thomas and Shurtlift] come up here, tell them to help us move the tree.' I turned around and started back [toward the fallen tree]."[12]

As he walked, Swainson's back was to the jeep. Sergeant Bruso had stopped somewhat ahead of him, and was waiting for Swainson to catch up, facing toward Swainson and the jeep. Swainson estimated he had moved between twenty-five and fifty feet ahead of the jeep when there was a tremendous explosion. The jeep had detonated a German "teller" mine buried just under the road surface. The mine, designed to take the tracks off a tank, contained eleven pounds of TNT.[13] An instant after it exploded, the jeep's cargo of munitions went off. Deanie, Thomas, and Shurtlift were obliterated.

Back in the village the Americans heard the huge blast. They immediately sent out a party, which reached the scene within minutes.[14] They found two survivors, Bruso and Swainson.[15] Swainson was unconscious. The blast had taken off one leg below the knee. His other lower leg was still attached, but badly mangled. The blast had also knocked him to the ground violently, breaking his jaw and a rib. Shrapnel had cut into both hands.

He awoke several days later in Verdun, in a public building that had been transformed into a U.S. military hospital.

The first thing he noticed was that he was in a bed with sheets, "which was a new experience," since he "had not changed clothes for about thirty days. I saw huge windows and thought, 'Where am I?' I even thought I might be in Heaven."

Then, looking toward the foot of the bed, he noticed that "there was nothing sticking up where my toes should have been. I picked up the sheet. I had no feet."[16]

Military surgeons had performed emergency amputations on both of his lower limbs below the knees. As a medical officer later explained it, the severe compound fractures in the relatively intact leg made its loss inevitable. The other leg was unsalvageable from the moment of the explosion.[17]

Swainson became aware that an officer was in the room, speaking to him, but it was difficult to turn his attention from the sight at the end of his bed. When he did, he realized that the officer was asking who had been with him on the road outside Thionville. His immediate reaction was, "The sons of bitches, they left me." The officer then explained to him that no identifiable remains could be found at the site, and the army needed to know who had died.[18]

By Thanksgiving Day Swainson was on a hospital train to Paris, which the Germans had surrendered in late August.[19]

At the hospital there they rolled us on litters into an operating room. There are two operating tables. The guy on the next table is screaming his lungs out because they have taken the dressing off and his whole thigh is opened up and they are cleaning it out. And I asked a question: how come you're not giving that guy anesthetic? You're gonna give me anesthetic, aren't you? And they said, "we are short." So they just held my shoulders down and cut the cast off and changed the dressing. It wasn't as painful as I thought it was gonna be.[20]

From Paris the army flew him to England, then took him by train to a U.S. military hospital in Wales, arriving November 27. Here he would stay two months, and two healing processes would begin. His broken bones and tissues would start to knit, and he would begin to reconstruct his identity, forming new expectations for the person he was now to become.

On December 2, weak and in pain, he wrote a letter.

Dear Dad,

I guess by this time you've gotten my Purple Heart and a telegram from the War Department.

I thought I would write to you and tell you what happened, and then you could do what you want about telling Mom.

It happened on the outskirts of Metz, we had taken two towns and they wanted someone to go along with [a] jeep to take ammunition and rations to one of the towns, well I volunteered. We came to a roadblock and started to remove it and then a barrage of 88's hit, right there and blew up some land mines.[21] I caught the full force of that blast, and three days later I woke up in a hospital in Verdun. Both my legs had been blown off below the knee[22], I had a broken jaw, a broken rib, a badly lacerated tongue, and shrapnel in both hands.

This writing is terrible I know, but my hand is still numb . . .

As soon as my legs heal up I'll be sent to the States, probably to Percy Jones Hospital at Fort Custer.

I had an operation on my legs yesterday and they found an abscess in my left thigh.

The pain is quite bad, but there are guys here worse off than me. . . .

I can't write much for a while, but tell everone [*sic*] at home to write, and Anne.

Your son,

Goad[23]

Carl's sister Terry was in England, serving as a nurse in the Canadian army. She managed to wangle three days leave, and took a train to visit her nephew, arriving December 28. She found him "with a beaming smile on his face when he saw me coming down the ward. It was a surprise for I didn't have time to call and say I was on my way." John told her that "there are lots of other boys here who are worse off than he is so he doesn't want any sympathy." He was afraid that his mother would "be worrying about him and be discouraged and he doesn't want that, for he intends to go back to school and educate himself for a self-supporting life ahead of him, and they told him he would be ready to go to school by Fall."[24]

Was this bravura designed to reassure his mother? Or was it a sign of an already-forming decision about his future?

Aunt Terry learned from the staff that John had suffered three hemorrhages in his right thigh soon after arriving, and the surgeons had been unable to find the cause until, in their third surgery, they located and removed a two-inch piece of iron chain link that had blasted into his leg, hit the thigh bone, and traveled upward ten inches, where it had wedged between the muscles and remained undetected.[25] John was keeping it for a souvenir, joking that he couldn't decide whether to "hand it in as scrap metal when he gets home or not."

He was having trouble sleeping. The doctors had just removed wires from his broken jaw, but instructed him not to open his mouth too wide for the next few months, until it healed. The shrapnel wounds in his hands made it difficult for him to grip anything for long. The doctors had also found what they called an "electrical burn" on his buttocks. This injury was a bit of a mystery, most likely caused by a piece of hot metal from the jeep.

Aunt Terry learned that John was "the youngest in the ward of 38 other patients and naturally they make a fuss over him. The nurse told me as sick as he had been, he never complained."

Boredom was always a problem, and the men looked forward to the movies that were shown twice a week, "But it's an orthopedic ward and there's so many up in fracture beds with traction splints on that he says he has to look at the pictures through the poles, ropes, splints, etc."

"He's lonesome naturally and he hated so for me to leave. He said, 'If you could just stay and talk to me.'" But after three days Aunt Terry had to return to her own hospital duties.

It was then that he again grasped a pen and, laboriously, wrote to his mother.

Dear Mom:

Well Terry left yesterday to go back to her hospital . . . I sure hated to see Terry leave. The two half-days she was here, time passed quickly. That's what I need more than anything else. That picture of you [presumably sent as a Christmas present] is the best picture that you've ever had, especially the smile. It makes it seem so real. I can remember seeing you smile like that. I'm going to send you a little prayer that I found in the Reader's Digest, when I first went to France. I cut it out and read it many times and hoped maybe you had read it too. It helped me a lot to think that you had said that prayer.

It's 9 P.M. New Year's Eve and I suppose the ward will be roaring around midnite. But this New Year's Eve the thing I'm most interested in is a good nite's sleep. Well, Mother, I'l [sic] write again soon. I don't want any of you worrying about me because I'm fine.

All my love always,

Goad[26]

One cannot help but notice the very different tones of Swainson's first two letters home. To his father, he describes what happened—the facts—in a man-to-man way, and signs "Your son, Goad." To his mother he speaks of his feelings, and signs with all his love.

By the end of January the army judged that John Swainson had recovered enough strength to endure a voyage across the Atlantic. He was put aboard a hospital ship bound for New York. On February 10 he surprised his delighted parents with a phone call from Halloran Hospital on Staten Island. He was on his way to Michigan, to Battle Creek, only 170 miles from Port Huron.[27]

In 1906 John Kellogg (brother of cereal entrepreneur W. K. Kellogg) had built a huge sanatorium in Battle Creek, hoping to prove his enema-centered health theories (his strange career was later satirized in the book and movie *The Road to Wellville*). In 1942 the U.S. Army, responding to the growth in worldwide casualties, had bought the sanitarium complex and rebuilt it into a 1,500-bed hospital for wounded combat veterans, specializing in amputation and rehabilitation from physical disabilities. They renamed it Percy Jones Hospital, after Colonel Percy Lancelot Jones, an army surgeon in the Spanish-American

War, the Mexican Campaign and World War I, and the pioneering organizer of the ambulance and mobile medical teams that saved countless doughboys' lives in World War I.[28] By 1945 it was the largest U.S. Army medical facility in the world, and by the end of the war its patient population was to peak at over 11,000.[29]

John Swainson long remembered his arrival at Percy Jones: "All these soldiers were milling around the main lobby, and everyone had at least one leg or arm missing—the hospital was an amputation center."[30] Pfc. Swainson was now among friends, and he found that made all the difference:

> A young person who loses a leg [in civilian life] is taken to a hospital. . . . There's nobody else around with legs off. Here I've got a ward with 40 or 50 people. It was actually helpful to see a guy in there maybe a month or two before you, and he's progressed so he's going down to physiotherapy and he's practicing walking and he'd be walking maybe with his butt sticking out and you'd say well, I'm not going to do that; I'm going to pinch my ass in and walk as normally as possible. You'd see this all the time. "I can do better" sort of thing. And you'd see the other type of person who gave up, wasn't going to try it, frowned all the time. So you got a sense of the whole thing that you don't get in your private little hospital.[31]
>
> There were 5,000 of us, mostly land forces, with all sorts of problems. That helped. You could see others getting better and learning how to adjust. . . . There was very little unnecessary sympathy. If you asked someone to get you a drink, he'd say "Go to Hell. Get your own drink."[32]

His sister remembered, "They were very much comrades, and when they got in wheelchairs and went out around the town, people would say, 'Oh, how did you lose your leg?' And they'd say, 'Oh, a goldfish kept nibbling away.'"[33]

Swainson's legs had healed from the explosion and field hospital amputations, but the surgeons were not finished with him yet. First they beveled the leg bones and did plastic surgery to erase major scars on the stump ends. Then they sent him to another hospital in Memphis, Tennessee, to repair damage to his back, caused when his rib was broken.[34] When he recovered from that, the doctors at Percy Jones performed reamputations on his legs, to equalize the stumps in preparation for fitting him with prosthetic limbs. Then, finally, he began the process of rehabilitation, of learning to walk again.

Swainson's own pride and competitiveness would have caused him to push himself, but the hospital provided additional incentives:

To get out of the hospital you had to be able to walk at least 10 feet without canes and be able to walk up and back down 3 steps without using the banister. I had two 30-day convalescent leaves. When I left for the 1st one I was using two canes. When I got back I was using one cane. When I got back from the 2nd 30 days I was not using a cane.[35]

As his physical skills improved, he took his place as a sort of upperclassman, helping and encouraging amputees who arrived, as he had arrived, with no idea what was coming.

One day he was talking with the young man in the next bed, trying to cheer him up. Swainson said, "We'll get fitted with prosthetics, we'll get the G.I. Bill, we'll get pensions, and it likely won't be that bad."

The young man gave him a look, and replied, "Maybe not for you, but being black, I don't have a prayer."

This simply had not occurred to John Swainson, who had grown up in Port Huron with little contact with minorities. Alan Zemmol, to whom Swainson related this story, said, "There was a sort of revelation to him all of a sudden. All of a sudden 'There's a kind of life out there that's different from what I know.' And he became very sensitive to other people's limitations, whatever they might be. . . . He had thought this guy was like him, that we'll all live happily ever after. . . . I think it had a tremendous effect on him."[36]

During his sojourn at Percy Jones, Swainson also met two badly wounded veterans who later became U.S. senators, Bob Dole of Kansas and Daniel Inouye of Hawaii. But the fellow patient who had the greatest impact on Swainson was Takaji John Goto.

"Tak," as he was known, was a "Nisei," a U.S.-born son of Japanese immigrants. Shortly after Pearl Harbor the U.S. government had begun rounding up Americans of Japanese descent who lived near the West Coast, sending them to internment camps in isolated locations. Over 110,000 people were forcibly relocated. Tak's family was placed at the Manzanar Camp in the Sierra Nevada mountains of California.

The U.S. War Department initially barred persons of Japanese descent from serving on active duty in the army, but a large group of Japanese-Hawaiian ROTC students petitioned to be allowed to serve. In 1943 the government relented and authorized the formation of all-Nisei combat units, to be assigned only to the European theater. Thus was formed the 442nd Regimental Combat Team, an all-Nisei unit. Tak volunteered.

In October 1944 the 442nd went to the rescue of a Texas National Guard battalion that had been surrounded by German forces in the Vosges region of France. The 442nd suffered over 800 casualties—nearly half its members—while rescuing just over 200 of the Texans.

It was during the later stages of that battle that Tak became a bilateral amputee.

At Percy Jones Swainson found in Tak a kindred spirit, "cheerful in the face of adversity" and determined to live a normal life,[37] and they became close. The discrimination Tak's family had endured—from their own government—only strengthened Swainson's dawning resolve to fight racial prejudice wherever he might find it.

Swainson's experience helping new amputees adjust at Percy Jones gave him an idea. In June he wrote an extraordinary letter:

> To: The Surgeon General, Washington 25, D.C. (Thru Channels)
>
> I, John B. Swainson, Pfc. ASN 36 882 974, Age 20, 95th Infantry Division, Machine Gunner, request the opportunity to go overseas on a morale tour for the purpose of demonstration of prostheses. I am a bilateral amputee 5½ inches below the knee.
>
> In my case I did not see a double amputation until arriving at Percy Jones, and I think that for the morale of the amputees overseas it would be beneficial for them to see the construction of a prosthesis and the demonstration of such.
>
> It is my understanding from the medical authorities here that I should be proficient in the use of my prostheses by 1 September 1945, and would be available for this assignment at that time.[38]

What is most striking about this letter from a twenty-year-old is not just the writer's self-confidence (making his proposal directly to the Surgeon General, before he had even learned to master his new legs), but the ability to generalize his experience to other new amputees in isolated hospital rooms around the world. If they could not come immediately to Percy Jones, why, he would bring the camaraderie of Percy Jones to them.

The reply came within a week—unusually fast for the army: Though "not[ing] with much pleasure your willingness to participate in a demonstration, overseas, of your prostheses," the army's answer was that "the European Theatre of Operations is undoubtedly clearing all amputees, and the Pacific area has offered no amputee problem to date, [and therefore] your request must be temporarily suspended."[39]

He used his first leaves to go home to Port Huron. His sister remembered, "He had artificial limbs from early on, but he used crutches at first. He wasn't that good at it at first, but he persevered. 'I'm gonna do it as well as you, and maybe a little better.' That was his attitude, I think, through life."

> When he was first coming home, he was not physically strong, and a few times he got kind of depressed about the whole thing. I don't think he ever took it out of our home. My mother would be the one to talk with him. My father was always on the road, selling.
>
> Sometimes they brought him home at night, when he'd had a little too much. Everybody was around, and he was getting a lot of attention. They were all near his age, all coming home from the Service.

Slowly, his strength returned. After leaving the canes behind, he worked to become so adept at walking that no one would notice. "After I left the hospital I found that a lot of people tend to treat a legless man like a freak."[40]

He would not allow that to happen to him.

Decades later, he recalled the central role that his rehabilitation had played in forming his character: If he hadn't been wounded, he told Huge McDiarmid, he would not have become a lawyer or gone into politics. "My mother used to say that, instead of getting an inferiority complex out of it, I got a superiority complex out of it, and that may be so. I had something to overcome, and I overcame it."[41]

CHAPTER THREE

The Best-Adjusted Veteran

As a high school student, Johnnie Swainson had not thought much about his future. There had been some talk about becoming a dentist. That was out now; too much time on one's feet. But now some kind of professional education was a necessity: "I had spent enough time in the hospital to know that I wasn't going to earn my living with my hands or my back. I certainly wasn't going to drive heavy equipment."[1]

And college was now a realistic prospect. Through the G.I. Bill, a grateful nation offered to pay the costs of college education for its returning veterans.

Swainson enrolled at Olivet, a small, private liberal arts school just twenty miles from Battle Creek. This choice allowed him to continue his active rehabilitation work while attending classes.

Swainson had received a double trans-tibial (below the knee) amputation in France. Later, after surgeons had performed a re-amputation to equalize the lengths of his stumps, he underwent a lengthy process of fitting of limbs, learning to use them, and re-training his leg muscles so as to walk with as normal an appearance as possible.

There had been few advances in the design of lower limb prosthetics since the Civil War. Most artificial legs were still made of solid wood, as they had been for centuries. Most also used a solid, nonarticulated foot (i.e., the foot could not move relative to the limb, as a natural foot would swivel on the ankle joint).

After the stumps had healed from the final surgery, a prosthetist wrapped each stump in bandages soaked in plaster-of-Paris. When it hardened, each plaster-of-Paris bandage was used as a mold for forming the socket end of a prosthetic limb. The socket would then be temporarily mounted on an adjustable artificial leg for walking trials; Swainson and his prosthetist would make adjustments on each temporary limb until they were both satisfied, Swainson with the legs' comfort and the prosthetist with their biomechanical soundness and the even distribution of weight on the stump.

New users of prosthetic limbs were (and still are) advised to try to keep their weight constant; "One of the greatest problems in obtaining good performance and maximum comfort is caused by over weight of the amputee. Fluctuations in body weight are reflected in the stump where changes in volume result in poor fit, discomfort, and consequently poor performance."[2]

The user would slip his stump into a sleeve or cuff, which surrounded the custom-fitted socket of the artificial limb. Some users preferred a rubber liner between the stump and the socket, for comfort. Others preferred a hard socket without a liner, for cooler temperature. The sleeve would then be tightened around the stump.

The battlefields of World War II produced such a large number of amputees that the National Academy of Sciences and Veterans Administration sponsored and coordinated a major research effort to improve prosthetics. This endeavor was just beginning when Swainson mustered out, but he was among the many veterans who were to benefit from the resulting improvements in prosthetic design over the years after the war. As the years went on, he would get new limbs periodically, and each would be better, more comfortable, and more functional than its predecessor. But the first pair was made of willow wood.[3]

In 1946 Olivet was entering the final phase of an experiment in using a tutorial system based on practices at Oxford University. Students were given a series of guided readings, which they discussed with their professor. Both the student and the professor contributed to periodic written reports on the subjects in the readings, and some of these reports have survived. They give glimpses of the developing outlook of young John Swainson as he first encountered new possibilities opened by the life of the mind.

His reaction to course readings on logic and deductive thinking was, "This course is very interesting and it really makes you think. I am very glad to have had the opportunity to take it."[4] Of course, logic and deductive reasoning are among the skills developed in a legal education, and the college's aptitude test had suggested that he had the potential to do well in law; late in his first year he changed his major from history to prelaw.

He found social psychology "one of the most enjoyable classes because it deals with the people whose society you must live in every day." More revealing was the professor's comment: "Student seems to apply social psychology to his extra-curricular activities."[5]

Perhaps most revealing of all was his comment on Margaret Mead's anthropology classic, *Coming of Age in Samoa.* Swainson observed, "The attitude the Samoans take toward some phases of sex and adolescence complies with my attitude toward those subjects. The discussions have been very welcome and interesting."[6]

At Olivet Swainson began dating Alice Nielsen, nineteen, a fellow freshman student. Reared in Detroit, the daughter of a Danish immigrant father and a Swedish mother, Alice had a cool intelligence, an artistic temperament, and classic, blonde Nordic beauty. A music major, she had worked in the classical music shop at J. L. Hudson Department Store in Detroit, and sang in the Detroit Civic Light Opera.[7]

He was surprised, and flattered, that she was interested in him.[8] He still thought of himself as small town, unsophisticated, one step up from working class. But his intelligence, energy, and sunny outlook were more appealing than he knew.

More quickly than either of them probably expected, dating turned to courtship and then engagement. On July 21, 1946, they were married. It is likely that their marriage was hastened by John's decision to leave Michigan, based on a physician's advice that his recovery was being hampered by the cold Michigan winters, and that it would be better for him to live in a warmer climate for several years.[9]

In 1947 they packed up their belongings and moved to Chapel Hill, North Carolina, and John enrolled at the University of North Carolina. Then, as now, UNC had one of the highest academic reputations of any southern institution, and its law school was one of the finest in the country.

After enrolling as an undergraduate, Swainson decided to take advantage of an accelerated program that allowed him to go to the law school without first graduating from college.

His classmates found John Swainson to be cheerful, active, and full of fun.

John Morisey, who later became general counsel to the North Carolina Municipal League, recalled, "We heard a lot about the problems of handicapped veterans. This kid was the best-adjusted veteran I ever saw." Morisey also learned that Swainson had a rule: "If he should happen to fall, nobody should try to help him arise. He did it himself."

The law school dean, Henry Brandis, marveled that Swainson "actually learned to jitterbug. . . . It was not very good jitterbugging, but it was fantastic that he could do it at all."

Wright Dixon, who later practiced law in Raleigh, said, "You appreciated and enjoyed his company. He had the gift of touching you with his happiness." Dixon also recalled that "John had a way of coming out on top. While in law school, we went on a deer hunt and although he did not get the deer, he was the man who butchered it, since he had done a lot of hunting in Michigan. Somehow, in dividing up the parts, he came out with the best venison steaks."[10]

Already he was developing the self-deprecating jokes about his disability (he refused to call it a "handicap") that he would use throughout his life. One classmate, Jim Blount, recalled a duck-hunting expedition on a day that turned out to be unseasonably cold—in the low twenties—and no one had brought warm clothes. "John on several occasions during the ride reminded us of what an advantage he had over us—at least his feet were not going to be cold."[11]

On one occasion Swainson was riding in a car with several classmates when a collision occurred. When the ambulance attendants arrived, they were visibly shocked to see what appeared to be the young man's legs twisted like pretzels. Swainson just smiled and said, "Don't worry about my legs. They'll come off."[12]

Although he was not an academic star (graduating forty-seventh in his class of sixty-five), the young veteran was as popular in law school as he had been in high school. In his senior year he was elected vice president of the law students association, and when the incumbent president graduated, Swainson served as president during his last semester.

Two sons were born to the Swainsons in North Carolina, John Stephen in 1947 and Hans Peter in 1949.

Several of Swainson's classmates recalled that after graduation in 1951 he made plans to take the bar exam and practice law in North Carolina, even renting an apartment in Raleigh. But then he changed his mind and returned to Michigan.[13]

There was a reason, and it tells us something about the fundamental attitudes that the young law graduate had formed even then.

A decade after his graduation, when he had been elected governor of Michigan, John Swainson was invited back to Raleigh to speak at the law school's graduation exercise. In his speech he noted in passing that the law school had admitted its first African American student ten years before—during his senior year.[14]

What he did not mention was that he had gone out of his way to welcome that student publicly, and provided some assistance with his early adjustment to studying law. As a result, John later told his family, a significant number of people shunned him.[15] This was a major reason for changing his plans and returning to Michigan.

The Swainsons settled in Redford Township, in western Wayne County outside Detroit, and John studied for the bar exam, which he took and passed in April 1952.

After passing the bar exam, a new attorney is formally admitted to the bar in a ceremony, usually conducted in a courtroom by a sitting judge. After receiving his passing grade, Swainson joined a large number of other new attorneys in a group admission ceremony in Detroit. Afterward, a group went across the street for a celebratory beer.

Among them was Frank J. Kelley, the son of the Democratic Party leader of Wayne County. Kelley, like Swainson, had a deep, booming voice and a sardonic sense of humor. The two initiated a conversation.

"He was very affable, and we got along quite well," said Kelley.

> Somebody had told him that I was involved in politics. He told me that because he had this terrible handicap with the legs, that he didn't think he could handle the physical exertion of practicing law, and that probably his best bet would be to get into public life, where he could make a contribution and it wouldn't be so physically demanding as running around as a lawyer.
>
> I said, "That's interesting," and he said, "I'm thinking of joining the Young Republicans." Then I went to work on him immediately when I heard that and I came up with seventeen reasons why I thought he should not be a Republican. He listened very patiently. I said, "Think it over."[16]

Another acquaintance of Swainson, Arthur Jenkins, invited him to a meeting of the Redford Republican Club, and even paid his membership dues. Swainson went to two meetings, "But the way some of the party leaders looked down on us, it wasn't for me."[17]

With a family to support, the young lawyer needed an income. He went to work for the Wayne County Social Services Department as a caseworker-investigator. He also managed to line up a part-time job working for Wayne County Juvenile Court judge Nathan Kaufman.[18] At the same time, he opened a small law office in the Cadillac Tower in downtown Detroit. There he met other young attorneys struggling to build their practices. One was Joe Pernick, who also had an interest in politics. Eventually, they formed a partnership.[19] To help build his practice, Swainson also joined every veteran's organization available to him.

Kelley invited Swainson to a meeting of the 17th Congressional District Democratic organization, the most powerful local party organization at the time. Swainson brought Joe Pernick. They met other young attorneys who were, like them, interested in changing the world. Swainson found these people "vibrant and alive, and interested." Among those at the meeting were a young married couple, both attorneys: Hicks and Martha Griffiths. The Griffths had been instrumental in creating the Michigan Democratic Party that elected G. Mennen Williams governor in 1948, and reelected him in 1950 and 1952. Now Martha Griffiths was preparing for a pioneering run for the U.S. House of Representatives in 1954.

Contained within the 17th Congressional District was a newly created 18th State Senate District, a result of redistricting from population shifts captured by the 1950 census. No incumbent state senator resided within the new district, and, with western Wayne County's suburbs rapidly growing, local Democratic leaders saw an opportunity to increase their representation in the Michigan Senate.

Kelley was an obvious choice. He was young, articulate, energetic, and his father was a longtime leader of Wayne County's Democrats. Importantly, he had the Irish name, which reliably added a few percentage points to the vote for any candidate in Michigan.

Kelley recalled being approached by Al Myers, the brilliant, abrasive chairman of the 17th Congressional District Democratic organization. But Kelley was planning to leave Wayne County for Alpena in northern Michigan; he wanted to be a small-town lawyer.

"I said, 'Why don't you run John Swainson for state senator? I mean, here's a guy, he's a war hero, lost both his legs for his country. He's a wonderful fellow. Why don't you run him?'

"And he [Myers] said, well he didn't have the good name.

"I said, 'With his war record he won't need the name. He'll make the name.'"[20]

Kelley was right. U.S. Senator Joseph McCarthy had been garnering heated national publicity by accusing Democrats of being dupes of the Communists and questioning their patriotism. The tactic had been adopted by other Republicans in races around the nation. Here was a Democrat who had given his legs for his country. No one could question his patriotism.

Swainson was interested. Politics was exciting, and it was a way to move up in the world. He agreed to run, and the district Democratic organization, in an unusual move, agreed to endorse him in the primary. In August Swainson defeated his primary opponent, Richard E. Manning, by 1,372 votes out of 26,780 cast. This victory put him on the ballot as Democratic nominee. The Republicans nominated Clarence Reid Jr., son and namesake of the incumbent Republican lieutenant governor Clarence Reid. Until 1966 the offices of governor and lieutenant governor were separately nominated and elected. Thus, the voters had the opportunity to elect a governor from one political party and a lieutenant governor from the opposing party, and did so from time to time, to the chagrin of both party organizations.

CHAPTER FOUR

A Party Reborn

FOR MOST OF THE FIRST HALF OF THE TWENTIETH CENTURY MICHIGAN WAS A REPUB-
lican state. From 1900 through 1946, the Republican candidate won eighteen
of the twenty-three biennial gubernatorial elections. Only one Democrat had
managed to be reelected governor—in 1914. In the quadrennial presidential
elections, only Franklin Roosevelt had managed to break the Republican hold
on Michigan's voters. In 1946, when Republican prosecutor Kim Sigler ran for
governor, even Wayne County (home of Detroit, the nation's fifth largest city),
had gone Republican.

Both houses of the Michigan State Legislature were under complete Republican control. After the 1946 election the State Senate had a Republican majority
of twenty-eight to four. In the State House the Republican majority was an
incredible ninety-five to five.

The Republican Party was well funded, for state Republican chairman Arthur
Summerfield, a wealthy Flint Chevrolet distributor, "levied an informal 'tax' on
all General Motors dealers in the state to finance Republican campaigns and
used the funds to maintain an efficient statewide organization."[1]

Strangely isolated from the national party's enthusiasm for the New Deal,
the Michigan Democratic Party was "weak and tainted with corruption."[2] The

state party organization served mainly as a mechanism for distribution of federal patronage from the Roosevelt administration.

But a new generation of young activists was returning to Michigan from World War II service, burning with reformist zeal and the confidence of youth. Some of them thought they saw an opportunity to make something out of the moribund Michigan Democratic Party.

One of these reformers was Neil Staebler. Staebler had grown up in comfortable circumstances in Ann Arbor, the son of a successful local heating oil supplier. A brilliant polymath, he graduated from the University of Michigan in 1926, then joined a group of students in a tour of the Soviet Union. Unlike many leftists who idealized the Communist state, Staebler saw the harsh dictatorship for what it was. But he also concluded that the USSR would develop into a major industrial competitor to the United States, and that its increasingly totalitarian political system would eventually challenge Western democracy around the world. He decided that he would make it his life's work "to bring our U.S. economic, social, and political system up to its potential."[3]

But there was no immediate prospect of starting this project, so he joined the family business.

During World War II Staebler enlisted in the navy. At age thirty-eight, he was a bit old for combat, so the navy decided to make use of his experience in the fuel business; he was assigned to estimate the fleet fuel requirements, and was kept in Washington.

Mustered out at war's end, Staebler returned to Ann Arbor, where he became active in the tiny local Democratic Party organization. He began to dream of constructing a new Democratic Party, one that would implement the progressive causes he espoused. At age forty, he embarked upon his life's work.

In 1946 Staebler traveled to Iowa for a meeting of the politically liberal American Veterans Committee. There he met a young lawyer from Grosse Pointe, Michigan, who shared his views on politics and the potential of government to help people.

Gerhard Mennen Williams, thirty-five, was an heir of the Mennen family, which had made a fortune in cosmetics. Tall and lanky, with a brilliant mind and nonstop work ethic, Williams was an academic star at a private prep school, then at Princeton University, and finally at the University of Michigan Law School, attaining his law degree in 1936.

Well aware that his privileged background afforded him opportunities that most could only dream of, Williams formed a religious conviction that he must use his gifts to improve the lives of the less fortunate.

He saw that Franklin Roosevelt was creating a new kind of activist government, and yearned to be part of it.

Williams sought out former Detroit mayor Frank Murphy, who had been elected Michigan governor as a Democrat in the 1936 Roosevelt landslide. Murphy, a lifelong bachelor, warmed to the idealistic young lawyer and his wife, Nancy, and helped secure Williams a job in the Michigan Attorney General's Office.

In 1939 Roosevelt appointed Murphy attorney general of the United States, and Murphy took his young protégé with him to Washington as his administrative assistant.

When the Japanese attacked Pearl Harbor, Williams obtained a navy commission and, at age thirty-one, went through basic training and officer candidate school, finishing near the top of his class. Then, as his biographer dryly put it: "Williams was fluent in French and German and had traveled extensively in Europe. Naturally the Navy assigned him to the Pacific theater." Williams served aboard several aircraft carriers, participating in the battles of Wake Island, the Marshalls, and the Gilberts.[4]

Upon mustering out in 1945, Williams again turned to his mentor, and Frank Murphy secured him a position as deputy director of the Detroit office of the U.S. Office of Price Administration. At the OPA office he met a young husband-wife team of attorneys, Hicks and Martha Griffiths, who shared his dream of a resurgent, progressive Michigan Democratic Party. The Griffiths invited Williams to join their small law office in Detroit, and he eagerly accepted.

Mennen Williams had been privileged to see politics practiced at the highest level, and he concluded that he could succeed in that world. He just needed an opening.

The opportunity came in 1947, when a vacancy occurred on the Michigan Liquor Control Commission, a bipartisan agency that regulated liquor licenses and retail sales of alcoholic beverages. Republican governor Kim Sigler was required by law to appoint a Democrat to the seat. He had not heard of Williams, but was told that the young lawyer had some governmental experience. Without giving much thought to the matter, Sigler appointed Williams, who began using the position to travel around the state, getting to know local leaders.

At the same time, Hicks and Martha Griffiths began taking Williams to Detroit-area ethnic clubs. They also introduced him to labor leaders around Detroit.

Organized labor had grown dramatically in Michigan in the 1930s and 1940s, and by 1948 over one-third of families in the state had at least one member in a labor union. But this growing interest group had stayed out of state politics: As Williams's biographer put it, "Most unions in the state were either politically inactive or inept. Prior to 1948, the Michigan Congress of Industrial Organizations (CIO), the umbrella group that represented most of the major industry-wide unions, including the United Auto Workers, distrusted both major parties and was officially nonpartisan in the state elections. It refused to endorse candidates or allow members to serve as delegates to political conventions in Michigan."[5]

But not everyone in organized labor shunned politics. August Scholle—universally known as "Gus"—was president of the Michigan CIO. A high school dropout who had mastered seven skilled trades, Scholle came to the attention of the legendary John L. Lewis when he single-handedly chartered unions for 20,000 workers in Toledo.[6] Lewis made him a regional director for the newly independent Congress of Industrial Organizations and brought him to Michigan.

A compact bundle of energy and intellect, Scholle realized early that labor's rights depended on who made the laws. He made it his mission to wipe out the malapportionment of legislative districts that had resulted from shifts toward a more urban population. He wanted create a legislature that was truly representative, a battle he fought in the courts for over a decade, and eventually won. He recognized the gains for labor that Roosevelt's election had made possible at the national level, and believed that organized labor in Michigan should participate in the political process, preferably with its natural allies, the liberals within the Democratic Party. But Scholle could not convince the rest of the labor leadership to change course.

Two events, little remembered today, changed their minds.

In early 1947 the newly elected State Legislature gathered in Lansing. With huge Republican majorities in each house and Republican governor Kim Sigler installed on the second floor of the Capitol, the way was open to enact the wish list of their backers, including Arthur Summerfield and the auto companies. Among the first items on that list were a series of bills known as the Bonine-Tripp amendments, which gutted the Workman's Compensation Act, impairing labor's hard-won rights for no-fault compensation of workers injured on the job. Governor Sigler signed the bills. This flung a gauntlet into the faces of union leaders, and showed them the consequences of eschewing competition in state politics, leaving the field to their adversaries.

The second event—actually a series of events—previewed what would happen if the progressive union leaders remained on the sidelines. Someone else had recognized the Michigan Democratic Party as a tempting takeover target: Jimmy Hoffa.

Hoffa had built Detroit Teamsters Local 299 into a powerhouse, which he controlled completely. In 1946 the Teamsters succeeded in electing their candidates to many county Democratic delegate positions, particularly in the Detroit area. One result was that in the spring of 1947, Hoffa's forces scored a surprising victory at the State Democratic Convention, electing John Franco chairman of the state party.[7] It is probable that Hoffa's goal was not to create a dynamic political party to win elections, but rather to get his allies into positions to influence the Truman administration's decisions on such legal matters as prosecutions of union corruption. In other words, he was more interested in electing a sympathetic Democratic National committeeman than a governor. But the other labor leaders didn't know that at the time, and Hoffa's reputation was anything but reassuring. Hoffa was constantly looking to expand his power, and he had aggressively pursued bringing Michigan food workers into the Teamsters, causing jurisdictional disputes with the CIO and creating increasing personal conflict with Gus Scholle.[8] Hoffa had been indicted in 1946 for demanding "fees" from independent grocerymen who refused to hire union drivers, and he made no secret of his head-busting methods of persuading those who refused to toe his line.[9]

The stage was set. Neil Staebler wanted to cleanse the Democratic Party of corruption and use it to guide Michigan toward humane and progressive policies. He needed troops and candidates. Mennen Williams wanted to be governor. He needed a strong Democratic Party. The CIO wanted protection in Michigan from its enemies—the Republicans and Jimmy Hoffa. It needed a winning presence in Michigan politics. It had thousands of potential troops.

Organized labor's concerns about Hoffa's designs on the Democratic Party were the immediate catalyst for a planned trip to Detroit by the U.S. assistant secretary of labor, John Gibson. Gibson was a former chairman of the Wayne County CIO and a close friend of Gus Scholle.[10] At Williams's suggestion, the Griffiths agreed to host a dinner so that Gibson could meet with Staebler and other liberal Michigan Democrats.

The dinner, which took place at the Griffiths' Detroit home on November 21, 1947, has assumed mythical status among Democrats as the beginning of the modern Michigan Democratic Party. Besides the Detroit and Ann Arbor contingents, liberals from Flint, Grand Rapids, Muskegon, and Three Rivers attended. After Martha Griffiths had served smothered chicken, the group adjourned to the basement for coffee. It was then that Staebler proposed creating Democratic Clubs in cities throughout Michigan as a way to channel the energies of liberal and anti-Hoffa laborites into gaining influence within the party.

Williams volunteered to run for governor in 1948, which he had wanted to do for some time. He and Staebler argued that his candidacy would give new party members a focus around which to organize. With the possible exception of Williams himself, nobody present expected Williams to actually win. Staebler thought it would take ten years just to remold the state Democratic Party into an effective organization.[11]

Nevertheless, Staebler, the Griffiths, and other attendees at the November dinner began establishing Democratic Clubs around the state. By spring there were clubs in Michigan's dozen largest cities, including Detroit.

Most significantly, Gus Scholle's constant warnings of the Hoffa threat finally got through to the CIO leadership. At the Michigan CIO Political Action Committee conference in March 1948, the committee unanimously agreed to work within the Democratic Party, in cooperation with the liberals, with the goal of remolding the party into a progressive organization. The means of doing so were spelled out: "We . . . advise CIO members to become active precinct, ward, county and congressional district workers, and to attempt to become delegates to Democratic conventions."[12]

The CIO resolution was a historic turning point in the relationship between unions and the state Democratic Party. However, implementing it would take time; precinct delegates had to elect state delegates, who then chose delegates to the national convention. Hoffa still wielded power over this process.

Thus, in the summer of 1948 at the Democratic National Convention, which nominated Harry Truman, the Michigan delegation elected George Fitzgerald as national committeeman. Fitzgerald was Jimmy Hoffa's personal attorney. With Hoffa's support, Victor Bucknell of Vicksburg entered the Democratic race for governor. Bucknell, forty-four, was a lawyer and member of the Democratic State Central Committee who had run for the Michigan Supreme Court, unsuccessfully, in 1946.[13]

The battle with the Democratic progressives was on. In Wayne County Scholle and the CIO organized the liberal-labor coalition's campaign. The coalition fielded a thousand candidates as Democratic precinct delegates. All of them were supplied with campaign literature in support of the liberal-labor slate, which prominently featured Mennen Williams's name.[14] Scholle and CIO attorney Tom Downs also organized a massive voter registration drive.[15]

The old-line Democratic leadership, fighting for its life against the liberal-labor coalition on one side and Hoffa on the other, sponsored a third candidate for governor, Burnett Abbott, a former U.S. congressman from Albion.

Leaving their children with a relative, in early August Williams and his wife Nancy began an unprecedented personal campaign that saw them stop in nearly every city and village in Michigan. Campaigning from dawn to midnight, and with no help from Democratic "regulars," Williams spoke to any audience he or his friends could find. He gave as many as thirty speeches a day.[16]

Williams could not afford to buy radio time (he had not yet come into his inheritance, and his wealthy family declined to help finance his campaign), so he stopped by every local radio station for an interview.

In Detroit Williams stopped at factory gates for every shift change, shaking hands with the workers as they emerged. His campaign particularly courted ethnic groups, including a major emphasis on civil rights for African Americans.

In the primary election, on September 14, 1948, 285,000 Democrats voted. Mennen Williams received 39 percent of their votes, enough to win the nomination by a margin of 8,000. But his real margin of victory was earned in Wayne County, which he carried by 12,000 votes.

Meanwhile, Governor Kim Sigler, running unopposed in the Republican primary, received 431,000 votes.

Sigler, a handsome, silver-haired lawyer and former cowboy, had first come to public attention in 1944 when he was appointed as special prosecutor to investigate corruption in the State Legislature. He aggressively pursued State Senate leaders, while carefully cultivating the press. The State Senate leaders felt betrayed—Sigler was a fellow Republican—and they struck back by creating a committee to investigate Sigler's conduct of his office.

The result was an internecine public battle, conducted via the newspapers. Sigler presented himself as a lone, honest prosecutor battling the forces of corruption, and his image grew to heroic proportions.

This drama culminated in the creation of a "public demand" that Sigler run for governor. He entered the race in March 1946 and in the June primary he easily defeated three rivals for the Republican nomination. In November he crushed his Democratic opponent, former governor Murray Van Wagoner, by nearly 300,000 votes.

Once in office, it would seem Sigler might have conciliated the legislative Republicans and their backers. Instead, he proceeded to alienate most of the remaining local and state Republican leaders; he often arrived late for local

Republican dinners and ignored local leaders. He seemed to believe that he had been nominated and elected without their support and didn't need it now.

As *Time* magazine put it, "Kim Sigler burned a little too brightly. During two years in office, he tramped on legislative toes, ignored party wheel horses, [and] dictatorially alienated members of his own cabinet."[17] According to Neil Staebler, "An important segment of the Republican Party leadership was eager to get rid of the incumbent Governor . . . The word was passed, 'Vote for this whippersnapper Williams. . . . We'll vote him out the next election, then we'll have the position back with our kind of guy.'"[18]

Whether the Republican leaders actually encouraged a vote for Williams is debatable, but they did very little for Kim Sigler. And Sigler did little for himself. The governor, a licensed pilot, flew around the state, but often made only one appearance a day, returning to Lansing each night. Williams, meanwhile, began his campaign with fourteen-hour days, then extended it to eighteen-hour days, scheduling no less than sixteen events a day, and as many as twenty-five.[19]

Williams got one final break. He needed a large turnout, and the weather on Election Day, November 2, 1948, was clear and relatively mild. In a shocking upset, Williams defeated Sigler by 163,000 votes, while Republican Thomas Dewey bested President Harry Truman by 35,000 votes in the state. Williams won 64 percent of the Wayne County vote.[20]

At the 1949 Democratic State Convention, the liberal-labor coalition completed its triumph. As one historian of the period put it, "The regular organization was not captured; it was destroyed and replaced with an entirely new one."[21]

In the 1950 gubernatorial election, the Republicans came roaring out of the gate. Former governor Harry F. Kelly represented a reasonably united party this time, and he came so close that it required a contested recount to establish that Williams had been reelected, by the thinnest of hairs: 1,154 votes out of 1,879,382 votes cast.[22]

Two years later, in the 1952 election, Williams did a bit better, defeating Fred Alger Jr.—after another recount—by 8,518 votes.

Williams's greatest challenge as governor was dealing with a legislature both houses of which were under firm, seemingly perpetual, Republican control. The 1948 election returned twenty-three Republicans to the State Senate and only nine Democrats. In the State House of Representatives, the balance was sixty-one Republicans to thirty-nine Democrats.[23]

A major foundation for the Republicans' domination was malapportionment of legislative districts. In the 1950 election the largest senatorial district contained

544,564 people, the smallest contained only 61,008.[24] But each district received exactly the same representation: one state senator.

The State Senate's districts had been established in 1925, based on the population distribution of the 1920 census. The ensuing years had witnessed dramatic population shifts from rural to urban and suburban areas, but the Republicans, naturally wishing to keep their control of the legislature, had never allowed a reapportionment.

The majority of the legislative Republicans were philosophically opposed to expansion of government services, and to the kind of activist, New Deal–style policies that Williams and his allies favored.

The revenues to fund Michigan's state government came principally from a sales tax, a small levy on corporations, and a series of "nuisance" taxes on such items as cigarettes and liquor. There was neither a personal nor a corporate income tax, and the Republicans opposed all attempts to add these new taxes, arguing that they would drive business from the state.

As Williams and his allies saw it, they had pledged to expand government services to help those in need, but the intractability of the permanent Republican legislative majority blocked fulfillment of their programs. When Williams could get the legislature to enact social programs, its Republican majorities refused to enact the taxes necessary to pay for them.

Therefore the Democrats took another tack. In 1952 the liberal-labor-Democrat coalition succeeded in initiating a ballot proposal to amend the state constitution to provide for reapportionment on a basis more reflective of the distribution of Michigan's population. The Republicans responded by placing their own, competing, proposal on the ballot; this would grant substantial reapportionment for the State House of Representatives (partly by increasing the number of seats), but freeze the existing, malapportioned, State Senate districts. In the 1952 election, the Republican proposal received more votes than its Democratic competitor, and was thus adopted as an amendment to the Michigan Constitution. This virtually guaranteed that the State Senate would remain in conservative Republican hands in perpetuity.

With Neil Staebler and organized labor improving the campaign organization and making the governor's reelection their top priority, Mennen Williams finally broke through to a big victory in 1954, defeating Republican nominee Donald S. Leonard by 300,000 votes.[25]

Democrats captured 70 percent of the vote in Wayne County, and swept all statewide offices for the first time since 1936.[26] However, because the State

Senate's districts were based primarily on geographic area rather than population, and Democratic voters were concentrated mainly in relatively few densely populated cities and suburbs, the Republicans remained the majority party in the Senate, twenty-three to eleven.

John Swainson benefited from the heavy Democratic turnout, squeaking in with 51.4 percent of the votes cast for state senator in the 18th District.

A Democrat was also elected to the second highest position in state government, as Lt. Governor Clarence Reid (the father of Swainson's opponent) was defeated in his reelection bid by Williams's former legal advisor, the mild-mannered Phillip A. Hart, who was immediately crowned by the press as Williams's heir-apparent.

CHAPTER FIVE

Legislator

On New Year's Day, January 1, 1955, John Swainson took the oath as an elected member of the Michigan State Senate. He was twenty-nine years old. And although the Senate was traditionally recognized as the "upper house" of the legislature, its members were elected to the same two-year term of office as the members of the State House of Representatives (the "lower house"). The sole difference was the size of their districts. He would have to seek reelection in only two years.

Swainson was a diligent state senator—he never missed a session of the Senate.

He worked on improving government and regulation, cooperating with Republican Bill Broomfield of suburban Royal Oak to investigate penetration of the debt management business by racketeers.[1]

He carried the governor's water loyally. He offered amendments to raise appropriations for state mental health services by $4 million, as requested by the governor. When the Republicans rejected the increases as unrealistic, he demanded a roll-call vote, to put them on the record.[2] When a $500,000 appropriation for college scholarships, proposed by the governor, was stuck in the

Senate Education Committee, he moved for discharge, forcing the Republicans to go on record against it.[3]

Swainson cultivated the press (*Detroit News* Capitol reporter Don Hoenshell would become a personal friend), but nonetheless generated opposition from news media that supported Republican positions. The *Grosse Pointe Press Review*, reflecting the conservative views of most of its readers, chided Swainson for his leadership in securing enactment of two important pieces of civil rights legislation, the Fair Employment Practices Act and the Equal Public Accommodations Act, both proposed by Mennen Williams. According to a July 26, 1956, op-ed piece, "Soapy," as Williams was known, had been "ably assisted by his 'team,' led by State Senator John B. Swainson of the 18th District, who does his bidding in the Senate, and by State Representative Edward Carey, international representative for the UAW-CIO . . . and spokesman for the Governor in the House. . . . Had it not been for the unceasing efforts of John B. Swainson in the State Senate and these members of the House . . . [the civil rights legislation] would not have become law."

Swainson would consistently advocate racial equality—which did him little good within his overwhelmingly white district. He authored a resolution calling upon U.S. attorney general Herbert Brownell to rule on whether it was lawful for federal funds to go to racially segregated schools. His support of the Fair Employment Practices legislation won him recognition from the NAACP.[4]

In the Senate he was a junior member of a party seemingly condemned to permanent minority status. Yet at the same time he was making a strong impression as a man with a future in statewide politics.

In 1956 the Teamsters Union, angered at his refusal to vote for several of the union's pet bills, decided to oppose him in the Democratic primary election. They ran Dudley T. Kavanagh, a real estate agent whose only apparent qualification for public office was that his middle name was "Thomas" and who could thus be advertised as "D. Thomas Kavanagh," a name similar to Michigan attorney general Thomas M. Kavanagh. Swainson was, once again, endorsed by the Democratic Party, as well as most major labor unions. He easily won renomination in the August primary, and went on to defeat Republican George F. Boos in the 1956 general election, with 51 percent of votes cast.

By 1956 Williams was becoming seriously interested in a run for national office, and he urged the organization to go all out for a victory that would be noticed by the national press and national Democratic leaders. The result was another 300,000-vote victory, this time over Detroit Mayor Albert Cobo. What made this particularly impressive was that Williams achieved this margin while Republican Dwight Eisenhower was carrying Michigan's presidential canvass by 350,000 votes over Democrat Adlai Stevenson.[5]

Williams's political future appeared to be bright. Because of his outspoken stands on civil rights, he was already nationally recognized as one of the party's leading liberal politicians. The 1956 campaign made him appear to be a strong vote-getter with ticket-splitter appeal. He began making plans targeted at the Democratic presidential nomination for 1960. His growing national ambitions were no secret to Michigan Democrats or, for that matter, Republicans.

On January 1, 1957, Inauguration Day, standing on the Capitol steps for Williams's oath-taking, Swainson drew a laugh when he told the governor, "After you win five times, they give this to you to keep."[6]

A week later Swainson danced the jitterbug at Boniface Maile's inaugural party (Maile, an attorney, was to serve as state and national commander of Disabled American Veterans and was a permanent fixture in Lansing, serving on the board of the Michigan Veterans Trust Fund for fifty years).[7]

Williams, always on the lookout for rising talent, quietly encouraged the young senator to take on the incumbent Senate Democratic leader, Detroiter Harold Ryan, for the leadership post. On the opening day of the session, several of Williams's aides stood watch outside the door as the Senate Democrats caucused. Ryan, who had held the position four years, lost it to Swainson by a six-to-four vote.[8]

The job itself was not enviable; it amounted to being the spokesperson for a powerless minority (Senate Democrats were still outnumbered by Republicans twenty-three to eleven) and taking on the extra work of rounding up the votes of cantankerously independent senators. If one wasn't careful, it was easy to come across to the public as an obstructionist, perpetually seeking to thwart the goals of the Republican majority.

But elevation to the leadership was a signal from Mennen Williams and his allies to the party: here is a Democrat with potential to rise. *Detroit Free Press* Lansing correspondent Owen Deatrick wrote, "Democrats in the Senate have high hopes for the new minority leader. They applaud his ability to bait the Republican majority without getting excited. He is considered in the front rank when the Democrats ever get around to shuffling the top leadership and start looking for a candidate for such spots as lieutenant governor."[9]

Paul Chandler, writing in the January 31, 1957, *Plymouth Mail*, observed that "the 'inside' information as of this moment seems to be that Gov. Williams will run again in 1958 for Governor, rather than as the opponent of Charles Potter for U.S. Senator. The reasoning is that a sixth term as Governor would leave Soapy on a stronger springboard to try for the presidency than would possession of a junior senatorship. Lt. Gov. Phil Hart is seen now as the opponent for Sen. Potter. And Democratic State Senator John Swainson of Plymouth is being groomed quietly to run as Lieut. Governor next time."

Chandler was correct on all counts, but nothing was guaranteed. The Senate leadership post provided Swainson the opportunity to demonstrate his political skills at a higher level, but the greater visibility also meant greater scrutiny of any stumbles.

The young senator encountered the dark side of his new visibility in February 1957, when he moved out ahead of his own party on the subject of a state income tax.

Swainson and his House counterpart, Rep. Ed Carey of Detroit, told reporters that they were drafting a proposal under which state taxpayers would pay the state of Michigan an amount equal to 5 percent of the income declared on their federal income tax return. This would be a means of getting a *de facto* progressive state income tax, a concept that was expressly banned by the Michigan Constitution. "In this way, we could get a graduated income tax without violating the state constitutional requirement," Swainson told Don Hoenshell of the *Detroit News*.[10]

Two former Senate Democratic leaders, Harold Ryan and Charles Blondy, quickly announced their dissent from Swainson's position. Blondy said, "It is unfortunate our minority leader got in this position. First we must do everything to reduce expenses in government . . . an income tax would be unpopular."

Swainson realized that he had gotten out too far ahead of his members. He cut his losses immediately, announcing that his statement had been merely his personal view, and the party's position was that "a corporation profits tax should be levied before consideration of any other form of taxation."[11]

In February a new Democratic senator, Basil Brown, learned that the Georgia State Legislature was considering a bill to bar racially integrated athletic contests. The University of Michigan was scheduled to host the University of Georgia football team for a game in October. Brown, who was of partially African American descent, demanded that the game be cancelled. Michigan's athletic director, Fritz Crisler, explained to Brown that the football schedule was arranged years in advance and that there were no plans for the Maize and Blue to play a return game in the state of Georgia.

Swainson and Detroit Democratic state representative George Edwards joined

Brown in demanding that the university cancel the game. The three of them appeared at a meeting of the university's Board of Athletic Control in Ann Arbor and made a statement. After they departed, the board voted to keep the Georgia game on the schedule. Since the university's independence was guaranteed by the Michigan Constitution, the legislature could not overrule its decision.

Swainson and Brown were to become close friends, sharing a rented house near the Capitol during the week.

In April Mennen Williams gave Swainson's prospects an indirect boost; he appointed Paul Adams to the post of attorney general to replace Thomas M. Kavanagh, who had won election to the Michigan Supreme Court. Michigan Democrats traditionally tried to nominate candidates for statewide office on a geographically "balanced" ticket. Adams was from Sault Ste. Marie in the Upper Peninsula. He would presumably run for a full term as attorney general in the 1958 election. The fact that an "outstater" filled this major office would leave the lieutenant governor slot available for a candidate from the Detroit area.

Swainson's reputation received another boost when the Detroit Free Press polled the Capitol press corps, asking each reporter to name the most effective legislators in each house from each party. The reporters were unanimous in naming Swainson and Harold Ryan as the most effective Democratic senators.[12]

In September the Swainsons moved from Redford Township to the charming western Wayne County town of Plymouth. Their house contained extra-wide doors and ramps to accommodate a wheelchair (which Swainson never used in public).[13]

The young state senator was still practicing law. In October 1957 he drew some attention from the local press when he represented Sam Zehra, an applicant for a coveted liquor license for his restaurant, before the Livonia City Council. Applications by eighteen others were also pending. The council granted only Zehra the license.[14]

Mennen Williams had gathered Democratic leaders to discuss the 1958 ticket at a private weekend conclave in May 1957.[15] No public statements came out of that meeting, but hints were dropped and signals quietly passed.

In December 1957 Lt. Governor Phil Hart celebrated his birthday with a modest party at his office. He blew out the candles on the cake and looked around the room, his gaze stopping on John Swainson. Hart revealed that his birthday wish was "that John Swainson will be the next occupant of this office."[16] That was a very clear signal. Two months later Hart announced that he was a candidate for the U.S. Senate seat held by Republican Charles Potter. Williams had decided to seek a sixth term as governor, but let Hart make his announce-ment first, probably to avoid the suggestion that Hart was Williams's puppet. At that time most observers believed that Hart was taking on the tougher race; he was facing an incumbent, while Williams had no prominent opponent on the horizon. The *Port Huron Times-Herald* quoted an anonymous Republican leader as saying that Williams's delay in announcing his candidacy was designed "to draw attention to Hart because he (Williams) felt he had no opposition and he wanted to do Phil a good turn."[17]

On the morning of February 17, a week after Hart's announcement, Swainson hosted a breakfast for the press and supporters. He stood and announced that he would seek his party's nomination for lieutenant governor. "My reasons for running for lieutenant governor are the same as my reasons for entering politics," he said. "I'm convinced that Michigan citizens deserve to be represented by people who are willing to demonstrate their concern for all of the people."[18] Asked for comment, Mennen Williams chimed in with low-key boilerplate: "Senator Swainson has done an excellent job as Democratic minority leader in the Senate and I have enjoyed working with him."[19]

Swainson continued his affiliation with his law firm while he campaigned for the office of lieutenant governor. One of his partners, Allen Zemmol, noticed that whenever Swainson was in the office, there seemed to be several black men in the waiting room. "They would go in and see John, and they would leave smiling. This went on, there must have been about twenty of these guys. So I asked him, what the hell is going on? I mean, who are these dudes? And he said, 'I was campaigning about a week ago and some guy came up to me and wanted to know if I could get him a job. Well, I discovered that the Wayne County drain commissioner had a bunch of non-civil-service labor jobs available. So I got this guy a job. But he apparently went and told all his friends, and I've been getting guys jobs all week long!' He got such . . . satisfaction out of getting these jobs."[20]

• • •

There is an old saying in politics: "Friends come and go, but enemies accu-mulate." Mennen Williams had been in office ten years, with his labor-liberal alliance in nearly complete control of the Michigan Democratic Party. But not all Michigan Democrats were liberal or unionists. There was a small group of dissidents who had concluded that the leadership had become a "dictatorship," taking orders from United Auto Workers president Walter Reuther and other labor leaders. They had formed themselves into the Democratic Club of Michigan, and they decided to run a slate of candidates in the August primary election.[21] Williams's opponent (his first primary opponent in ten years) was William Johnson, a radio station owner in Ironwood in the Upper Peninsula. Swainson's opponent was William Mohardt of Detroit.

In the August primary, Williams and Swainson swamped their opponents, each getting over 75 percent of the vote. But the public dissension was an early sign that the powerful machine that Neil Staebler had built was developing stress cracks.

Williams expected to win the 1958 general election in a cakewalk, against first-time Republican gubernatorial candidate Paul Bagwell, who had never held public office. After that, Williams planned to leave his loyal lieutenant governor in charge as he traveled the nation piling up support for the 1960 Democratic presidential nomination.

Swainson's Republican opponent was Donald A. Brown, an attorney and state representative from Royal Oak, a suburb of Detroit.

Williams decided that Bagwell was a Republican Party sacrificial lamb, and he therefore did not need to put in his usual energetic campaign. Instead, Williams devoted substantial time and resources to campaigning for other Democratic candidates.[22] But Bagwell surprised everyone, campaigning aggressively, challenging Williams to a televised debate, and scorching the governor when he turned down the challenge.

The result on election day was a relatively narrow margin for Williams. While Democrat Phillip Hart defeated incumbent U.S. senator Charles Potter by 172,000 votes and Democrat James Hare was reelected secretary of state by 300,000 votes, Williams defeated Bagwell by only 139,000 votes, getting 53 percent of the total.[23]

Swainson won by almost exactly the same margin, garnering 53.3 percent.

On January 1, 1959, John Swainson took the oath as Michigan's lieutenant governor. His new job would entail little power, but much visibility. His only official duty was to preside over the Michigan State Senate, with the power to cast a vote only in the event of a tie vote, which was extremely unlikely, since the Republicans remained solidly in the majority, twenty-two to twelve.

The narrow margin of Williams's reelection victory had not changed his national plans. He embarked on a series of trips designed to test the waters and garner support for a presidential bid in 1960. Whenever Williams left Michigan, Swainson became acting governor. In September 1959 Williams departed on a month-long trip to Europe, to strengthen his foreign affairs experience. He left instructions for Swainson and a loyal staff who could reach him by telephone or cable in case of emergency. Despite Williams's efforts to control events in the state even while absent, as the *Detroit News* reported, "There are those who believe that Swainson would use his authority without hesitancy in a pinch."[24] Every time Williams left the state, press attention automatically focused on the acting governor. Swainson didn't have to actually *do* anything. He merely had to look and sound gubernatorial, which he did.

The 1958 reelection campaign turned out to be the first in a series of missteps by the usually infallible Mennen Williams.

Williams next embarked on a series of out-of-state appearances designed to showcase him to national Democratic leaders, but he failed to impress them.

Finally, Williams determined to put an end to the ten-year stalemate between the governor and the legislature over Michigan's fiscal structure. As Williams's biographer put it:

Republicans had resisted Williams's repeated demands for a corporate profits tax while the governor had managed to dramatically increase state spending by borrowing funds to pay for his programs. Both sides, however, recognized that the stalemate was leading Michigan toward a day of reckoning, as continued budget deficits would eventually push the state into financial disaster.[25]

A 1958 recession had caused serious unemployment in the automotive industry, and undermined Michigan's tax revenues to the extent that the state government projected a deficit of over $110 million for 1959. Williams proposed, again, a corporate profits tax. But he added an even more provocative proposal: a graduated state personal income tax.

Republican legislators refused to consider the governor's proposals. They offered instead an increase in the sales tax, combined with borrowing from the Michigan Veterans Trust Fund.

Even knowing what was coming, both sides refused to compromise. Each thought the public would blame the other for the stalemate. The result was inevitable. In April the state government ran out of spendable funds and withheld paychecks from state employees. The "payless payday" generated headlines around the nation, and many of the news stories awarded at least equal blame to the governor. Damon Stetson wrote in the *New York Times*, "The reasons why Michigan, one of the nation's wealthiest states, has reached a point where it cannot pay its employees are both complex and controversial. The simplest explanation is that expenditures over the last three years have exceeded incoming revenue."26

Time magazine commented that "Soapy Williams tore off the kind of statement that has become the bane of (1) his friends, (2) his own presidential hopes and (3) his state. The Republicans, he stormed, had voted for 'payless paydays . . . cutting off welfare funds . . . the destruction of our universities.' Old Guard Republicans, who engineered the senate defeat, were indeed rather pleased at the prospect of once popular Democrat Williams standing before the nation as a flat-broke Governor.27

The net result was the extinction of any meaningful chance at the presidential nomination for Williams. As 1960 dawned, Williams faced the necessity of choosing between the only two political courses left open to him: either run for a seventh term as governor or campaign zealously for the Democratic presidential nominee, in hopes of appointment to a national office.

No one knew what Williams's choice would be. And until he made that choice known, no Democrat could begin openly organizing a campaign to succeed him, for Williams was still The Champ to both the Democratic leadership and the rank and file. Anyone so bold as to start a gubernatorial campaign before Williams had made his decision would be read out of the party.

However, no penalty attached to quietly making contingency plans and encouraging speculation. And so speculation began to bubble up about two Democrats who had been elected to statewide office and were believed to be interested in the top job should it become available: James M. Hare and John B. Swainson.

CHAPTER SIX

The Primary: A Major Upset

ON TUESDAY, MARCH 3, 1960, MENNEN WILLIAMS ASKED FOR FIFTEEN MINUTES OF time on Michigan radio and television stations to announce his decision on another run for governor. Barely restraining his emotions, Williams told the audience that he would not seek a seventh term, but hoped to work for the cause of world peace in some national office.

The next day Michigan's secretary of state announced he was a candidate for governor.

James M. Hare, forty, had served as Michigan's elected secretary of state since 1955. A former public school attendance officer and political science professor, Hare had been a Michigan leader of the liberal Americans for Democratic Action. He had come to public notice when, as the appointed manager of the annual Michigan State Fair, he had kicked out some of the seamier shows and made the fair more attractive to families.

To the public, and to many Democrats, Hare appeared the obvious choice. He had the name recognition that went with six years as secretary of state; his name was prominently displayed on every local secretary of state branch office, and on numerous official documents relating to the everyday life of Michigan residents. He had served six years administering a major department of state government, with reasonable efficiency and without scandal. He had won reelection by a greater margin than any other Democratic officeholder.

The secretary of state also had by far the biggest patronage organization of any state official. State law required at least one branch office in each of Michigan's eighty-three counties, but under the patronage system, the organization grew to a high of 270 branch offices,[1] each presided over by a Hare-appointed branch manager who received a cut of the fees generated by serving Michigan motor vehicle owners. As a matter of course, each branch manager was expected to support Hare's political campaigns and raise money to finance them. Thus Hare, unique among potential candidates for governor, had an existing statewide political machine, ready to spring into action at short notice.

Swainson, in contrast, had served four years in the state senate and one two-year term in the relatively insignificant office of lieutenant governor. He was still very young, at thirty-five, and he tended to look even younger in photographs. He had no organization at all.

Clearly, Hare had the advantage in the public, quantitatively measurable metrics.

But inside the Democratic Party there were other measures, less quantifiable but just as real.

The branch manager machine empowered Hare with an independence that he did not hesitate to exercise. When Governor Williams had made the state income tax his main issue against the Republicans' sales tax, Hare had not joined him—unlike Swainson. When Gus Scholle had loudly opposed electing a constitutional convention from existing legislative districts, because the delegates were certain to perpetuate legislative malapportionment, Hare had not joined him—but Swainson did.[2]

And it was not only on these very public, deep-gut issues that Hare had hung back. The office of secretary of state was almost purely administrative. Its bread and butter was the provision of essentially nonpolitical services to the public. The occupant of that office could maintain his electability by providing those services efficiently and cleanly. He had no need, indeed was not expected, to take positions on issues—positions that would alienate large groups of voters who were otherwise satisfied with his administration.

This was how James Hare conducted his office. It was a method designed to make him essentially unbeatable as long as he ran for reelection as secretary of state, and that was a major reason why Jim Hare had outpolled Soapy Williams in the 1958 election.

But a Democratic primary for governor was very different.

The unpartisan detachment that had allowed Hare to cruise along without alienating any major groups had also left him without any strong allies.

Intraparty politics is a clannish business, and clans tend to remember who was with them when it counted. Swainson had been a loyal and effective ally of Williams and the labor-liberal coalition in every battle since he had entered the State Senate in 1955.

Swainson was also seen, particularly by the local labor leaders, as a regular guy, a guy it was fun to have a beer with. He didn't talk down to them. Hare, on the other hand, was viewed as somewhat aloof.[3]

On the day that Hare announced his candidacy, Swainson issued a statement, but it was not quite the announcement that his supporters expected. Before determining his "own future course in public service," he said, "I hope to confer with representative local leaders throughout Michigan for their helpful counsel."[4]

Swainson's statement set off a flurry of rumors that he was considering not making the race. The speculation on his plans had him running instead for secretary of state, or awaiting appointment to a vacant judgeship in return for leaving the field to Hare.[5]

Actually, Swainson had every intention of running. But he could not declare himself immediately. While Hare had everything in place ahead of time—and thus could announce immediately—Swainson needed a little time to get commitments from leaders engaged in the intricate, behind-the-scenes dance that Williams's announcement had set in motion. The statement was shrewdly calculated to keep any fence-sitters from jumping on the Hare bandwagon until Swainson could get the commitments he needed. Most of what he needed was from labor, and labor leaders had talked each other into believing that Williams was going to run again.[6] It was only after Williams had made his announcement that it was possible to discuss their political support in any meaningful way.

There was another reason why Swainson had to quickly take soundings. Neil Staebler and Mennen Williams had privately asked him to sit this one out. As Staebler put it in his memoirs, "Mennen and I tried to arrange a pact between [Swainson and Hare] for an orderly succession to avoid a primary battle. Jim had been in office for six years and was better known statewide, so we endeavored to persuade John to run for lieutenant governor again."[7]

The vote-getting powerhouse that Staebler had patiently built over twelve years had never had to endure a primary for the governorship. Of course there had been disputes, including disputes over nominations for statewide office. But they had been settled quietly, behind closed doors, the losers often conciliated with promises of future rewards. Staebler had been able to suppress prolonged public battles that threatened to set factions openly against each other. A gubernatorial primary would be—by definition—a prolonged public battle, and there was no way Staebler could be sure that the party would reunite in time to win the general election.

But John Swainson would not agree to step aside, and Neil Staebler would not—perhaps could not—force him.

One of Swainson's first talks was with Gus Scholle. They met for one and a half hours, privately.[8] No public statement was issued by either man after the meeting, but its purpose neither required nor allowed a public statement. It was probably clear to Scholle by the time of their meeting that a consensus was emerging among top labor leaders and the Democratic Party leadership: during the primary campaign, both groups of leaders would maintain official neutrality. Hare, confident of winning the nomination, had actually *asked* that the top labor leaders maintain neutrality, fearing that if they endorsed him, his Republican opponent would use those endorsements against him in the general election.[9] But *local* leaders would remain free to support whom they wished, and this possibility was almost certainly discussed by Scholle and Swainson.

Swainson had already chosen the person to manage his campaign. John "Joe" Collins was a protégé of Neil Staebler, who had recruited him while Collins was a student at the University of Michigan, to unify feuding Democrats in Jackson County, Collins's home. Collins had accomplished the mission and become chairman of the county party organization. Only twenty-five, and just getting started in the insurance business, Collins had energy, enthusiasm, and few enemies. He had already managed a statewide campaign, for the University of Michigan Board of Regents. He also had a good relationship with Staebler, which could compensate for Staebler's coolness toward Swainson.[10]

In fact, Collins recalled, "Very quietly back then I got a lot of help from Neil Staebler—just on the names of people who could get the job done, that kind of thing. It was in the context of who would do some work, not necessarily [who] would be for John. I would ask him, for example, 'Who is good in Cass County?' if I was going up there the next day."[11]

The campaign began with no money. Joe Collins recalled:

I went back to Jackson. At that time I had a very good friend, Sam McNally, who was a regent at the University of Michigan. I had managed his campaign for the board of regents and I had met a lot of people in that campaign. . . . He was a farmer, an Andy Griffith type of character. Well, I got Sam and a Republican here in town, Glen Trolls, to put up $900. This was to buy the first handout cards so that John would have something to put in people's hands as he went around. On the front was a picture of his family and on the back was a biography of John.

On Saturday, March 5, in a dinner speech to the Eaton County Democrats, Swainson announced his candidacy:

> Principle and program will matter in the next few years. Experience will be needed in these critical times. Both my legislative and administrative experience have given me the necessary background and qualifications to help guide our state to meet the important and pressing issues of the '60s. That is why I choose, in all humility, to announce here tonight that I shall seek the Democratic nomination for Governor of Michigan.

Three days later the *Detroit News* published the results of a poll it had commissioned. Market Opinion Research, an experienced polling firm, had conducted the poll at an unspecified date before Mennen Williams had announced his decision not to seek reelection. The poll matched several leading Democrats, including Hare and Swainson, individually against Paul Bagwell, who was considered the likely Republican candidate.

Hare led the field. The poll showed voters preferred him to Bagwell by a margin of 55.1 percent to 42.4 percent, with 2.6 percent expressing no preference. Swainson also led Bagwell, but the margin was much narrower, 49.1 percent to 47.2 percent, with 3.7 percent expressing no preference.[12]

That Hare would come first was no surprise. His name was well known; he had already won three statewide elections. He had avoided supporting his party on a number of divisive issues and thus his appeal with voters in a general election-style poll.

But Hare and Swainson were not competing in a general election. They were competing in a primary, with very different dynamics than a general election.

As the Detroit *Free Press* put it, Hare had "deliberately divorced himself from . . . [Williams in] the tax battle last year [and] in doing so, he alienated large segments of the party who feel that he should have stood behind the Governor."[13]

Hare's people would try to use the *Detroit News* poll to show that Hare had the best chance of beating Bagwell (who was clearly headed for renomination against a token opponent). But this was no hindrance. Swainson and his supporters could make the argument that the poll showed that *either* Hare or Swainson would beat Bagwell, so labor should go with the candidate who best represented its interests, and that was clearly Swainson.[14]

Swainson appears to have recognized from the start that his record on issues important to party and labor activists was his greatest asset. Of nearly equal importance, he was already known and trusted by many local union leaders. Two of these leaders were Russ Leach, head of UAW Tool and Die Local 155, and Harry Southwell, head of UAW Amalgamated Local 174 in the Detroit area. They were strong supporters from early on, and they had the contacts with other local leaders—and knowledge of union politics—to give Swainson the opportunity to cement the support of a broad network of locals, especially in the Detroit metropolitan area. Swainson himself still had to close the sale in each case, but his enthusiasm and energy, as well as his "regular guy" personality, made this task easy. The local leaders could not help but contrast Swainson with the phlegmatic, pipe-smoking Hare.

Eventually, Hare and Swainson were joined in the primary by Ed Connor, a member of the Detroit City Council and former state representative, with ties to organized labor. Connor had neither the name recognition nor the statewide contacts of his rivals, and was never a major factor in the Democratic race.

The Michigan AFL-CIO invited all three Democratic candidates to address its May convention. Swainson was well received there and benefited from Leach's political savvy: "Acting on Leach's instructions," Swainson "entered the convention hall at the rear and proceeded down the middle aisle. Also following Leach's direction were several hundred delegates, who immediately pressed toward Swainson from both sides of the aisle with outstretched hands."[15]

The *Ionia Sentinel-Standard* reported that "Swainson . . . was hoisted to the shoulders of two hefty delegates and carried around the convention floor."[16] According to the *Petoskey News Review,* "Swainson's backers stole the show with a noisy, eight-minute demonstration that overshadowed convention introductions of his rivals."[17]

On July 6 Leach announced that the presidents of nine major Detroit-area locals (including six UAW locals) were formally endorsing Swainson. He predicted that 75 percent of the tricounty (Wayne, Oakland and Macomb Counties, i.e., metropolitan Detroit) labor movement would back Swainson.[18]

After months of preparation, Leach invited 205 Detroit area local union presidents to meet at his local's union hall on Eight Mile Road on Tuesday, July

12. These leaders represented two-thirds of all the union locals in the Detroit metropolitan area. Leach, Southwell, and Paul Silver (president of UAW Local 351) urged the leaders to push their own locals to formally endorse Swainson.[19]

The result was dramatic. One week after the meeting, Swainson's campaign announced that twenty-eight locals, with total membership of 108,400, were formally endorsing him.[20]

While Joe Collins organized local groups of supporters around the state, Swainson campaigned. Although his disability prevented him from matching the frenetic pace of Mennen Williams's early campaigns, he still drove himself doggedly. An example was Saturday, April 23. He began the campaign day with an 11:30 A.M. speech to the Bowling Tournament of the Polish National Alliance in Detroit, then did coffees at four homes in Detroit, one per hour starting at two in the afternoon. At 7:30 P.M. he dropped by a wedding reception in Detroit, then was driven to the downtown Detroit annual banquet of the Detroit Real Estate Brokers Association, where he was a featured speaker.

He left the banquet after his speech and traveled to an officers' installation ceremony for the Eagles (a Polish service organization) in Grosse Pointe at 9:45. He then made a 10:00 P.M. appearance at a testimonial dance for a Macomb County Democratic leader.

His evening was far from over. He left the dance at 10:45 to go to the annual Spring Frolic of Communications Workers Local 4012 in Pontiac. At 11:45 he left the Frolic to go all the way back to downtown Detroit for an appearance at the annual dance and card party of the Lapeer Parents Association, which he left at 12:45 A.M. to go to the dinner dance of the Southwestern Political Club in Detroit.[21]

Alice Swainson took lessons in public speaking, and hit the campaign trail on her own. On one occasion she was surprised to find herself sharing the stage with Jim Hare and Ed Connor, Swainson's primary opponents.[22]

On both Memorial Day and July 4 Swainson marched in three local parades. This was, of course, standard practice for politicians, and Swainson did not draw any special attention to himself. But, as his law partner Alan Zemmol put it, "[It] was like walking on stilts. So if he lifted a heavy object or went any kind of long distance, it started to have its effect. And he would do those things, but at great pain." Rest periods had to be built into his campaign schedules to afford him relief.[23]

In the August 2, 1960, primary election, Hare carried fifty-eight of the eighty-three counties, but Swainson carried all six in the Detroit metro area and won the nomination by 274,473 votes to Hare's 205,086 (Ed Connor received 60,895 votes).

Looking at the vote totals, Dudley Buffa observed that Swainson's margin over Hare in Wayne County was greater than his margin over Hare statewide. He concluded: "Wayne County gave Swainson the Democratic nomination; and the secondary leadership of the UAW, set free to follow their own counsel by the union's policy of non-intervention, gave Swainson Wayne County."[24]

In the Republican primary Paul Bagwell, by now unopposed in his second run for governor, received 480,361 votes, slightly more than Swainson and Hare combined.[25] The race was on.

CHAPTER SEVEN

The General Election: A Squeaker

PAUL BAGWELL, FORTY-SEVEN, AND JOHN SWAINSON, THIRTY-FIVE, MAY HAVE BEEN THE most articulate pair of rivals ever to contest the office of governor in Michigan. Each spoke in complete sentences, perfectly parsed.

Bagwell was, in fact, a professional rhetorician. A champion debater at the University of Akron, he went on to coach debate at Michigan State, where his varsity team won gold medals at national competitions. He was appointed head of the speech department at age twenty-nine.[1] In 1959 the university appointed him as its director of scholarships.[2]

Born on a farm in North Carolina, Bagwell, like Swainson, played high school football. But at age sixteen he contracted polio, and thereafter Bagwell's ability to use his legs was also limited. He had to wear braces and use a cane to walk.

Bagwell graduated from the University of Akron, becoming active in the local Republican Party. He also became a civic leader, eventually attaining the presidency of the U.S. Jaycees.

At Michigan State he continued in Republican politics, heading Michigan Citizens for Eisenhower and running for state auditor general in 1956. He lost, narrowly, but received more votes than any other statewide Republican candidate.

In the context of the 1950s Michigan Republican Party, Bagwell was a liberal, practically an insurgent. He supported opening up the party and expanding it beyond its base of rural and business conservatives, and he recruited other young moderates to leadership positions in the party, incurring the wrath of the GOP old guard. In 1959 the personification of that old guard, Arthur Summerfield (serving as U.S. postmaster general) attempted to oust Bagwell's choice for state GOP chairman, Lawrence Lindemer, but was blocked by Bagwell ally Henry Ford II.[3]

In 1958, with Mennen Williams and the Staebler-led Democratic machine at its apex, no Republican of stature was interested in running for governor, and Bagwell easily captured the nomination.

Surprising the leadership of both parties, Bagwell put on an aggressive campaign and came much closer to defeating Williams than anyone had expected. This made it impossible to deny him the nomination in 1960.

Maury Crane, hired by Bagwell in 1953, and later to serve as director of Michigan State University's Library of the Human Voice, recalled Bagwell as "a delightful, charming man. He was charismatic and had a euphuistic, flowery speaking style . . . he believed in oratory."[4] However, the Lansing State Journal noted that although Bagwell was "a polished platform speaker in the college debate tradition, some critics have said they feel he is lecturing at them."[5]

Although he trailed Swainson in the initial public opinion polls, Bagwell went into the campaign with several advantages, The first was the public image of "the mess in Lansing" as a result of years of bitter failures to reform Michigan's antiquated and inadequate patchwork of taxes. Bagwell could argue that as an outsider he brought a new approach, and could work with the Republican legislature, whereas Swainson was likely to continue Williams's record of bitter partisan gridlock.

Bagwell's second advantage was that two referendum proposals were to be on the November ballot, and polls showed that a majority of voters agreed with Bagwell's unequivocal support of each proposal.[6]

The League of Women Voters and George Romney's Citizens for Michigan had succeeded in their drive to place a constitutional convention on the ballot. Michigan's need for constitutional reform had become so obvious by 1960 that virtually nobody opposed the concept. But many Democrats, led by Gus Scholle, felt that a "con-con" (as it was universally abbreviated), with its delegates elected from existing legislative districts, would inevitably write a new state constitution that perpetuated the malapportionment of Michigan's existing legislature.[7] The anti-con-con Democrats, including Swainson, argued that piecemeal reform was preferable, via a series of amendments to be drafted by the legislature and placed before the voters. But the Democratic Party was divided on this issue. Both Mennen Williams and James Hare had endorsed the con-con.

The second referendum proposal was to amend the state constitution to allow the legislature to increase the state sales tax from 3 percent to 4 percent. Bagwell supported it. Polls indicated that a majority supported the sales tax increase and opposed enactment of a state income tax, which Williams had proposed.[8]

Shortly after Swainson won the nomination, Neil Staebler weighed in with his advice on how the Democrats could dodge their disadvantages on these issues. Although he was an idealist on moving Michigan's policies in a progressive direction, he was a hardheaded realist (his opponents would probably say "cynic") when it came to winning the elections necessary to enact those policies.

Regarding con-con, Staebler advised:

It is important that we do not get tagged in the public mind as being opposed to constitutional reform. Many people have a vague impression as a result of the tax stalemate and recurrent use of the phrase "mess in Lansing" that there is something wrong with the state government, and that change is needed.

While the newspapers and the Republicans will do everything possible to make "con-con" *the* issue, I do not think the average voter understands it nor is deeply concerned about it. The danger to us lies in the possibility that Bagwell and the Republicans will use it to pre-empt the "reform" label.

On the tax issue, Staebler observed:

1—Bagwell is endorsing the sales tax increase . . . 2—Historically, our Party and Legislative positions have been opposed to the sales tax increase. 3—The sales tax increase, according to the polls, is less objectionable to the voters than an income tax.

The Republicans will do everything they can to turn the State campaign into a referendum on sales tax vs. income tax. Already they are saying: "a vote for a Democrat is a vote for an income tax."

It is my judgment that if we openly campaign for an income tax it could cost us the election. . . . The position, by candidates, might be stated something like this:

"There is no question that the State needs the money. Even the Republicans admit this. As for me, you know where I stand. I don't think the sales tax is the right answer. . . . But whatever the people decide, we Democrats will accept your verdict and get on with the job of building Michigan. . . . If the sales tax is turned down . . . what Michigan really needs is a complete overhaul and reform of the tax structure, including relief for small business, elimination of those obnoxious nuisance taxes on consumers that the Republicans are so fond of, and an easing of the property tax burden on home-owners."

Avoidance of issues was to be complimented by emphasis on personalities:

We must establish the closest possible identification between Jack Kennedy and John Swainson, developing and exploiting their many remarkable similarities, i.e., both are young; but seasoned and experienced in government; both are war heroes; both are dynamic, new political personalities.[9]

John Swainson would stick to Staebler's script with few deviations throughout his campaign.

But before he made any public statements on the issues, he had to heal the wounds opened by the primary campaign and make sure he would lead a united Democratic Party into the general election.

After his primary victory, he took a vacation, returning to Lansing August 8.

The State Democratic Convention was scheduled to take place only three and a half weeks after the primary, and it would be Swainson's first test as new leader of his party.

The candidates for governor and lieutenant governor had been nominated in the primary election, but all other candidates for statewide office were to be selected at the party's August convention. Although he was now ex officio party leader, the candidate for governor could not simply dictate to the rowdy delegates. But he could exert a powerful—often decisive—influence on their choices.

Swainson's first decision was what to do about his defeated rival, James Hare:

What do I do regarding the secretary of state, who would have to receive his nomination to continue as secretary of state at the convention of which I would be the prime figure? And I could have indulged myself, I suppose, in some hurts or imagined hurts from that primary campaign . . . and suggest that somebody else be nominated. I think that would have been a tragic mistake . . . so, after considering this for some time, we asked Jim Hare if he would again be a candidate for secretary of state.[10]

Before the State Democratic Convention opened, Swainson met with a group of congressional district chairs, soliciting local Democrats' views on the issues, and what his campaign would need to do in each district.[11] Then, on August 27 he appeared before the convention's Platform Committee. He was obviously mindful of the fact that Williams's and Hare's endorsement of con-con represented the views of many Democrats, but also that Gus Scholle's opposition represented the views of those who had supported him in the primary. Swainson asked that the committee endorse a resolution favoring constitutional reform, but remaining neutral on con-con. The committee complied.

Afterward, Swainson held a news conference, telling the press that "he personally would urge citizens to vote against a constitutional convention . . . however, he would not campaign actively against it." Responding to a question, Swainson said the campaign's main issue would be "revision of the tax structure" and his first priority was to defeat the ballot proposal to increase the sales tax. Beyond that, he had no specific proposal for new taxes. However, he added, "I'm on record for the income tax concept. We need a continuing source of revenue for a growing state."[12]

On August 27, some 3,000 delegates cheered and marched up and down the aisles of the Grand Rapids Civic Center as Mennen Williams bade them good-bye and introduced John Swainson as their new leader. All incumbent Democratic state officials were renominated without opposition, including Hare. The convention adopted all of Swainson's preferred platform planks without serious dissent.

Now he had a reasonably united party. But he still had to blend his band of "dedicated amateurs" with the seasoned veterans of Mennen Williams's campaigns, while minimizing hurt feelings. To Joe Collins, the challenge was that

the Williams people were together for six elections. And the day we started to get organized [for the general election], Sid Woolner [Williams's state campaign coordinator] did the same job he had been doing for five years. And Helen Berthelot did the same job she had been doing for twelve years, probably behind the same desk. In their minds, probably with some justification, that was the only way you ran a campaign. But in the general election one of the big differences [with Williams's campaigns] was that John had no preexisting organization. He knew people, because he had been every place, but he did not have an organizational structure. And so it was a lot of time on the road. Helen, as an example, her visualization of running a campaign was to sit at that desk with a telephone so that you could coordinate everybody's efforts. So the fact that I was on the road all the time, she thought that was crazy. But she did not realize that John wanted a network of people who were his people.[13]

Berthelot, who had served as Williams's campaign manager in several successful elections, became the Democratic Party's overall campaign coordinator. Her perspective on things differed from Collins's: "The only hard part was overcoming the suspicion of some of John Swainson's staff. Joe Collins . . . was an astute politician, but he didn't have much experience in campaigns at this level. Joe was friendly, and I had no problems with him—except that he believed he could be of more help to John in the field. Joe never spent any time in the office after 6:00 P.M., so his staff left also. Several times I tried to explain to him that many of the worst emergencies arose in the early evening. He was quite content to let me handle them."[14]

The Michigan Democratic campaign formally kicked off on Labor Day, Monday, September 5. Following a tradition begun in 1948, the party's presidential candidate was to appear in Detroit's Cadillac Square, joined by local candidates. Polls indicated that Michigan's twenty electoral votes were up for grabs, and John F. Kennedy needed them.

John Swainson had not attended the Democratic National Convention in Los Angeles, at which Kennedy had won the nomination, but he and Kennedy had met before, briefly, in 1959, when Kennedy had addressed Michigan Democrats at the Jefferson-Jackson Day dinner, the major annual fund-raising event.

On Labor Day Kennedy delivered his speech to an excited crowd of 60,000. Then he and his staff repaired to the presidential suite at the downtown Book Cadillac Hotel. Both Kennedy and Swainson needed to build rest periods into their campaign schedules, and this was Kennedy's down time. Swainson joined the crowd of people milling around the hospitality section of the suite. It was a warm day, and all the bodies made it even warmer in the suite.

Kennedy was in the master bedroom. Upon learning that Swainson had arrived, he called out, "Come on in, John." Grateful to get out of the overheated hospitality room, Swainson entered the bedroom. Kennedy, who changed his clothes several times a day, was fresh from a bath, sitting nude under a sheet on the bed, sipping from a bottle of beer, awaiting a steak he had just ordered.

The two of them chatted, Swainson said, "as any two persons would chat about finding themselves in the same sort of occupation, which is gaining votes."[15]

On this Labor Day Kennedy and Swainson were to spend the entire day together, traveling in a motorcade to speak at the State Fairgrounds, Pontiac, Flint, and Muskegon, and beginning a mutual admiration that lasted until Kennedy's death. Swainson was to form

> an identification with him, much more so than a political identification. I felt almost like I would toward an older brother . . . I felt a camaraderie . . . there was an understanding. You're talking to a person who has the same background of having been in the service, having been in the legislative body, having done the same things you've done. You don't have to draw large discussions and identifications or anything, you know what [each other were] talking about. . . . There was an identity.[16]

Kennedy and Swainson did, indeed, share some important characteristics, which each of them would have recognized. First was their relative youth, and the almost unprecedented political success each had achieved at their respective ages (Kennedy, at forty-three, became the youngest person to be elected president). But it went much further. Each knew the pain of wartime battle wounds, and each of them made light of them, when he referred to them at all. Each had disciplined himself to overcome physical infirmities.

Both men were highly intelligent, and each spoke in a dignified, highly articulate manner. Each displayed a self-deprecating wit. Both were pioneers of a new generation in politics, with a new style that seamlessly integrated dignity and humor. And both had an eye for the ladies.

It would be easy to assume that Swainson was merely deluding himself that Kennedy (whose dazzling charm was his greatest asset) reciprocated his admiration. But as we shall see, Kennedy's affection for Swainson was real.

Kennedy was to make two more campaign swings through Michigan, on October 13–14 and October 26. On the latter occasion Kennedy and Swainson rode side by side in a convertible past cheering crowds, "looking as youthful and happy as two college football stars coming home from the big game."[17] Between campaign stops in Hamtramck, Mt. Clemens, Roseville, and the State Fair Coliseum, the two candidates spent eight hours together, much of it in private conversation. This intimacy was not forced upon Kennedy, who was well known in his circle for ruthlessly jettisoning boring companions, no matter their political importance.

Swainson's Labor Day appearances with Kennedy undoubtedly helped the younger man by exposing his winning personality to the thousands who came out to see the presidential candidate. But these appearances were part of the state and national parties' campaigns, not Swainson's. He did not launch his own campaign until September 8, when he and Mennen Williams addressed 350 Democrats at a rally at the new junior high school in Plymouth. The rally was nearly an hour late in getting started, because of glitches in a television taping by all the statewide Democratic candidates.[18]

Swainson and his newly-put-together team had not tackled a campaign of this magnitude before, and he—and they—had to go through a shakedown period (it probably would have helped if they had started earlier). Inevitably, he—and they—suffered comparisons with the experienced Williams and his equally experienced campaign staff.

A week after the campaign kickoff the Detroit *Free Press's* Robert Boyd reported that Swainson was "driving hard, putting himself through exhausting 14-to-16-hour days, making speeches, shaking hands, and bucking up party workers around the state." But Boyd also observed that in spite of Swainson's own hard work, the campaign was "still in low gear" and "his campaign machinery [was] new and still sputtering. In some places it suffers from the bruising primary battle against Secretary of State James Hare."

Swainson's days were indeed long. On Wednesday, September 14 the *Free Press* reported that he began the day by addressing a breakfast meeting of young Democratic business and professional people in Grand Rapids, then shook the hands of workers at union halls and factory gates in Owosso, and "ended a 15-hour day of campaigning with an appearance at the Saginaw County Fair."[19] The next day, in what the *Free Press* called "a grueling, 17-hour day of campaigning," he began before dawn at the gates of the Saginaw Gray Iron Foundry, shaking hands with as many of the 3,000 arriving workers as he could. He then spoke at a local high school, opened the local Democratic headquarters, toured several other enterprises, and addressed a luncheon meeting of the Saginaw Optimists Club, before making the 150-mile drive to Niles, where he ended around ten o'clock at night. On Friday, September 16 he began with a 9:00 A.M. breakfast in Dowagiac, spoke to a truckers' convention in Traverse City at noon, taped an interview at a Detroit television station at 5:30, spoke at an 8:00 P.M. Detroit meeting of the Wayne County Polish Clubs, and finished the day with a 10:00 P.M. appearance at the Fall Festival Dance of Local 681 of the Dearborn Federation of Teachers.[20] The next day, a Saturday, he took the morning off, then attended scheduled events at 11:30 A.M., 2:00 P.M., 6:30 P.M. and 10:30 P.M.[21]

Swainson had little choice but to put in these horrifically exhausting days. It was expected that a campaigner would run hard, and failure to do so would have been noticed; it was as though extreme physical and mental stamina (or self-discipline) had become part of the standard for high public office. His opponent had no choice, either.[22]

But Swainson had to meet an additional expectation. Mennen Williams had been the supercampaigner, shaking every hand in sight, calling square dances, doing the polka, giving as many as thirty speeches a day. Very few human beings could match that level of energy. And Swainson's disability, though he never mentioned it and did his best to conceal it, imposed its own limitations.

His friend and law partner Allen Zemmol said about these limitations:

> Although John appeared to get around very well, he really did need help from people. I remember when he was campaigning, whenever I was with him, I made whoever did the scheduling give him at least two hours to be off his feet and lay down. Because, while he looked like he could do extremely well, and did, it took its toll. I mean, I saw those stumps that looked like hamburger from being rubbed raw.[23]

Joe Collins, who managed the campaign and traveled with Swainson, recalled:

> John might have 14 engagements on the average day. At night he would go into the hotel room and right into the bathroom, take his legs off and go into the hot, hot bath with salts because he would have not only swelling but abscesses on his stumps. Sometimes those abscesses would have to be [lanced] just to get them to empty out. He would do that himself, and he would do it day after day. . . . And never any complaints.[24]

The candidates readily agreed to a series of debates, or joint appearances. Each had something to gain. Bagwell's people believed that he was the more polished debater and his maturity would contrast well with Swainson's youthful appearance. Swainson's supporters had no doubt that he had much the more dynamic personality and demonstrably greater knowledge of the issues facing government.

Their first face-to-face confrontation took place September 20 in Lansing and was televised. Each made a thirty-minute speech, and then responded to questions from a moderator. The *Detroit News* described it as "a mild debate, gentlemanly throughout." Predictably, Swainson argued that Michigan's unemployment rate was caused by a "stagnating national economy," while Bagwell blamed "irresponsible political leadership in the governor's office and the domination of labor bosses."[25]

Swainson outlined an eight-point economic development program that included expanded port development, a commission to study automation, and a state-local loan program to help finance industrial expansion. Bagwell proposed to send a task force of leaders to recruit manufacturing plants from other states. Swainson responded, "I resent it when Tennessee sends a raiding party to Michigan and I don't think we should do the same."

Bagwell's only harsh attack was aimed at the AFL-CIO. He quoted a union pamphlet that claimed that "the people voting against you are the bankers, the merchants, the car dealers, the big industries, the utilities—all of the fat cats who make money whether you have a job or not." Such language would be understandable, Bagwell said, if it came from Soviet leader Nikita Khrushchev, "but it is not understandable coming from an organization which has taken over a political party to achieve the social goals it can't get at the bargaining table, even by the threat of a strike."[26]

William Milliken, who would later serve fourteen years as Michigan's governor, was then a young Republican state senator. He recalled:

> I was there and Bagwell was a good debater. He kept referring to John Swainson as "Johnny," and I kept wishing he would refrain from doing that. Finally, after one more such reference, while making his last point, Swainson pointed his finger at Bagwell and referred to Bagwell as "Paully," and it brought the house down. I think it was the *coup de grâce*. He won the debate on that point alone.[27]

Bagwell and Swainson were to make five more joint appearances, three of them televised. By most accounts the only one that produced more than polite restatements of positions was their last, on October 27, at the Detroit studio of WWJ-TV. After Swainson repeated his standard line about supporting "total tax revision" but opposing both a sales tax increase and an income tax, Bagwell said, "He has given no answer at all. The state is deep in debt. The treasury is empty. My opponent is still ducking what he stands for." In response to a question, Bagwell repeated that he favored the one-cent sales tax increase, but if the voters rejected it, he would reluctantly recommend a flat-rate income tax; "As much as I would dislike to do so, I would be forced to do this to save the State from financial chaos." Later, he added, "I don't know what kind of a secret tax Johnny proposes."[28]

Bagwell's new aggressiveness was probably in response to the publication, three days earlier, of a poll commissioned by the *Detroit News,* showing that Swainson had increased his lead over Bagwell to eleven percentage points (54.4 percent—43.4 percent) with less than two weeks remaining before the election. Swainson was even running ahead of John Kennedy in Michigan.[29]

The joint appearances provided the electorate with little enlightenment, and not even much entertainment.

But the fact is that there was little about which the two candidates could debate. Aside from con-con and the sales tax increase, there were few substantive issues between them. Bagwell, who was a moderate to begin with, went out of his way to court union members (exemplified by his opposing the enactment of "right-to-work" laws that would prohibit collection of union dues from workers who did not join the union). Swainson, for his part, went out of *his* way to show that he was not the antibusiness, union drone that the Republicans depicted, often mentioning that he supported reduction of local taxes on machinery and inventory, and a shift to business taxation based on ability to pay (though he gave no specifics).

While disagreeing on the proposed sales tax increase, both Swainson and Bagwell favored "total tax revision," with a state income tax as a last resort.[30]

Bagwell dwelt on Michigan's economy, referring to a list of forty companies that had left Michigan, and a loss of over 80,000 manufacturing jobs in the past decade. He argued that this decline was the result of business-hostile state policies dictated by the unions.[31] Swainson brushed this aside as a "smear" on Michigan's reputation, which itself was hurting the business climate.[32]

In a nutshell, Bagwell wanted the election to be a referendum on the Michigan economic climate and the Williams administration's twelve years of deadlock with the legislature. Swainson wanted the election to be a personality contest.

Election day, Tuesday November 8, dawned cloudy in most of the state. Occasional light rain was expected, mixed with scattered snow in western areas. This was not bad weather for Michigan in early November, and it dampened voter turnout not at all. The people came out in unprecedented numbers, drawn by a presidential election that was expected to be very close.

In fact, the election set a record never since matched in Michigan: 72.7 percent of the voting age population went to the polls, a total of 3,381,097.[33]

Swainson campaigned at factory gates in the morning, then went to his home precinct in Plymouth to vote. He and the family had dinner privately at home.

Then, leaving two-year-old Kristina with a babysitter, John and Alice Swainson took the two boys with them to the Swainson election night headquarters at the Henrose Hotel in downtown Detroit. Bagwell, his family, friends, and supporters would spend the evening at the Jack Tar Hotel, across the street from the Capitol building in Lansing.

After the 8:00 P.M. closing of the polls, the results began to trickle in, then cascaded in a series of large and small data lumps from Michigan's mix of cities, small towns, and farm areas. It soon became apparent that things had changed since the opinion polls were taken; this was going to be a very close election.

At 2:30 A.M. Bagwell's vote-watchers reported that projections showed him carrying 33 percent of the Wayne County vote and 58 percent of the outstate vote. It looked like a winning combination, prompting Bagwell to exclaim, "We're in like Flynn!"[34] At roughly the same hour Swainson was getting similar news from the staff at state Democratic headquarters, based on the television news reports. He believed he was going to lose.

At that moment Helen Berthelot returned from the Wayne County clerk's office, where she had been granted special access to get the latest returns as they came in. Overhearing the staff member, Ed Winge, giving Swainson the bad news, she grabbed the phone. "John," she said:

> I don't know where Ed got his report, but it is way off. I just came back from the County Building. We are winning heavily enough in Wayne County to go over the margin we need to overcome the outstate vote. . . . The TV reports are behind. The County Building can't have given them the latest figures yet. When I left we were way ahead, and some of the downriver reports were not in, and Hamtramck was not in either [these were heavily Democratic areas]. Go to bed and get some sleep. You will have to make a victory statement in the morning.[35]

Swainson, tired but buoyed by the news, stayed up a while longer in hopes that Bagwell would make a concession statement. None was forthcoming, so at 3:00 A.M. he went to bed.

In Lansing Bagwell was still up. At 5:30 A.M. state Republican chairman Lawrence Lindemer told him, "We are completely confused by the reports we are receiving." Various sources now were showing Swainson leading Bagwell by 53,000, 63,000, and 108,000 votes, but nobody knew if they included the Hamtramck vote. Turning to the reporters, Bagwell said, "I can't make a statement at this time. I am going to sit up all day and all night if necessary."[36]

Bagwell's suite was still crowded with friends and supporters at 6:40 A.M.

when he was given further vote totals, which showed that he had lost. Finally, he issued his concession. "Lt. Governor Swainson has clearly won the race for governor," he said, adding, "I have stated repeatedly I would never run again for governor. I have had enough experience running second."

In fact Swainson's final victory margin was tiny. He received 1,643,634 votes to Bagwell's 1,602,022, or 50.64 percent of the total votes for both candidates.[37] Swainson finished behind James Hare, John Kennedy, and Senator Pat McNamara.[38]

The next morning, Alice Swainson, a Michigan State Police bodyguard, and Margaret Halava (Mennen Williams's appointments secretary and a friend of the Swainsons) gathered in the living room of the candidate's suite. Presently the bedroom door opened and a short figure emerged, wearing an equally short bathrobe. John Swainson, walking on his stumps, smiled and said, "Good morning. OK, so I won. Now what do I do?"[39]

CHAPTER EIGHT

Governor, Year One: Stumbles

LATTIE COOR WOULD LONG REMEMBER THE NIGHT HE ARRIVED IN MICHIGAN. COOR was just twenty-four, a graduate student at Washington University in St. Louis, Missouri. He had begun work on a research project, assisting three professors who were comparing the relationship between public schools and politics in three states. Coor was assigned to gather data on Michigan, but he was having difficulty getting state officials to return his calls, so he decided to pay a visit to the state capital.

He arrived on a cold night in late January 1961. After checking in at the Jack Tar Hotel in downtown Lansing, he saw the gleaming white Capitol dome, illuminated by flood lamps, just across the street. With nothing else to do, he decided to walk over for a closer look.

He found an entrance and walked into the building. Following direction signs, he climbed the stairs to the Senate chamber. He gained admittance through unlocked doors, but the Senate itself was empty. He crossed to the opposite wing of the building and looked in on the House chamber. It, too, was empty.

Returning to the central rotunda of the vast building, he figured he might as well have a look at the governor's office, or as close as he could get. To his surprise, the outer door was also unlocked, so he walked in.

A quarter-century later, Coor remembered it vividly: "Again, I saw no one, so I went further inside. Then, I saw: sitting behind a huge desk with two secretaries standing next to him, was this kid."

"I barged in. He said hello and asked what I was doing in town. So I told him. I described the project and my role in it."

At some point early in their conversation, Coor realized two things: this kid was the governor of Michigan, and they were hitting it off. Then John Swainson said, "I could use somebody like that on my staff. Come back tomorrow." Coor heard himself say, "I'll work for you for free."

The next day, wondering if he had been dreaming, Coor returned to the governor's office. He was hired as an assistant to the governor, without compensation, and was given an office in the basement. Within days he was writing a draft of Swainson's upcoming speech to be delivered at the February Democratic state convention.[1]

Swainson was in no position to turn down a competent volunteer. The penurious legislature had appropriated money for only two political appointees in the Governor's Executive Office: an executive secretary (the position is today known as "chief of staff") and press secretary, each to be paid $13,000. These were called "unclassified" positions, in contrast with most government jobs, which were filled by competitive civil service examinations in the "classified" service. Everything else—and everyone else—had to be paid out of the $154,000 the legislature had appropriated for "other salaries, contractual services, supplies . . ."

This was a legacy of Mennen Williams's long-running battle with the legislature. Williams, knowing he would have to give up funding of important programs to get funding of adequate staff, had decided instead to hire the people he wanted as private employees and pay them out of his own considerable fortune (Swainson, lacking Williams's personal resources, would eventually use the proceeds from a large fund-raising dinner to supplement his staff).[2]

In fact, Swainson used a time-honored executive branch maneuver to pay his first announced appointee. Following his election in November he announced that forty-four-year-old Robert Derengoski, who had come to Lansing to serve as an assistant attorney general, would become his legal advisor, but would remain on the attorney general's payroll.

He hired forty-two-year-old Margaret Halava as his personal secretary. She had served as Mennen Williams's appointments secretary, and was a close friend of the Swainsons.

In December he hired Mitch Tendler, thirty-five, as his executive secretary and Thaddeus "Ted" Ogar, forty-three, as his press secretary. Tendler, a former high school English teacher, was a longtime Swainson supporter and had served in the Williams administration as deputy state racing commissioner. Ogar had been editor of the Michigan AFL-CIO News for over a decade.

Swainson created a new position for Jordan Popkin, a thirty-three-year-old Massachusetts native who had come to Michigan to work in hospital budgeting and ended up working for Mennen Williams. Popkin and Swainson had shared a Lansing house during the week for the past two years.[3]

Neil Staebler had decided that the time had come to move on after ten successful years guiding the Michigan Democratic Party. Tradition held that a sitting governor had the right to name the party's chairman. Swainson floated the name of Al Meyers, the brilliant but abrasive chairman of the 17th Congressional District organization.

The reaction of party activists was immediate and negative. As Joe Collins put it, Meyers

> had the brains to be state chairman and he was a hard worker. But he was abrasive and he could not tolerate people he felt were less intelligent than he was.
>
> The minute the press put that out, it was like the flag going up the pole. You either shoot or salute. Well, there were more shooters than saluters and the phones were ringing every place. People were saying this would be awful for John. So . . . John had a meeting with Al and told him "Al, this just won't float. I'm getting criticism from everybody, which I don't need getting started here."

Swainson asked Collins to come to a meeting at his house on a Saturday morning at ten. When Collins arrived,

> Gus Scholle, Roy Reuther and a couple of others were there, and a couple of people from John's office. Gus took the leadership, actually. Obviously, they had all gotten there at nine o'clock and talked this all through. They said, "John's got a problem to replace Al as the state chairman." This would have been January or February of 1961. The convention was [to be] in March of '61.
>
> The issue really was, who knows the Swainson people around the state? The staff was very small. And I had done all the traveling. And so, would I consider being the state chairman?

Collins accepted.[4]

Since 1945 the state of Michigan had provided a "summer residence" for use of the governor on Mackinac Island in the strait between Michigan's Upper and Lower Peninsulas. But when it came to a year-round home, the state's first family was on its own. In January the Swainsons took a two-year lease on a home at 4305 Appletree Lane in the Lansing suburb of Delta Township and moved the family in, renting out the Plymouth house.[5]

While the world of politics might not have been her first choice, Alice worked hard to be a supportive political wife. When John was running for governor, she gamely sat for interviews. When she was Michigan's First Lady, she gave well-prepared speeches and kept herself informed on the issues.

As a friend, Vicky Seide, put it, "She did what she had to do and did it well."[6]

An accomplished musician and painter, Alice Swainson was most comfortable in the arts. When the Swainsons entertained friends, she would sometimes bring out her guitar and play popular folksongs.

As he prepared to take office following the election, John Swainson faced a peculiar fiscal matrix, with opportunities for both success and instability.

The voters had approved the constitutional amendment to allow the legislature to increase the state sales tax from 3 percent to 4 percent, by a vote of 1,241,558 to 1,216,504. As puzzled as anyone else by the results of the election, Swainson reflected, "I campaigned against the sales tax increase and a constitutional convention and yet they elected me and approved both issues. It is hard to know what to think."[7]

The voters had also returned a fifty-six to fifty-four Republican majority to the State House of Representatives, to go along with the twenty-two to twelve Republican majority in the State Senate.

In 1960, following their long stalemate with Governor Williams and the payless state paydays, the legislature had finally enacted a series of temporary excise tax increases on beer, liquor, cigarettes telephone charges, and hotel room charges (collectively known as "nuisance taxes"). They provided $55 million a year in desperately needed revenue, but they were due to expire June 30, 1961.

Swainson and his backers had opposed both the nuisance taxes and a sales tax increase, partly because they viewed both taxes as regressive—falling mainly upon those with the least ability to pay—but also because neither sales nor excise taxes provided any assistance to cities. All of the revenues went directly to the state government. Any state financial assistance to cities remained at the discretion of the legislature; given continuing rural dominance of the upper house, any such aid was likely to be sporadic and grudging.

During the campaign Swainson had made it plain that he favored replacing Michigan's jury-rigged tax structure with a system based on ability to pay for both individuals and businesses. Although he had never expressly described this as an "income tax" (the closest he came was using the phrase "income tax concept"), everyone knew what a tax based on ability to pay meant.

On November 19, the governor-elect went into a bit more detail, describing his favored tax principles. It was not a detailed plan, but an outline.

He reluctantly accepted the verdict of the voters who had chosen to raise the sales tax: "On election day the people of Michigan indicated their acceptance of this form of tax increase and . . . it is my clear responsibility to recommend to the legislature speedy implementation." The sales tax, however, would "not solve the problems of local units of government [cities and counties] nor . . . meet the problems of Michigan business."

Therefore, as governor he planned to propose exemption or reduction of local personal property taxes (of which businesses paid $200–$250 million a year to local governments,[8] substituting an "equitable" state tax, and returning the lost revenue to local governments. He further proposed to enact new state taxes to supply more revenue to local governments which were increasingly "hard-pressed by rising demands for services."[9]

He also proposed to give local governments express authority to levy new forms of taxation besides the property tax.

Following his announcement, Swainson took Alice and the children to Florida for a badly needed ten-day vacation.

Upon their return, Swainson's staff set up a series of meetings with Michigan leaders of business, government, and labor. Swainson discussed the state's fiscal and economic problems with Henry Ford II, Detroit mayor Louis Miriani, L. L. "Tex" Colbert of the Chrysler Corporation, Robert McNamara, the new president of Ford Motor Company (who was about to be drafted by President Kennedy as secretary of defense), state revenue commissioner Clarence Lock, John Gordon, president of General Motors, George Romney, president of American Motors (and leader of Citizens for Michigan), Gus Scholle, and Leonard Woodcock, vice president of the UAW.[10]

He was hoping to develop a consensus around a tax reform package that would fit the description he had announced before his departure for Florida, a description that had been left purposely vague. He was also hoping to translate the good personal relations he had with many of the senior legislators into an effective working relationship, a relationship that had eluded Mennen Williams.

However, there was the little matter of the sales tax amendment.

It is rare that any electorate votes to authorize increasing its own tax burden, but Michigan voters had done just that. State politicians of both parties recognized that the government badly needed the estimated $120,000,000 in new revenue that a one-cent sales tax increase would produce. The 1960 fiscal year, only half over, was projected to create a $64 million deficit by July, according to Senate Republican leader Frank Beadle.[11]

Even though both Williams and Swainson had opposed the amendment—with its implied rejection of a state income tax—they recognized there was nothing to gain by defying the expressed will of the people. With the support of Swainson and leaders of both parties in both houses, Williams called a special session of the outgoing legislature for early December, to consider a one-cent sales tax increase.

On December 7 both houses passed a one-cent increase in the state sales tax, to take effect January 1, by overwhelming margins. Williams signed it immediately.

The sales tax increase would complicate Swainson's professed task of seeking comprehensive tax reform. It both removed the fiscal pressure on the legislature to increase revenues and solidified the Republicans' opposition to an income tax. It did not, however, deflect Swainson's intent to remold Michigan's fiscal structure.

On February 1 he presented his special message on fiscal reform to the legislature. For the first time, he spelled out specific proposals. The major features were these:

- Repeal of the Business Activities Tax (Michigan's main business tax), regarded by the business community as particularly onerous because it did not distinguish between large profits and small or no profits.
- Exemption of food and drugs from the 4 percent sales tax, which fell disproportionately upon lower income individuals.
- A 3 percent income tax on individuals and corporations.
- Express authority for cities to levy an income tax of up to 1 percent.

Swainson's hopes were high. He believed that he had developed a decent working relationship with the business leaders, and that they were not averse to his tax reform package, which was more favorable to business than Williams's proposals had been. When he spoke to the Detroit Economic Club in March, he was well received. He believed that this would help him with the Republicans in the legislature.

The new governor was also doing his best to build on his good relations with legislators of both parties; he knew most of them well from his days as a state senator, and most of them liked him personally. He kept up these contacts, lunching with Republican legislators at the Lansing Press Club, and giving them free access if they needed a meeting. In March Detroit Free Press political writer Ray Courage gushed, "This has been the longest political honeymoon between a Democratic Governor and a Republican Legislature that anyone can remember. And if it lasts for the remaining 645 days of Swainson's term, he won't have any trouble getting re-elected."[12]

It all appeared to be working when the legislature enacted a Swainson proposal to put a constitutional amendment on the ballot to establish a Greater Michigan Authority to use the state's credit to help finance local industrial development.

And then it all fell apart. In a matter of three months Swainson alienated both Democratic and moderate Republican legislators, and his entire 1961 legislative program went down to defeat.

It began with money—taxes and the budget. The law required that a state budget be enacted by May. Swainson and his party had consistently supported spending increases to keep up with the state's burgeoning education needs. Demands on the state's colleges and universities were exploding as the number of young people graduating from high school and seeking further education ballooned. The state college enrollment in September 1961 was projected to grow by 7,000 over the previous year, and the college presidents were asking for a $20 million increase just to serve new students. The state also needed an infusion of at least $7 million to continue construction on several half-completed buildings, and Republicans were unalterably opposed to borrowing to complete them, a possibility Swainson had suggested. There was insufficient time to attempt passage of the complex tax reforms that Swainson had proposed, and no legislative support whatever for additional temporary taxes.[13]

That left the politicians with only one possible way out—extend the nuisance taxes that were due to expire June 30.

This was politically risky for legislators of both parties, the Democrats because their party had officially opposed the temporary nuisance taxes from the start, and the Republicans because they had pushed the new taxes through on the promise that if the people voted to authorize the one-cent sales tax increase, the nuisance taxes would be allowed to expire.

But on April 5 seven moderate Republican senators stuck their necks out and introduced a bill to extend the life of the nuisance taxes. By April 14 they were joined by a group of moderate Senate Democrats.[14] Together, the two groups appeared to have enough votes to get an extension of the nuisance taxes passed by the Senate. If the extension passed the House as well, then the governor would come under enormous pressure from the state's educators to sign it.

John Swainson made his decision. On the evening of April 14, after the newly allied Senate Republican and Democratic moderates had finished a celebratory dinner together, the governor summoned the Democratic senators to his office. He told them he would not support the extension, and he pulled them out of the coalition.[15]

The Republican moderates, who had risked their own careers to support the extension, were enraged. "We were taken for suckers," charged one of them, John Stahlin of Belding.[16]

The damage wasn't over. On the morning of April 19 a delegation of educators, led by Superintendent of Public Instruction Lynn Bartlett, met with Swainson. Every major education organization in the state was represented. The educators' priority was not the state's tax structure; their priority was finding enough money to service the growing student body, and there was now only one way to do that. One by one, they gave Swainson their arguments and their predictions on what would happen without new revenues.

The governor emerged from the meeting and executed a 180-degree political turn, saying that he "would give thoughtful consideration to any proposals to extend the nuisance taxes, . . . providing that the governor's minimum appropriation recommendations are realized." He appeared to believe that this pronouncement would part the curtains for the reemergence of the coalition of Senate Republican moderates and Democrats. But the coalition was a broken egg; it could not be reassembled.

John Fitzgerald of Grand Ledge, one of the Republican moderates in the Senate who had attempted to work with Democrats to extend the nuisance taxes, put it succinctly: "The Governor's realization that something needs to be done came one week too late."[17]

In fact, Swainson's pulling the Democrats out of the budding coalition had not only angered the moderate Republicans, it had thrown them back into the arms of their conservative brethren for the remainder of the session. They would not extend the nuisance taxes or vote for appropriations anywhere near the figures Swainson had requested. His budget requests would be dead on arrival, and the state's education and mental health systems would be underfunded as a result.

But Swainson's turnabout on nuisance tax extension also hurt him with his own party's legislators. He had yanked them out of their newborn alliance with moderate Republicans, which angered the Republicans and made it harder for the minority Democrats to get anything at all from the majority. And then he had changed his mind, after the damage to them was done. They would not forget it.

The next stumble occurred over what came to be known as "the Milk Bill."

The introduction of waxed paper milk cartons in the 1950s had coincided with the rapid rise of supermarkets to disrupt the economics of the milk industry, in which "milkmen" delivered milk house-to-house in glass bottles. Many in the traditional dairy industry complained that the supermarkets were using milk as a "loss leader," pricing it at or below cost in order to attract shoppers into the stores. The United Dairy Workers Union, seeing its members' livelihoods at risk, allied itself with management in pushing for legislation that would effectively fix the retail price of milk at cost plus eight cents per gallon, to be enforced by a new state bureaucracy.

Democrats and Republicans joined to sponsor the bill. Swainson's aides described it as "similar to one the Governor sponsored."[18] It passed both houses by large margins and was sent to the governor.[19] But consumer groups raised an outcry, and on May 12 the House took the unusual step of recalling the bill, taking it off the governor's desk and sending it back to committee. Swainson seemed to agree with the recall, saying, "This bill, I believe, was an attempt to rectify some trade practices, but it probably went too far."[20]

But the Dairy Workers Union pressured House Democrats to reconsider, and in June they supported repassage of the bill; it was brought back, and again passed and sent to the governor's desk. On June 13 Swainson lunched with representatives of farm groups. They later reported that the governor had discussed how the provisions of the bill would work "when the bill became law."[21] Since the bill had passed both houses of the legislature, the only remaining step necessary for it to become law was the governor's signature, so this seemed tantamount to a promise to sign it into law.

Michigan Farm Bureau lobbyist Stan Powell confirmed that Swainson "repeatedly made comments which seemed to imply that that there was no question but that the bill would receive his approval and become law."[22]

The next day the governor vetoed the Milk Bill, leaving several Democratic legislators "flabbergasted," according to the Detroit Free Press. Outraged Dairy Workers Union leaders hung black crepe over the entrance to their Detroit headquarters.[23]

Even before the nuisance tax and Milk Bill mishaps, there were signs that Republicans in the legislature were not going to let their personal affections for the new governor deflect them from challenging him. One of the earliest such signs was an unemployment compensation reform bill that the House Labor Committee sent to the full House at the end of March.

In 1959 the Michigan Supreme Court had decided Park v. Employment Security Commission,[24] which came to be known as the "Ford-Canton" decision. The UAW had initiated a local strike at a Ford forgings plant in Canton, Ohio. When the parts manufactured in Canton ceased to arrive at Ford assembly plants in Michigan, the assembly plants had to cease operations, and their employees were laid off.

The employees applied for unemployment compensation, asserting that they were indisputably unemployed, and that their unemployment was not the result of any labor dispute between them and the company. The company disagreed, pointing out that the statute prohibited benefits to workers who were laid off because of "the existence of a labor dispute in the establishment in which he [the employee] is or was last employed." The company argued that the Ohio forging plant and the Michigan assembly plants were part of one "establishment."

A majority of the Supreme Court ruled that the employees were entitled to benefits. This set off a firestorm among Michigan manufacturers, who feared that the UAW and other industrial unions could use the employers' money—instead of the union strike fund—to pay workers idled by the union's own decision to strike. Millions of dollars were at stake, as was the balance of power between labor and management.

The Republicans had introduced bills to repeal the Ford-Canton decision in 1959. The bills had easily passed the Senate, but had been stopped in the House.[25]

Now, in 1961, the Republicans had a one-vote margin in the House, and they decided to use it to try again for repeal. They sweetened the bill a bit by raising the annual amount of wages on which employers would be required to pay compensation, but this did not lessen the opposition of the Democrats. The issue of overruling the Ford-Canton decision was a partisan litmus test. Virtually all Republicans supported it, and virtually all Democrats opposed it.

From the moment the bill was reported out of committee, Democratic leaders in the legislature publicly urged Swainson to veto it if it passed. Yet he was strangely silent. He was well aware that a veto of the bill would disappoint the business community, and he needed their support for his tax reform program, so he allowed them to believe that he was considering signing the bill. He even granted a request for a personal meeting with business leaders, who did their best to persuade him to sign. Then, as the legal deadline approached by which the governor had to either sign or veto a bill, he vetoed it on June 6, 1961.

Business groups did not hold back in expressing their anger. Michigan Chamber of Commerce vice president Harry Hall said, "Gov. Swainson has vetoed the hopes of thousands of employers who had expected him to place the public interest ahead of petty partisanship involving a political debt to union leadership."[26] Michigan Retailers Association vice president Richard Cook said, "We are bitterly disappointed in the governor, and fear for the future of our state under obviously dominated leadership."[27]

Swainson's handling of the unemployment compensation bill veto destroyed most of the goodwill he had gone out of his way to establish with the business community. He never got it back.

By the end of his first year in office, Governor Swainson had vetoed seventeen bills passed by the legislature. *Detroit Free Press* political writer Ray Courage wrote that Swainson was

> disillusioned by Michigan's big business leaders when—after lengthy pre-inaugural sessions with them—they failed to rally in support of his tax reform program. He was frustrated by the Republican-controlled Legislature which paid little heed to his attempts at cooperation and killed virtually everything in his legislative program.[28]

Lansing State Journal political columnist Willard Baird noted that the young governor had cut back his press conferences from an initial two a day to two a week, ending a practice begun by Governor Wilbur Brucker in 1931. To Baird, Swainson's first year as governor was "a disappointment to many of his Democratic friends."[29]

Some of Swainson's first-year problems were exacerbated by the inexperience and small size of his Executive Office staff. Swainson himself was aware that his office needed better management, and he contacted Joe Collins for suggestions. Collins, in turn, called Wayne County Democratic chair David Lebenbaum, who suggested they talk to a young Detroit attorney who had just ended a term on the state Liquor Control Commission: Zolton Ferency. Collins mentioned Ferency to Swainson, who "remembered Zolton positively, so he was open to the idea. Zolton came [to Lansing] and there was a luncheon. Then what was discussed was mainly not so much Zolton's background as what he saw in the job. And by the end of the lunch John was satisfied and Zolton was satisfied and that was it."

Ferency took over as executive secretary on April 21, 1961, and remained in that position for the rest of Swainson's term as governor. Collins's assessment was that "from every quarter he did an excellent job. If he had problems anyplace, it was with the other staff, because when Zolton said this was the way it was going to be, that was the way it was going to be. He was a strong manager. Nothing slipped through to John, which, quite frankly, John was looking for."[30]

Where Swainson could implement new policies without legislative concurrence, he acted. One of the few subjects on which he could have an impact was equal opportunity. Like Williams, Swainson strongly believed that people should not be denied the opportunity to fulfill their potential just because of their color. Consulting with the state Fair Employment Practices Commission, in May 1961 Swainson issued a Governor's Code of Fair Practices for the state government. It banned racial discrimination in recruitment, hiring, and promotion of state employees, and required all state agencies to cooperate fully with the FEPC. The Michigan Employment Security Commission, which referred job seekers to potential employers, was ordered to refuse discriminatory job offers.

The governor did not merely promulgate an order; he followed up. Seven months after issuing the code, Swainson called a meeting of all state agency heads, and quizzed them about their employment practices in the presence of the executive director of the U.S. Commission on Civil Rights, who noted that this was the first meeting of its kind in any state.[31] To further ensure that the state's hiring and promotions would be nondiscriminatory, Swainson appointed the first African American, Robert Greene, to the state Civil Service Commission in 1961.[32]

Swainson also backed aggressive action by the state Fair Employment Practices Commission. He fully supported the commission's extensive February 1961 investigation of employment practices in the State Highway Department, and publicly praised the independently elected highway commissioner, John C. Mackie, for speedily implementing the FEPC's recommendations.[33]

In April 1961, following allegations of widespread employment discrimination in Michigan's horse racing industry, Swainson asked the FEPC to investigate. The FEPC found that most jobs in the industry were filled by referrals from three unions, and most of those referred were friends or relatives of existing employees, the overwhelming majority of whom were Caucasians. In March 1962 the FEPC held a series of meetings with the State Racing Commission, the racetrack associations, affected unions, and concessionaires. This process resulted in a declaration of policy by all constituent groups and organizations in the racing industry that employment was to be open to all, regardless of race, and the constituents undertook to implement specified steps to implement the policy. These steps were implemented beginning with the 1962 racing season.[34]

In early 1961 President Kennedy had nominated Michigan Supreme Court justice Talbot Smith for lifetime appointment as a federal district judge. The nomination cleared the U.S. Senate, and Smith declared his intention to resign in October. This would create a vacancy on the Michigan Supreme Court, the first to be filled by Governor Swainson.

Swainson asked Michigan auditor general Otis Smith to ride with him on a trip to Grand Rapids (about sixty miles from Lansing).

Smith, an African American, had migrated from the South to Flint, graduated from Catholic University Law School in Washington, D.C., and had established a law practice, becoming involved in Democratic politics with the encouragement of Mennen Williams. Eventually, Williams had appointed Smith chairman of the state Public Service Commission, the body that regulated the rates of public utilities. In 1959 the elective office of state auditor general became vacant, and Williams appointed Smith. The following year Smith ran for the full term and won, becoming Michigan's first African American elected state official.

During their ride to Grand Rapids, Swainson asked Smith what he thought about the Supreme Court vacancy. Taking the question at face value, Smith named several Detroit area trial judges who he thought would do well on the Supreme Court. But the governor had an objection to each of Smith's proposed nominees, "Every one I'd name, he said, 'He's not well. He doesn't want it. He's got a problem.' I finally said, 'There must be somebody down there. They're electable. They have great credentials in Wayne County where you need the vote.' He said, 'How about you?'"

Smith asked for time to think over this unexpected offer. At thirty-nine years of age, he questioned whether he was seasoned enough to join the Supreme Court. But an old attorney mentor in Flint gruffly reassured him, "Well, Smith, you can't do any worse than some of those old guys up there already. You might as well try it." So Smith accepted, becoming the first African American justice on the Michigan Supreme Court.[35]

Swainson had never forgotten how alone and discouraged he had felt after the loss of his legs, or how the other amputees at Percy Jones Hospital had both challenged and inspired him to do the work necessary to recover and lead a normal life. Now he put the word out among his staff and friends: if you learn of anyone who has lost a limb recently, let me know—quietly.

His secretary, Margaret Halava, witnessed the result:

> He had access to knowledge when somebody in the state would lose a limb, if it was just a farm boy in a mowing accident. John would be notified, and we would work it into his schedule, and he would just show up at the hospital with no advance notice to the family, or the hospital or the public, especially to the press. It was never in his [official] schedule. He never wanted it advertised. He just wanted to go in and talk to the young man or young woman, or older man or whoever it was, and tell them about his experience and what can be done. And he would take his leg off and show them the prosthetic and explain to them that the advancement of the technology was happening so that they would be able to function just as well as he could. He would get up and put it on and then do a few little dance steps, to show them.
>
> Many times he would spot somebody in a crowd and he would send the state police over to find out about them and get some information, and later on he would show up at their home . . . and let them know that you, too, can get around. He never wanted that publicized. . . . He got letters for years afterwards from people, thanking him again for taking the time to share his experiences with them.[36]

Zolton Ferency recalled, "He would maybe read about someone in the newspapers or hear about it from the State Police. He always seemed to know when some kid fell under a train somewhere, and next thing you know he would be over there at the hospital talking to him. He never, never once, mentioned it in public."[37]

Swainson would continue these visits after he left the governor's office. In 1963 twenty-three-year-old Kevin Farley was sitting in a wheelchair at his home in the small town of Leslie, recovering from a freak electrical accident that had destroyed both of his legs, "feeling down and out and blue and discouraged and depressed and with no hope at all." A car pulled into the driveway, unannounced.

Farley recognized the man who had only recently vacated the governor's office, as he got out of the car, walked up and rang the doorbell. Swainson came in, expressed his sympathies, and showed Farley his artificial legs and his stumps. Then he said something that Farley never forgot: "You've got two ways to go, my friend. You can continue the way you are and society will take care of you. Or you can get up on artificial legs and make something of your life." Farley returned to active life, eventually becoming supervisor of the State Capitol's document room. Of Swainson, he said, "He laid it right on the line. It was the best thing that ever happened to me."[38]

Swainson also used the governor's chair to continue in his role as a one-man social services center, utilizing his detailed knowledge of government and his extensive personal network to help ordinary people with their problems. Lattie Coor saw this at first hand. "He would never turn away a phone call or a request," said Coor. "He kept a pocket full of notes that he had written, and which he would give us, to help people."

> He would say, '"Let's do something about this,' often with specific suggestions. He knew a lot of people and he knew who the players were in both public and private agencies. And he would suggest that you call a particular person.
>
> One afternoon during the winter I received a call from a family in Jackson, and they told me that their heat had been turned off. In fact, it was a collect call. Swainson walked in and asked what was going on. We told him. He said, "Call so-and-so at the Salvation Army," and had other detailed instructions, a complete plan to help this family.

Swainson's propensity to help anyone in need could, at times, cause problems. Always an early riser, he began showing up at the office before anyone else, including the switchboard operator. Occasionally, another early riser somewhere in Michigan would call the governor's office before it was officially open. Swainson would answer the phone. His secretary, Margaret Halava, would learn the result:

> He'd say, "The governor speaking." And he'd start talking to whoever was calling, whether it was a constituent with a problem—and listening to their problems, commenting on it, be very polite, and take copious notes and promise to look into it. Or—and this is where we trembled—"I will fix this."
>
> He did that on a couple of occasions and it created all kinds of problems

when he gave a firm answer that he would fix this. Well, the department or the area that it covered was so far out of being able to be fixed that it took a lot of commenting and explaining.

He said, "You can't stop me from answering the phone."

That left only one alternative, Margaret Halava recalled: "We finally changed our switchboard operator's schedule so she came in earlier."[39]

CHAPTER NINE

Governor, Year Two: Almost

THE GREAT MAJORITY OF SUCCESSFUL POLITICIANS RISE LOCALLY. THEY BEGIN AS mayors, school board members, state legislators, their achievements rippling through small ponds. Most never go further, but some impress their colleagues or regional party leaders enough that they advance, incrementally, to greater responsibilities. Only a few, through lucky timing, boldness, and shrewd understanding of the moment, manage to rise to the very top. But even so, they bring themselves to the attention of the public purely in the context of the public offices that they hold and seek. This was the story of John Swainson.

There is another, rarer, path: that of the star, the achiever who attains regional, national, or even international acclaim elsewhere, in a highly visible leadership role, then becomes "available" for elective office. Think U.S. Grant and Dwight Eisenhower. When the star is finally persuaded to run for office, there is an aura of near-inevitability.

George Romney was a star.

Born in 1907, Romney was president of American Motors Corporation (AMC), the successor to the Nash and Hudson automotive manufacturers. In the 1950s he had launched a major national advertising campaign for the company's new "compact" car, the Nash Rambler. The theme of the campaign was the gutsy underdog—AMC—taking on the Big Three U.S. auto companies and their "gas-guzzling dinosaurs."

Romney had decided that he himself would be the campaign's major spokesperson. Thus, many of the national newspaper and magazine ads featured photos of his square-jawed, rugged face and quoted his words.

The campaign succeeded brilliantly. By 1960 AMC held 7.5 percent of U.S. automobile sales, its highest share ever. And whether intentionally or otherwise, the campaign made Romney the best-known industrialist in America.

During World War II Romney's age and family status had exempted him from the draft, but he had played a major role in coordinating the U.S. auto industry to war production. He found that he enjoyed public service.

Romney's opponents, competitors and negotiating partners consistently underestimated him. He often came across to them as naive, but he was actually an optimist who believed that his unbending determination could overcome barriers that more experienced operatives considered insurmountable. And more often than not he ended up understanding everything he needed to understand.

However, Romney did have one seemingly rigid bias. He believed that industrial labor unions like the UAW exercised too much power within American industry, harming its efficiency and competitiveness. He was not shy about expressing this view and, as a result, many union leaders did not trust him, and a few despised him. Among the latter group was Gus Scholle.

By late 1956 Romney's name had become well known throughout the United States. When the president of the Detroit Board of Education asked him to accept the chairmanship of a citizens committee on the future of the financially troubled Detroit Public Schools, he accepted.[1] The committee worked for eighteen months and produced a lengthy report with detailed recommendations, one of which was that the Detroit Public Schools raise nearly $200 million in order to keep up with the needs of a growing student body.

The school board accepted the committee's recommendations. As a start at raising the needed funds, the board proposed a $60 million bond issue, to be on the ballot for the April 1959 election. The voters had only recently rejected a much smaller bond issue, and the chances for this new proposal did not look good.

Though he was a not a Detroit resident (his home was in suburban Bloomfield Hills) Romney decided to campaign for the bond issue, putting his reputation on the line. On the Sunday before the election he and his sometime adversary, UAW president Walter Reuther, appeared together on Detroit's WJBK-TV to explain why the bond issue was important to Detroit's future. The next day the voters approved it by a margin of nearly 60 percent. George Romney had launched his public career.

Romney's work on the schools report and the bond issue had earned considerable public acclaim. He decided to turn his energies to a wider arena. The seemingly permanent warfare between Democrats and Republicans in Lansing had led the state government into fiscal near-disaster and payless paydays, and hurt Michigan's national image. Traditional partisan politics seemed incapable of producing a solution.

Yet a group of dedicated citizens, working outside the traditional political system, had been able to overcome a similarly intractable situation in financing the Detroit Public Schools. Why not apply this method to the "mess in Lansing"? Within three weeks of the successful bond election, Romney brought together a small group of community leaders to discuss creating an active, but nonpartisan, approach to solving the problems of the state as a whole. Thus was born Citizens For Michigan.

The organization conducted its first meeting in Lansing in June 1959. In September the organizers elected Romney as chairman.[2] Big business was prominently represented by Robert McNamara of Ford Motor Company, Edward Cushman (vice president of American Motors), and Joseph Brady (vice president of Citizens Mutual Insurance). Wisely, Romney also persuaded *Detroit News* editor Martin Hayden to join.

Big labor was also invited and, over the opposition of Gus Scholle, some union representatives did participate.

CFM eventually grew to a membership of 5,000.[3] Its leaders were well aware of suspicions that it was a front for Romney's political ambitions, and they adopted a policy against supporting any candidate for public office. They also limited financial contributions to the organization to no more than $100 a year from any individual.[4]

CFM formed committees on various governmental subjects. These committees performed studies, heard from experts, and eventually made recommendations. Out of this body of work emerged the two principal positions most closely identified with CFM: the first was that Michigan should adopt a flat-rate corporate and individual income tax. The second, which had originated with the League of Women Voters, was that Michigan's government should be reformed from top to bottom by calling a constitutional convention.

"Con-con" supporters gathered enough signatures to place the proposal for a convention on the 1960 general election ballot. As we have seen, the voters approved it. However, the exact method of choosing delegates was left to the legislature.

Romney expressed a strong preference for a nonpartisan convention, but in this case Romney really was naive; given the legislature's role, that was never a realistic possibility. The legislature instead provided for partisan election of a total of 144 delegates, one for each State Senate district and each State House district, and the resulting convention, unsurprisingly, looked a lot like the legislature itself in its party composition. Roughly one-third of the delegates elected in September 1961 were conservative rural Republicans, one-third were moderate Republicans, and one-third were Democrats. Romney was elected as a Republican delegate from suburban Oakland County, but when the convention met in October his desire to be elected its president was thwarted by the conservatives, and he had to settle for one of three vice-presidencies.

The legislature itself washed its hands of con-con, failing even to appropriate funds to establish preparatory study groups. Governor Swainson stepped into the breech, naming his own preparatory commission and persuading the Kellogg Foundation to fund it.[5]

As 1962 began, Swainson received his second opportunity to fill a vacancy on the Michigan Supreme Court. In November 1961 thirty-three-year-old Jerome Cavanagh had been elected mayor of Detroit. Having been elected partly on a promise to change the culture of the Detroit Police Department, Cavanagh persuaded a liberal Democrat, Justice George Edwards, to leave the Supreme Court and accept the job of police commissioner. Edwards resigned from the court in January and Swainson appointed attorney general Paul Adams to the court. This then presented Swainson with the opportunity to appoint an attorney general to serve out Adams's term.

In what may have been his most significant appointment, Swainson chose Frank J. Kelley. Kelley, the son of former Wayne County Democratic leader Frank Kelley, had befriended Swainson the day they were admitted to the bar, and had introduced him to the Democratic Party in Wayne County. Kelley had since moved to Alpena, where he was active in civic affairs. Thus he possessed both a northern Michigan residency and a Detroit Democratic pedigree, both of which would add strength to the Democratic ticket, as would his Irish name. Additionally, Kelley had a strong, dynamic personality that came across on television.

Kelley went on to serve as Michigan attorney general for thirty-seven years, pioneering aggressive enforcement of consumer protection and environmental laws, winning ten statewide elections and mentoring several generations of lawyers and politicians.

As he entered his second year in office, Swainson's focus remained on fiscal reform. On January 26 he once again presented his reform program, in a special message to the legislature, asking enactment of a 3 percent income tax on personal and corporate income, abolishment of the business activities tax, and an exemption for food and drugs from the 4 percent sales tax. The governor estimated the package would produce an annual net revenue increase of $71 million.[6] Swainson had reason for hope; Republican State Senate majority leader Frank Beadle had signaled that the Republicans should give "serious consideration" to an income tax, if one were introduced.[7]

On February 1 the Swainson package of tax bills was introduced in the House.

Meanwhile, Detroit mayor Jerome Cavanagh began preparing his own package of proposed legislation, to authorize new city and county taxes, in anticipation that legislative action, if any, on Swainson's proposals might come too late to help Detroit out of its own increasingly difficult fiscal situation. The city was facing a projected deficit estimated at $46 million, and Cavanagh was required to present a city budget by April.[8]

Swainson, already facing the prospect of competing Republican tax proposals, did not appreciate yet another one from a supposed ally. He called Cavanagh's proposal "a retarding factor to state fiscal reform." Cavanagh lashed back that the city would not receive enough money under the governor's tax plan, and that the legislature might not enact the plan in time to help the city.[9]

On February 10 George Romney, saying that he had fasted and prayed for twenty-four hours before making the decision, announced his candidacy for the Republican nomination for the office of governor. Gus Scholle was predictably unimpressed, saying Romney was "trying to put on an act of having a pipeline to God in order to become Governor of Michigan."[10] Swainson was already a candidate for reelection. He had casually disclosed that decision at an October 1961 Democratic dinner, and reiterated it at an end-of-year news conference in December.

On the evening of February 28, taking a breather from the stress of legislative relations, the governor climbed into the back seat of his State Police–driven sedan for a special trip to Port Huron. The trip was timed so that he would arrive at the Blue Water International Bridge, which connected Port Huron with Sarnia, Ontario, near midnight. The bridge's construction had been financed with bonds, which were repaid over a quarter-century by tolls charged to motorists using the bridge. The bonds had been fully paid off and the authorities had decreed that tolls were to cease at the end of February.

The governor's father, John Carl Swainson, had left behind his life as a traveling salesman for the less strenuous job of toll collector at the bridge, but that job was about to disappear, and John Swainson wanted to be the last person to pay a toll to his father. At midnight the big sedan pulled up to the booth. The governor handed the toll taker the fare and said, "You're out of work, Pop."[11]

In the Senate, the income tax bills were stuck in the Tax Committee. But on April 5, seven Republican moderates joined with eight Democrats to launch the first successful Senate discharge petition since 1912, forcing the bills to come to the floor for a vote. Senate Republican leader Frank Beadle spoke in favor of discharge. In the House, Republican leader Allison Greene predicted that if the income tax reached the floor, it would probably pass.[12]

The governor asked to speak to a joint session of the legislature, and, after some delay, the legislative leaders agreed. Swainson, sensing that the culmination of his political career was within reach, was conciliatory. "I am not concerned with who gets credit for doing what has to be done. And if, as some feel, it is blame rather than credit . . . I am prepared to accept such blame," he told them.[13]

But even as the young governor seemed within reach of his goal, the even younger mayor of Detroit was reaching desperately to stave off a fiscal disaster. Jerome Cavanagh's own appeals to the legislature and the governor had failed to produce a timely result. April had arrived, and with it the city's budget deadline. As Cavanagh viewed things, even if the governor's plan were to be enacted, it would fall far short of supplying Detroit's financial needs.

On April 7 the mayor appeared before the Detroit City Council and proposed a city income tax of 1 percent, to be levied on both Detroit residents and non-resident commuters who earned their income within the city. According to the *New York Times,* "Mayor Cavanagh said a city levy was his second choice but that the State Legislature had not given clear indication of what course it would take in providing additional funds for either the state or local governments. 'The City of Detroit cannot wait any longer in taking appropriate steps to meet its emergency needs for a new source of tax revenue,' he said."[14]

The suburban reaction was immediate. To outraged cries of "no taxation without representation," John T. Bowman, a Democratic member of the House from suburban Macomb County, introduced a bill to prohibit cities from placing an income tax on nonresidents. This was to be forever after known as "the Bowman Bill." A similar bill was introduced in the Senate, and the bills sailed through both houses.

On April 16 Senate majority leader Beadle announced that a tax plan had been worked out and agreed to by the governor, the Republican chairman of the

House Taxation Committee, the Senate Democrats, and moderate Republicans. It included a 3 percent personal income tax and a 5 percent corporate income tax. Swainson said, "For the first time in many years a majority of the legislature has been united on a program which attempts to meet obvious and compelling needs of the people of Michigan." Detroit Democratic representative Joseph Kowalski referred to a possible compromise tax package "acceptable to both Detroit and Bowman."[15]

Asked for a statement on the tax reform package, George Romney declined.[16] The governor held his breath.

After several days of procedural wrangling the Senate began debate on the income tax bill on Monday, April 23. Deliberations went into the evening, then into the night. The governor took up residence in the office of the lieutenant governor, T. John Lesinski, following the proceedings on a loudspeaker—part of the lieutenant governor's equipage for his constitutional role as presiding officer of the Senate. As the night wore on, Swainson met with senators, staff members, and Gus Scholle. At one point he even provided parliamentary advice.[17]

The Senate recessed at midnight, then reconvened at 12:01 A.M.

Senator John Smeekens, a die-hard income tax opponent from the small town of Coldwater,[18] did his best to filibuster, speaking against the tax for hours and insisting that the Senate clerk, Beryl Kenyon, read the entire forty-three-page, 10,000-word bill aloud, instead of the customary "considered read" waiver. Amid acrimonious arguments, Beadle resigned as majority leader.[19]

During the night, as the proceedings were covered live by Detroit television reporters, telegrams streamed in from supporters and opponents of fiscal reform. One was from Citizens For Michigan, urging the Senate to pass an income tax.

As dawn broke, Swainson sent coffee and doughnuts down to the Senate floor.

Finally, at 10:45 A.M., the Senate voted on the income tax bill. It passed, eighteen to fifteen.

Romney finally spoke, congratulating the coalition members on putting the State's interest above local and partisan concerns.

A tired but jubilant Swainson told reporters, "It's been a long day. But it has been an enormous day. . . . Many said it would be impossible to achieve an income tax. It is proved not impossible. Michigan has been united by this bi-partisan effort."[20]

His celebration was premature.

On Thursday the Detroit City Council enacted Mayor Cavanagh's nonresident income tax, lobbing a grenade into the fragile Senate alliance. Under enormous pressure by the major auto manufacturers, two Republican senators, John Stahlin and Thomas Schweigart, announced that they were leaving the income tax coalition.[21]

On Friday one more Senate supporter of the income tax, Haskell Nichols, announced that he would change his vote.[22]

Monday the Senate again met into the evening. By then the Senate Republican moderates were in a stampede to abandon the income tax. A motion to reconsider the previous vote was carried by a margin of eighteen to fifteen, which brought the income tax bill back to the floor, its shrinking group of supporters awaiting the *coup de grâce*. This was swiftly administered via a motion to table the bill, which passed nineteen to thirteen, with one senator absent. The Michigan income tax was dead. And so was any chance of compromise on the Bowman Bill, which was now on the governor's desk. He had one week to decide whether to veto or approve it (after that, it would become law without his signature). If he vetoed it, he would anger suburbanites. If he approved it, he would anger Detroiters.

On May 7 he vetoed it, saying, "I have been advised that . . . this legislation is of such great political moment that . . . my decision could well alienate great blocs of votes. . . . I will not allow any considerations of political rise to deter me from a decision I believe to be right, just and responsible." Pointing out that cities and suburbs have common interests, including common tax problems, he spied the cause as "legislative neglect of metropolitan problems, unfair treatment by the legislature of our metropolitan areas. . . . How can the State, with integrity, obstruct local efforts to solve local problems that the state, itself, helped create?"[23]Amid this turmoil, the constitutional convention approved a final draft for submission to the people, freeing George Romney to begin his active campaign for governor.

Romney had his work cut out. On May 14, 1962, three days after the constitutional convention finished, a *Detroit News* poll showed that 48.9 percent of the voters preferred Swainson, to 42.9 percent for Romney.[24]

Because of the fact that self-identified Republicans were a minority statewide in Michigan, Romney decided to set up two parallel campaign organizations: Romney for Governor, to identify and turn out Republicans, and Romney Volunteers, to solicit independents and Democrats.[25] Romney's campaign staff believed that in order to win they needed to turn out the entire Republican base, plus get nearly all of the independent voters. Thus it would be critical to organize get-out-the-vote drives in heavily Republican areas, but this, in itself, would not be sufficient. As Dr. John Dempsey, one of Romney's senior advisors, noted:

> The campaign would have to be directed most of all to the Independent vote in the major counties . . . in the major urban and suburban counties where the largest Independent vote is found. . . . Every effort should be made to make the campaign a battle between George Romney and John Swainson, and not between the parties. And Romney should attack all through the campaign, never defend.[26]

The state Republican organization initiated an extensive voter identification project, designed to identify and register every Republican who was eligible to vote.[27]

The Romney Volunteers eventually grew to an estimated 60,000 members.[28] Chaired by Dr. Dempsey, the Volunteers had a "firm and inflexible rule that every chapter and every volunteer would support only one candidate: George Romney. It was felt that . . . to support other candidates would reduce the appeal of the movement and would in the end cause it to compete with the Republican Party."[29]

On July 4 Swainson marched, by invitation, in the City of Wyandotte's traditional Independence Day parade. Romney was not invited, but he arrived early, walking the parade route ahead of the marchers, introducing himself to spectators.

Two weeks later Romney invited himself to the annual UAW retirees picnic at Belle Isle. Union leaders were not amused, but Romney received a polite receptions from the retirees and their families, and even a cordial welcome from a group of American Motors retirees.[30] Romney knew that the press would record his presence, and he was willing to take the risk of a hostile reception in order to make the point that he was his own man, and not antilabor.

On July 18 the Michigan Supreme Court launched a thirty-pound shell into the political waters. In a four-to-three decision, the court declared that the Michigan Senate's malapportionment violated the U.S. Constitution's Fourteenth Amendment equal protection rights of voters; the justices canceled the August 7 State Senate primary election.[31] Although the court ordered the legislature to attempt to agree on a reapportionment plan by September, the only realistic alternative available on short notice appeared to be an at-large election, in which all Senate candidates ran statewide.

The case had been brought by Gus Scholle. All of the justices who voted for the primary election's cancellation were Democrats (Kavanagh, Souris,

Smith, and Black) and all of the dissenters were Republicans (Carr, Kelly, and Dethmers). To many Republican activists, this looked like an attempted coup, because Republicans were unlikely to keep control of the Senate in an at-large, statewide election.

With the state lurching toward a constitutional crisis, the governor asked for public service television and radio time. On July 19 he addressed the people, explaining the court's decision and its ramifications. But then he went further, equating Michigan's reapportionment foes with the "white supremacy advocates in Alabama and Tennessee who fought desperately in the courts to maintain that supremacy—and lost. The oil-rich barons of Oklahoma and the factory farmers of Wisconsin who fought to retain their power—and lost."[32]

Swainson's television address enraged rural and conservative Republicans, who now saw him as using his public office and the public airwaves to further a conspiracy with Scholle and the Democratic justices to destroy the Republican Party in Michigan.

The Republican conservatives thus far had been mistrustful and lukewarm toward Romney, the politically moderate newcomer. But now he saw a wonderful chance to unite them around him, at no political cost. He was offered free time by the television stations to respond to Swainson, and he grabbed it. Two nights after Swainson's address, Romney spoke to the people. He scoffed at the prospect of each voter having to elect thirty-two state senators, calling it "Russian roulette" and raising the prospect that all thirty-two senators might come "from a single county and a single political party."[33] Romney proposed instead that the legislature submit the issue to the people at the November election.

Meanwhile, three Republican state senators who were also defendants in the Scholle case petitioned the U.S. Supreme Court for a stay of the Michigan court's order. Since the U.S. Supreme Court was in summer recess, the petition was sent to Potter Stewart, the U.S. Supreme Court justice who handled emergency petitions from within the Sixth Circuit, which included Michigan.

Stewart was on vacation in Franconia, New Hampshire. He commandeered a courtroom in nearby Littleton. There, Whitney North Seymour, a past president of the American Bar Association, presented the argument for a stay on behalf of the Republicans. Michigan's attorney general Frank J. Kelley and two assistants argued against a stay. At the conclusion of the hearing, Stewart granted the stay, to allow the Republicans time to file a petition with the full U.S. Supreme Court, and for the full Court to decide whether to take up the case when it reconvened in October.

Thus the constitutional crisis ended as suddenly as it had begun. The thirty-pound shell was defused. But the waves it had created rolled on. John Dempsey believed that

> the Michigan Court's decision had a major effect on the outcome of the campaign . . . While many, and perhaps most Democrats in the urban areas applauded the Governor and the Court, their votes were safely "for" Swainson even before the Court ruled. It was with the suburban and rural voters that the Democrats most needed advances, and these groups felt that the decision threatened their representation.[34]

Moreover, the *Scholle* decision gave Romney his opportunity to become the defender of the rural and conservative Republicans, thus gaining their support, but without having to change his moderate-to-liberal philosophy, which would have alienated the independents without whose votes he could not win.

Neither Romney nor Swainson faced a contest for his party's nomination, and it was clear that each was to be the nominee from June 17, when they filed their petitions to be placed on the ballot. No one else filed for governor. However, they were not the official nominees until August, when the uncontested primaries designated them as the legal candidates. And it was not until August 25 that both parties held their state conventions, nominating candidates for the offices of lieutenant governor, auditor general, and secretary of state. It was then that the campaign began in earnest.

Delivering the main speech at the Republican convention in Grand Rapids, Romney tore into the Democrats and their labor allies; referring to the *Scholle* decision, he said: With John Swainson in the driver's seat and Gus Scholle supplying the gas, their special interest steamroller nearly flattened the voting rights of every citizen in this state. . . . They organized a power play behind a distorted and twisted interpretation of judicial decision in a grab for complete political domination as brazen as this or any other state has ever seen.[35]

Romney also challenged political extremists, challenging the Democrats to expel far leftists and going out of his way to attack the far-right wing of his own party, represented by the John Birch Society.

In contrast, the Democrats—for once—had a relatively quiet and peaceful convention, in Detroit, renominating all incumbent state officials without dissent.

A private poll for Romney by Walter DeVries in August found that 60 percent of voters expressed themselves as "dissatisfied" with the way things had been going in Lansing, with only 7 percent saying they were "satisfied." John Dempsey regarded this result as "an astounding fact . . . in this state, with an unemployment rate lower that for several years previous, with no acute financial problem at the moment, and with the beginnings of an economic boom dimly visible."[36] However strong the dissatisfaction, it did not translate automatically into a preference for Romney. A *Detroit News* poll released September 30 showed the two candidates in a virtual tie, 49.7 percent for Romney to 47.5 percent for Swainson.

On Friday, October 5 President John F. Kennedy flew in to Detroit Metro Airport. After a brief speech at the airport, JFK was driven to the Sheraton Cadillac Hotel in downtown Detroit, where he spent the night. The next morning Kennedy addressed a large crowd in front of the hotel, telling them, "One of the most interesting political phenomena of our time is to see Republican candidates in various states who run for office and say, 'elect the man.' You can't find the word 'Republican' on their literature, and I don't blame them. But we write the word 'Democrat' in large letters."[37] Kennedy and Swainson then traveled by motorcade to Hamtramck. The *New York Times* estimated that as many as 100,000 people saw Kennedy in Detroit. The president, Swainson, and Neil Staebler then flew to Flint and Muskegon, where Kennedy again spoke to large and enthusiastic crowds.

Kennedy was aware that his own pollster, Louis Harris, who was also working for Michigan Democrats, had recently found Swainson to be running behind Romney, 53 percent to 47 percent. During a meeting at his hotel with Frank J. Kelley, when they were briefly alone, the President told Kelley that some of his own aides had pressed him to cancel his Michigan trip, because Swainson's campaign was a lost cause. Kennedy told Kelley he had refused, telling them, "This guy lost both his legs in the war. He campaigned for me. You think I'm going to let him down?"[38]

The perceived success of the 1960 televised debates between Nixon and Kennedy were changing the face of American politics. The public had begun to expect televised debates at the state level, and the local television stations saw them as a way to provide, or appear to provide, a public service.

Swainson had done well in his debates against Bagwell in 1960, and he had lost none of his mastery of detail or sparkling personality. Some of Romney's advisors were leery of putting him into a situation in which they thought he would be at a disadvantage. Yet, in the end, they concluded that televised debates were inevitable. They decided to agree to no more than three, to be made available statewide.[39]

Under the rules agreed to by the candidates, the debates would be highly structured. All questions would be posed by a panel of reporters, answers were limited to one minute, and the entire program was limited to thirty minutes. This would permit little time for substance.

The first televised debate took place October 9. Swainson won the coin toss and opened. His statement reflected a new theme; instead of attacking the Republican legislature for blocking all progress, he spoke positively, of promises he had made and kept, of making government more efficient, of improving the state's mental health system and strengthening public education, and, with President Kennedy, of lowering Michigan's unemployment rate to its lowest level since 1955.

Romney in his opening statement claimed that Swainson's employment figures were misleading, that "two years ago there were 81,000 more people employed in Michigan than there are today." He attacked the rosy picture Swainson had painted; taxes were up $70 million, the state's deficit had increased by $14.8 million, spending had increased by $100 million.

Romney then turned to what he saw as his strongest issue.

I know what we have to do in Michigan. We have to put an end to the partisan bickering and the blaming of others. We have got to have spending reform and we have got to have tax reform . . . and we have got to go out and re-sell Michigan. And to do that we have got to have new leadership and a new approach that will bring unity and progress.

Romney's own advisors believed he lost the first debate, that he had looked nervous and hesitant.[40]

The second debate, eight days later, was a far different story. In fact, it produced arguably the most dramatic encounter of the campaign.

It was Romney's turn to make the first opening statement, and he attacked. Until last week, he said, Swainson had been complaining about how bad things were and blaming others. Then, suddenly, "He did a complete flip-flop on the condition of our state. . . . Now he says everything is rosy." Romney then recited a series of statistics to show that employment was down while state spending was up. "When my opponent took office two years ago, our biggest unsolved problems were these: we needed more jobs, and we had a real money mess. Today, we still need more jobs, and we have a bigger money mess, more debt, even higher taxes."[41]

Swainson replied that Romney was unhappy at the outcome of their first debate. "He is unhappy, I think, because he has no platform, no program, and his record of political leadership has been a failure." What the state needed was more appropriations for education, medical care for the aged, better retraining for the unemployed, and improved unemployment compensation. And these benefits to Michigan were on the way. "But now that the battle is almost won, my opponent wants to lead the victory parade." Yet Romney "cannot even lead his own party, let alone the people of Michigan."[42]

Then, according to the *Detroit Free Press,* Swainson said that "Romney, as a newly proclaimed party head and vice president of the Constitutional Convention, should have done more to promote fiscal reform by the state legislature."[43]

At this Romney was visibly provoked. He shot back, "During the period when he said I should have been responding to the situation in the Senate, I was occupied with positions of leadership." Then, turning to face his opponent, Romney said:

And John Swainson, I'd like to say this to you as directly as I can: that what you are really saying is that you thought I as a private citizen should step over and do your job as Governor as well as serve as a delegate to the Constitutional Convention and as well as to head up American Motors and the other activities in which I was engaged. And this is one of the biggest admissions of failure on your part that you could possibly cite. It simply meant you couldn't handle your own job, so you want me ——(time expired).[44]

Swainson, appearing unmoved by Romney's attack, responded without hesitation.

All during 1961 there was a program before the legislature. . . . Certainly, if he does believe in citizen participation, he should have made himself available to the Taxation Committees of either house of the legislature. This is a citizen's duty. In fact, in 1962 when we were having the long debates, and some very serious consideration being given to solving the problems of Michigan in the fiscal area, an official invitation was issued to Mr. Romney.

It would have only taken 100 yards' walk either way either from his hotel room or from the Constitutional Convention, to support that program or oppose that program. At least we would have known where he stood. The fact of the matter is the opportunity for leadership was there. The man was lacking.[45]

Swainson's campaign had received regular reports from Louis Harris, John Kennedy's pollster. In mid-October Harris sent Swainson a confidential report. Harris noted that "we have seen Governor Swainson go into an early lead against George Romney, only to slip slightly behind, then further behind." The current prospects, as of the first week of October, were better: "The narrow gap is closing and Swainson appears to be coming on."[46] In September Romney had been ahead 49 percent to 43 percent with 8 percent undecided. Now Romney was leading Swainson 49 percent to 46 percent, with 5 percent undecided. Swainson was now within three percentage points of Romney.

Harris found that when he did not refer to Swainson and Romney by name, but instead asked voters whether they would vote for "the Republican or Democratic candidate for Governor," the results were dramatically different: 46 percent indicated they would favor the Democrat, 38 percent the Republican, and 16 percent were undecided. Though Harris did not expressly say so, Romney's decision to advertise himself mainly without party identification had been wise.

On October 21 the *Detroit News* published results of its poll, taken before the second debate. It showed Romney ahead, 52 percent to 47.3 percent.[47]

Both Swainson and Romney kept the grueling schedules expected of candidates for governor, but it was Romney who, at age fifty-five, displayed an energy that recalled the early campaigns of the young Mennen Williams. On Saturday, October 27 he flew to Cadillac and Ludington, then to Escanaba, Marquette, and Iron Mountain in the Upper Peninsula. At each stop he addressed a well-organized campaign rally, speaking directly to 10,000 people from widely scattered areas in one day.[48]

Romney spent Sunday at home (he did not campaign on Sundays). The following Monday he left his Bloomfield Hills home at 5:00 A.M. Traveling by motorcade with other Republican candidates, he greeted arriving workers at the gates of three factories in Pontiac and Oxford, then drove to Lapeer, where he spoke at a restaurant and a state mental health facility. Next he spoke at a restaurant in Davison, then at a campaign rally in Flint. Next came a speech in Montrose and another in Saginaw. At 11:30 he held a news conference at the Romney Volunteers headquarters in Saginaw, then stopped at a nearby shopping center to shake hands with shoppers.

At 12:20 P.M. he spoke at Hemlock, then moved on to a cattle auction at Breckinridge. Next was a street corner rally in Alma and a student rally at Alma College. At 2:45 he greeted General Electric workers at a shift change in Edmore, then addressed a Republican rally. He then spoke outdoors in Lakeview, Howard City, and Newaygo.

At 6:20 the motorcade pulled into Muskegon, where, finally, Romney could have some private time. No public events were scheduled until 8:00 P.M., when he did a press conference and radio and television interviews. Then it was on to Walker Arena for another speech to a large crowd. Then he retired for the night at the Occidental Hotel.[49]

On October 26 the two candidates met for their final televised debate. *Detroit News* political writer Don Hoenshell characterized its tone as one of "restraint and serenity."[50] Neither candidate said much of substance, and neither attacked the other. Undoubtedly, both were restrained by the fact that the nation was in the middle of the Cuban missile crisis, which had caused President Kennedy to cancel a planned second campaign trip to Michigan. In his opening statement Swainson apologized to Democrats in Macomb and Genesee Counties for having canceled campaign appearances to attend meetings on civil defense in Lansing.

On the Sunday before the election—November 4—the *Detroit News* published its last preelection poll. It showed Romney still ahead by 50.9 percent to Swainson's 48.4 percent. Since the October 21 *News* poll Romney had slipped a full point and Swainson had gained a full point.[51]

On Monday night—election eve—both Swainson and Romney appeared on purchased television time. Swainson's program was a two-hour "telethon" shown on one station in Detroit. Romney's program was only thirty minutes, but it was shown on six stations throughout the state.

Early on the morning of election day John and Alice Swainson voted at the Plymouth Township Hall. After voting, the governor was driven to Dearborn, where he shook hands with workers at a Ford plant. Then he went to the Henrose Hotel in downtown Detroit, which would be his election night headquarters, as it had been in 1960.[52]

Romney flew to campaign appearances in Bay City and Port Huron before ending the day at his headquarters hotel, the Pick-Fort Shelby, also in downtown Detroit.

That evening as the returns began coming in, it was soon clear that something new was happening. Turnout was much higher than normal for a nonpresidential election. In Dearborn, the largest Wayne County suburb, Romney was leading. Swainson had taken Dearborn by a six-to-five ratio in 1960. In the Oakland County suburb of Southfield, Romney led by a ratio of eight to five, a larger advantage than the five-to-three margin Bagwell had in 1960. In Wayne County as a whole, the governor's advantage was reduced from the previous 67 percent to about 60 percent.[53]

Shortly before midnight Romney appeared before his cheering supporters. "With over two-thirds of Wayne County in, we are running four to five percent ahead of the 1960 Republican vote," he said. "We are getting 33 to 40 percent. It certainly looks like this should do the trick."[54]

He was right. In 1960 the Detroit metropolitan area of Wayne, Oakland, and Macomb Counties, containing approximately half the state's voters, had given Paul Bagwell 39.5 percent of their vote. In 1962 they were giving George Romney 43.6 percent.

By 2:00 A.M. the tricounty totals were in, and enough of the outstate results from Republican areas had been tallied to give Romney the lead. The Democratic leaders knew that Romney would not relinquish that lead.[55]

Swainson's followers at the Henrose Hotel clung to their hopes in spite of the numbers. At 4:00 A.M. the governor came down to the ballroom for the last time, thanked them, and told them it was over. Then he went to bed.[56]

The final vote for governor was Romney 1,420,086, Swainson 1,339,513. The total votes cast—2,764,839 including minor party candidates—broke the Michigan record for a nonpresidential election. Romney received 51.36 percent of total votes cast, to Swainson's 48.45 percent.[57]

Romney had no coattails. He was the only statewide Republican candidate elected. All of his running mates went down to defeat, including the candidate for lieutenant governor, Clarence Reid.

Neil Staebler was elected to the one-term statewide office of congressman-at-large (statewide only because of the legislature's inability to agree on apportioning a new congressional district in time for the election). He said that it was the veto of the Bowman Bill that caused Swainson's defeat. "We had to have 64 percent [in Wayne County] to win," said Staebler, but the Romney vote in Wayne County suburbs was so high that it held Swainson's total in the county to 61 percent.[58]

The next morning John Swainson slept late in his twentieth-floor suite at the Henrose. Emerging from the elevator at 12:30 P.M., Swainson said he was "relieved. I can live like a human being for a while now." He also agreed with Staebler that the Bowman Bill was the biggest single factor in his defeat.[59]

The Swainson's had brunch with their son Steve, then headed home.

CHAPTER TEN

You Know You're No Longer Governor When...

AS HE DEPARTED THE HENROSE HOTEL LATE ON THE MORNING OF NOVEMBER 8, John Swainson's reaction to his first electoral defeat was philosophical. "I've dropped a few balls before," he told a supporter. "You just have to pick them up." In answer to a reporter's question about what had defeated him, Swainson agreed with Neil Staebler that his veto of the Bowman Bill "was the biggest single thing."[1] Later, he said, "When 1,340,000 people vote for you, there is no feeling you have been rejected. Any governor must face hard decisions and then at an election face the consequences."[2]

The aftermath of the defeat wasn't all serious. Press secretary Ted Ogar produced a small book of photographs with facetious captions, called "Who Was in Charge Here?" Only 100 copies were printed, and the book was given to Swainson staffers and friends at a combined Christmas-farewell party. One photo was of U.S. senator Hubert Humphrey looking at Swainson incredulously, with the caption, "Governor, you mean you went for an income tax in an election year?" Swainson had attempted to send a Christmas card to every person in his card file, which virtually all governors do, so another photo in Ogar's book showed Alice Swainson saying to John, "But 12,000 people don't send Christmas cards to *us*."

The defeated candidate rarely let on that he had been affected. Instead, he deflected any expressions of sympathy with quips, such as "You know you're no longer governor when you get into the back seat of a sedan and it doesn't move" and "You know you're no longer governor when you take off your coat and it just falls on the floor."[3]

Two days after the election, Swainson departed Lansing on what his staff said was a vacation trip to Florida, exact destination unspecified. But the actual destination was Washington, D.C. President Kennedy fitted the lame-duck governor into his schedule between a 10:30 meeting with his science advisor, Jerome Wiesner, and a noon meeting with his national security advisors. At 11:00 A.M. Swainson was ushered into the Oval Office, where he spent thirteen minutes with the president. The meeting was not a secret in Washington—it was on the president's official schedule—and the press immediately began to speculate that the youthful governor and the president discussed the possibility of a job in the Kennedy administration. Swainson's office issued a statement denying that any job had been discussed. The only purpose of the visit, it said, "was to express personal appreciation for [the president's] great assistance and cooperation in helping Michigan to move ahead."[4]

In fact, there was no need for the president and the governor to discuss any specific job. Each would have understood that Swainson was simply seeking reassurance of Kennedy's continued goodwill. The simple fact that the president fit Swainson into his schedule conveyed that reassurance.

In December Swainson announced that he would form a law partnership with Congressman John Dingell, Detroit attorney Ken Hylton, and his former partner Allen Zemmol, to conduct a general practice in the Cadillac Tower in downtown Detroit.

Then U.S. Sixth Circuit Court of Appeals judge Thomas McAllister announced that he would retire as of January 1. McAlllister was from Grand Rapids, and it was traditional to replace a U.S. Court of Appeals judge with a person from the same state.

A federal judgeship is a lifetime appointment, made by the president with the advice and consent of the U.S. Senate. Swainson indicated his interest to the White House, and was told to send a statement of his qualifications. It appears that he did so, sending copies to Michigan's U.S. senators, Patrick McNamara and Phillip Hart.

According to a later account by Swainson, the president called him in early December. During their conversation Swainson said, "I asked that I be given consideration for any job that might develop on the federal bench, but Mr. Kennedy questioned the wisdom of my getting out of politics."

After reflecting on the president's words, Swainson in the last week of January "wrote Mr. Kennedy saying he intended to stay in Michigan and remain active in party politics."[5]

Swainson's account appears confirmed by a short note from the president dated February 5, 1963:

Dear Governor:

I appreciate very much your letter of recent date and I am happy to learn of your decision. We need a strong voice in Michigan and I know of no one better qualified to help the Democratic Party in that State than you.

. . . looking forward to seeing you sometime soon, I am

Sincerely,
John F. Kennedy[6]

Why would the president call John Swainson and ask him to reconsider his wish to become a federal judge?

The likely answer involves a growing split in the Michigan Democratic Party and Senator Patrick McNamara's view of Swainson.

Although the Constitution provides that the president shall appoint federal judges and the Senate shall "advise and consent" on such appointments, the process that has evolved over time is more complicated. When the president has an opportunity to appoint a federal judge from a state, the person who chooses the appointee is that state's senior U.S. senator from the president's political party—in Michigan, Senator McNamara. This practice applies to all federal courts except the Supreme Court. All members of the U.S. Senate understand this rule and guard the privilege of choosing judges zealously against any threats.

At the same time Swainson was expressing his interest in the federal judiciary, Joe Walsh, a former UAW publicist and Swainson campaign speech writer, was about to achieve his dream job—working in the White House as an aide to presidential appointment secretary Kenneth O'Donnell. But aides to Senator McNamara, Neil Staebler, and Michigan party chair Joe Collins viewed the prospect of Walsh advising the White House on Michigan politics as a disaster, the result of a power play by the UAW. Joe Collins phoned a friend at the Democratic National Headquarters and told him that the Michigan Democratic

Party didn't want Walsh in the White House. McNamara called the White House directly with the same message. The result was that the job offer was withdrawn, ignominiously for Walsh and the UAW.[7]

Thus, the president would have been well aware of the bitter feud stirring within the Michigan Democratic Party. Although he liked Swainson personally, he was not about to inject himself into a family fight, much less go to bat for Swainson in a lost cause, which his nomination for a federal judgeship over McNamara's opposition would surely be. Moreover, Kennedy would have risked alienating a liberal senior senator of his own party, whose votes he would need on many matters of great importance to his national programs.

This is surely the reason why Kennedy called Swainson and asked him to reconsider, and then wrote him a thank-you note. Both men understood that Swainson was taking one for the team, and there would be other opportunities for him after feelings calmed down in Michigan.

But why was Michigan's senior Democratic U.S. senator opposed to Swainson's bid for the federal judgeship?

According to a lengthy, multisourced Detroit *Free Press* story,[8] Neil Staebler and Joe Collins had advised Swainson to call both the president and Senator McNamara regarding his interest in the federal judgeship. Swainson spoke to the president, who advised him to write a letter stating his qualifications. But when Swainson spoke to Senator McNamara, he "apparently made no flat request for a judgeship appointment."[9] Thus, when McNamara received his copy of Swainson's letter to the president, he thought that Swainson was going over his head and seeking the appointment directly from the president. Offended by this cheek, McNamara quietly made it known that he would block the appointment if Kennedy submitted it. Collins then called Swainson, who was vacationing in Mexico, and advised him that he had better talk to McNamara or the judgeship would slip away. Swainson interrupted his vacation to fly to Washington, where he had a long talk with the senator over lunch. But McNamara was unmoved. According to a "closely involved third party," "John did everything but ask Pat for it, and I guess that's what Pat was wanting."[10]

The *Free Press* story, however, does not add up. If Swainson's motivation to contact McNamara was knowledge that McNamara was offended by a perceived breach of protocol, then Swainson would have brought it up in their conversation. There was no reason not to.

Could it be that McNamara had another reason for opposing Swainson, a reason he did not care to disclose?

In 1977 Remer Tyson wrote a lengthy feature article about John Swainson in the *Detroit Free Press.* Tyson's article revealed, for the first time, that in 1962 an FBI bug

> is said to have recorded the mention of Swainson's name in a conversation then among a group of men that the FBI had identified as top underworld leaders in Michigan. The mob leaders talked about how they had paid off Swainson for doing them political favors while he was in office, according to the transcripts of the FBI tape recordings. The transcripts were sealed in a court case and never made public generally, but some reporters have what is purported to be copies of them . . .
>
> Swainson said he learned of the suppressed transcripts . . . in July 1975. He said he did not know the men who supposedly engaged in the conversation about him and had never had any sort of dealings with them.[11]

At the time the recordings were made, it was unlawful to divulge their contents to anyone but criminal justice professionals. Yet Vincent Piersante, commander of the Detroit Police Department Intelligence Bureau, who worked closely with the FBI in its investigation of organized crime, believed that the FBI divulged the contents to Democratic Party leaders, including Mennen Williams.[12] Given the fact that the FBI is a federal agency, whose budget must be approved by Congress, it also seems likely that the FBI would also have disclosed this transcript to Senator McNamara.

The bug was installed at the Detroit office of Detroit Mafia captain Anthony Giacalone, and Piersante was given a copy of the transcripts. In Piersante's recollection, the transcripts included Giacalone quoting Swainson as being willing to do business. Piersante did not mention Giacalone saying that they had actually done business with Swainson.

What are we to make of this?

First, no evidence of corruption in the Swainson administration has ever come to light. No federal, state, or local prosecutor ever brought any charges of corruption against Swainson (or anyone on his staff) for any actions during his time as governor.

Second, Giacalone's statement that he had talked with Swainson may well be true—it is consistent with Swainson's well-known inability to turn away anyone who wanted to talk with him—but no evidence has come to light that indicates they had any kind of ongoing relationship. As his law partner Allen Zemmol said

He never judged people, which was a terrible mistake on his part. He was totally nonjudgmental. Everybody was, you know, decent, as far as he was concerned. Even when, to any other person you would say watch your step, this guy is going to be very bad . . . he did not recognize that if you are a public figure holding public office, some nasty people are going to . . . attempt to latch on to you.[13]

Third, it is well documented that organized crime leaders are prone to exaggerate their influence. For example, New Orleans crime boss Carlos Marcello was secretly taped by the FBI as part of its "BRILAB" investigation, bragging, "It takes time to get where I'm at. To know all these people—governors, business, the attorney general, they know me. . . . I had [Louisiana] Governor McKeithen for eight years." "Maybe I can make a phone call to the attorney general." "I got the only man in the United States can tell 'em [the Teamsters leadership] what the fuck to do." Former prosecutor Vincent Bugliosi concluded after interviewing experts on organized crime in New Orleans that "there is no evidence to support the degree of power and influence he [Marcello] suggested in the BRILAB tapes."[14]

Finally, it is indisputable that the cause of the FBI's aggressive action against organized crime—after years of denial that national organized crime organizations even existed—was U.S. attorney general Robert Kennedy. Kennedy took a personal interest in the fight against organized crime and its attempts to corrupt political leaders. It is nearly inconceivable that Robert Kennedy would later allow his brother to ask John Swainson to consider a federal regulatory appointment, if the Justice Department was aware of any *credible* evidence that Swainson was corrupt. Kennedy would have access to more than just a raw intercept. He would have access to the experts who could evaluate this evidence and tell him whether there was anything to it.

Whatever the reason for McNamara's opposition to a judgeship for Swainson, intraparty relations were not about to calm down; events were moving in the other direction, toward an open split.

Each odd-numbered year the Michigan Democratic Party held a state convention in February to nominate candidates for statewide offices to be filled at the spring election (State Board of Education, highway commissioner, university trustees) and to elect the state party chairman.

As the delegates assembled in Grand Rapids on the evening of Friday, February 1, two factions were fighting for control of the party machinery. One faction, led by Neil Staebler, consisted of virtually all of the statewide officeholders, including the two U.S. senators. This faction supported reelection of Joe Collins as state chairman. Although Collins had managed Swainson's 1960 campaign, he was seen as more a Staebler protégé than a Swainson man. He had led the party through a successful election in 1962, with all statewide candidates winning except Swainson.

The other faction consisted of Swainson and a number of UAW officials, including vice president Leonard Woodcock and community relations director Mildred Jeffries. In the past the UAW usually had been content to leave active politics to Gus Scholle, but in the 1962 election many UAW people had actively participated in the Swainson campaign, which had caused some resentment among the Democratic Party activists, who believed that the UAW had contributed to the loss of the state's most powerful office.

The Swainson-UAW faction wanted either Zolton Ferency or Swainson himself to run the party. As the date of the convention neared, Swainson told his friends he was not interested. Four days before the convention, Ferency declared his candidacy.

Gus Scholle was not a member of either faction, but he personally favored continuation of Collins in office.[15]

As the convention opened, the labor caucus met and found itself hopelessly divided. As a result, the caucus followed Gus Scholle's suggestion and took no position on who should lead the party, leaving each member free to support whichever candidate he or she wished.[16]

John Swainson was not in Grand Rapids. He was in Detroit's Lakeside General Hospital with an acute bronchial infection. But he was in contact with Ferency's supporters by phone.

The election of the state chairman was scheduled for Saturday afternoon.

On Saturday morning Swainson's law partner Kenneth Hylton invited all of Collins's major supporters to a meeting at his suite on the sixth floor of the Morton House Hotel, three blocks from the Civic Auditorium, site of the convention. Their understanding was that Swainson wanted to get the two factions together to try to work out their differences. Neil Staebler later said that Swainson himself telephoned him to stress the importance of the meeting.[17] Those attending included U.S. Senator Phillip Hart, Lt. Gov. T. John Lesinski, Attorney General Frank Kelley, Secretary of State James Hare, and two Staebler aides.[18]

The meeting was to begin at 11:30 A.M. and invitees were told that Swainson had checked himself out of the hospital and was on his way. Noon came and Swainson did not appear. The attendees attempted to exchange pleasantries as some of them sipped on beers. At some point Allen Zemmol, who had been hosting the group along with Hylton, slipped away.

When Swainson had not arrived by 1:00 P.M., inquiries were launched. After a few minutes, T. John Lesinski, "anger all over his face and chewing his cigar furiously,"[19] sputtered to the group, "We've been double-crossed."[20] Swainson had bypassed the waiting leaders and was at that moment addressing the convention. He had gone directly from the hospital to the convention hall and, escorted by Zemmol, walked slowly from the back of the hall up the aisle to the stage, to the sound of tumultuous cheering from the delegates, who had read that he was hospitalized.

Swainson then delivered a rousing speech. He attacked Romney's support of "this very fraudulent new constitution," which was to be on the ballot at the upcoming April election. He told the delegates that he had wanted a federal appointment, but had decided to withdraw his name from consideration so that he could stay in Michigan and work to strengthen the party, but not as chairman. "You all know whom I want in that job!" he concluded, to a roar of approval.[21]

Joe Collins was on the convention floor. He sensed the convention moving toward Ferency. Looking around for his major supporters, he could find none of them (no one had notified him of the Morton House meeting). It was suggested to him that his supporters were absent because they could no longer support him.[22] Collins decided to give up. He asked for the microphone and advised the convention to elect Ferency by acclamation.[23]

The incident was a gift to the media. It was reported in gleeful headlines ("Swainson 'Trick' Dumps Collins" in the February 3 *Detroit News;* "No Trickery In Coup, Says Swainson" in the February 4 *Detroit Free Press*), and was ever after known as "the Morton House Coup."

Most of the officeholders at Ken Hylton's suite did not take the matter very seriously, but Lesinski never forgave Swainson, and Neil Staebler declined to accept Swainson's public apology for what Swainson said was a lapse by an aide, who was supposed to inform those waiting for him at the hotel that he was not coming. But Alan Zemmol confirmed the *Detroit News* account, and Swainson himself never went beyond this brief statement, which sounds more like an attempt to salve the victims' wounds.[24] In any event, Swainson had no regrets. He wrote to Lattie Coor, "The victory was sweet. We're back in, but there are a few chafed people."[25]

The year following his defeat was to be somewhat unsettled for John Swainson and his family.

In January the ex-governor opened a temporary office in the Michigan National Tower, across the street from the State Capitol building. There he went through his accumulated papers. In October, before the election, the Swainsons had purchased a large house on Lansing's stately Mar-Moor Drive,[26] but had also kept their house in Plymouth.

Uncertain where they ultimately were going to live, they decided to send both of their boys to private boarding schools. Steve, fifteen, went to the Leelanau School in Glen Arbor, Michigan. Peter, eleven, was sent to the Mohawk-Cragsmoor School in Cragsmoor, New York.[27] Kristina, not yet in school, remained with her parents.

By June the law partnership in Detroit was flourishing. Swainson told Lattie Coor it was "both active and lucrative."[28] Swainson had an "imposing, walnut-paneled office, nearly as big as the Governor's office in Lansing" on the twenty-ninth floor of downtown Detroit's Cadillac Tower.[29] He commuted from Lansing in a leased Ford Thunderbird, and stayed two to three nights a week in a small apartment at the Park Shelton on Woodward north of Detroit's office district.

He kept the door open for another run for governor. "I don't think the public investment in me should be cut off," he told *Free Press* politics writer Tom Shawyer, to whom he showed his card file containing names, addresses, and other information on 12,000 people whom he had dealt with in his political career. He spent a part of each day telephoning and writing political allies.[30]

In May he traveled to Washington and met with President Kennedy for over forty-five minutes.[31] According to Swainson's 1970 oral history interview with the John F. Kennedy Library, the president and Kenneth O'Donnell asked him to consider appointment to the U.S. Securities and Exchange Commission. Swainson told them he would think about it, but was not really interested. According to his oral history, he was still

> both physically and psychologically depressed from that very strenuous [1962] campaign, and I was sort of getting reacquainted with the family. Our children were quite young at the time. I didn't feel I wanted to move them into the Washington situation. If I were going to consider anything, I was more attracted towards perhaps an opportunity to serve . . . in the capacity of ambassador . . . or consul.[32]

He was still mulling over a rematch with Romney. In June he told his friend Doris Jarrell that he was "waiting until after the fall [legislative] session to make any real determination." But he was ambivalent, and a little wistful at what he had already missed: "The boys came home from school . . . and we all had a chance to be together at the lake over the long Memorial Day weekend. This is the first time the family has had the opportunity to be together on Memorial Day for nine years, and I must say that not being in public office does have some compensations."[33]

By September he was "very interested" in running again, and announced that he would make a decision by January 1. He revealed, for the first time, that during the 1962 reelection campaign he "had a good deal of difficulty with [his] legs."[34] His decision would "depend entirely on my doctor's advice pertaining to my ability to make another statewide campaign."[35]

Late in the fall he asked Lattie Coor if he would be available to help in a 1964 campaign, but Coor, back at St. Louis University, had made the decision to pursue his academic career in earnest, and was about to be married. He declined, with regret. Swainson understood. He told Coor, "Alice and I . . . often wonder what course our lives would have taken had we made other decisions. We, of course, have absolutely no regrets, but sometimes reflect on our present situation."[36]

In December Neil Staebler, whose statewide congressman-at-large seat was about to disappear, indicated for the first time that he was leaning toward running for governor even if Swainson got into the race.[37] Staebler had always insisted that he would only run if no other major candidate was willing to take on Romney. But his thinking had evolved. The *Lansing State Journal* observed, "Union-backed Swainson forces took over party leadership nearly a year ago, ousting Staebler's protégé John J. Collins from the party chairmanship. A desire to restore a broader-based control in party circles is seen by many as a major influence in Staebler's decision."[38]

On the day after Christmas Swainson checked into Ann Arbor's University Hospital for a thorough, two-day series of examinations. His self-imposed January 1 deadline rapidly closing in, he scheduled a news conference for Saturday, December 28. Zolton Ferency said, "There is so much interest in this thing that we're thinking of selling tickets to the announcement, to help pay off the party deficit."[39]

Ferency's quip wasn't entirely specious. The news conference, held in Detroit, was packed.

Swainson stepped to the podium and revealed that the physicians had found a previously undetected fragment of shrapnel in one of his leg stumps, and they had concluded that he could not undertake an arduous campaign. Therefore, he would not be a candidate for governor in 1964.[40] Neil Staebler would be unopposed for the Democratic nomination to take on Governor Romney.

Now what? For the first time in a decade, he was not a candidate for public office. President Kennedy's November 22 assassination had deprived him of not just a friend, but of any realistic prospect for a federal appointment.

He still loved politics, and he still had the card files. He wasn't retiring from politics. But for the time being, he would just have to accept a less exciting life. He would put his energies into his law practice, into building a nest egg.

In January 1964 the Swainsons sold their Lansing home and reserved a twenty-first-floor apartment at the newly built Lafayette Towers in downtown Detroit, not far from John's law office. To provide space for times when the family was together, they began looking for a cottage. In April they found a site on Lake Michigan's shore near Manistee in the northern Lower Peninsula. There they built a cottage. Swainson's sister Carroll and her husband, veterinarian George "Doc" Whitehead, went in on the property with them.[41]

In June the Swainsons bought a 167-acre farm in rural Washtenaw County, near the village of Manchester. The farm included a white clapboard house, two barns, 140 sheep, and "scores of chickens," according to the *Lansing State Journal,* which reported that the Swainsons would use the farm for vacations and extended weekend stays until they could move in later in the year.[42] They bought the property on a land contract, and Swainson's status as a disabled veteran exempted him from paying property taxes.[43] The Plymouth house was still leased to a tenant, but they would sell it a year later, when the lease expired.[44]

With Swainson having dropped out of the race, Neil Staebler's nomination for governor was secure. Now, to have any chance against the larger-than-life George Romney, Staebler needed a united Democratic Party. He purchased this unity by promising to give up his position as national committeeman to Swainson. It was a fair gamble for both sides. If Staebler could defeat Romney, he would remain the leader of the party in Michigan, and the White House would still have to consult him on federal patronage in Michigan. If, on the other hand, he lost, then the White House would have to consult Swainson. It was assumed that President Johnson would be reelected and would win Michigan in a landslide, perhaps even large enough to carry Staebler into the governor's office.

The bargain was executed at the Democratic National Convention in August in Atlantic City. John Swainson was elected Democratic national committeeman from Michigan. His friend Mildred Jeffries was reelected national committee-woman. Lyndon Johnson was nominated for a full term as president.

As he returned to Michigan from the convention, John Swainson's place seemed assured. He was making a good income in a successful law practice. He was back in politics, if not as a candidate at least as a patronage chief. His formerly divided party was on the mend. He was planning the renovation of the old farmhouse in Washtenaw County, with an eye to making it his home in 1965.

And yet, he was not quite satisfied.

The law firm was doing well, and he was bringing in plenty of business. But it was not always the kind of business he wanted. His law partner Alan Zemmol remembered:

> People would seek out our firm because they felt that he had connections with someone that might be helpful to them, which is not unusual. . . . And there were occasions when people wanted things done, things which he felt uncomfortable [about], and wouldn't become involved with, for example, seeking pardons or lobbying for certain positions, the things he did not feel comfortable doing.

Moreover, the economics of law practice dictate that unless one is a personal injury lawyer (which Swainson was not), the path to a good income is to represent mainly vested interests—established institutions or wealthy individuals. That was not John Swainson. And, as he told his friend, political writer Don Hoenshell, "he would feel uneasy appearing before a judge he appointed while governor."[45]

Then, at a moment when Swainson seemed to have few immediate options, fate opened a new one. On August 27 Wayne County circuit judge Miles Culehan died.

Formerly a circuit court vacancy would be filled by appointment of the governor, and George Romney's nonpartisanship did not extend quite so far as to offer a judgeship to the leader of the Democratic Party. However, the new constitution (which Romney supported) had gone into effect on January 1, 1964, taking the appointive power away from the governor and providing that all judicial vacancies were to be filled by election.[46] And even though judicial elections were nonpartisan, Wayne County was still heavily Democratic, and heavily pro-Swainson.

The special election would be held in April 1965, for the balance of the six-year term. Swainson knew that it could draw a crowd of Democrats who understood, as he did, that this was an unusual opportunity. He put out the word that he was considering seeking the office. The point was to scare off other potential candidates from declaring early, before Swainson had made up his mind. It worked. In Wayne County no one known as a Republican stood a chance of winning, and no Democrat wanted to run against the popular ex-governor.

On November 20 he announced his candidacy, saying, "My schooling and training were for the law. I have helped enact and administer the laws of this state. Now I seek the honor of interpreting that law."[47]

One other candidate filed to run. Seymour Markowitz, twenty-seven years old, was two years out of law school and living with his parents. He believed that "Swainson has too many allegiances. He couldn't just drop out of politics—even though he said he did—because he's Mr. Democrat in Michigan." Markowitz admitted that Swainson was "a good man. I even voted for him myself."[48]

Eventually, the State Board of Canvassers ruled that Markowitz had not obtained enough lawful signatures to earn a place on the ballot,[49] leaving Swainson the sole candidate. In April 1965 he was duly elected as a judge of the Third Judicial Circuit of Michigan.

The circuit court is Michigan's "trial court of general jurisdiction," meaning that it possesses legal authority to conduct the trial of every kind of case which the constitution or laws of Michigan do not expressly assign to any specific court.

In practice this has meant that circuit judges have authority over three major types of litigation: criminal felonies (i.e., crimes punishable by more than a one-year sentence); major civil damage suits (e.g., personal injury and medical malpractice suits, and business disputes); and divorce (with attendant issues such as child custody, alimony and child support).

In most areas of the state a judicial circuit is composed of one county, and a judge is often publicly described as, for example, an "Ingham County Circuit Judge." However, this is incorrect. Circuit judges are state officials, not county officials, and they exercise the judicial powers of the state. It just happens that they are elected, in most cases, by county.

Wayne County contains within its boundaries the city of Detroit as well as numerous smaller municipalities, and is by far Michigan's most populous county. By virtue of that fact, the Third Judicial Circuit (coextensive with Wayne County) elects the largest group of circuit judges.[50] In 1965, when John Swainson took the oath, there were twenty-one.

In the executive and legislative branches, where John Swainson had grown up, it was axiomatic that one used his or her official powers to aid friends and allies, and to punish enemies. Legislators voted for bills that would aid their supporters. As governor, Swainson had vetoed bills that would harm the interests of his supporters. This was perfectly normal and expected.

But a judge was governed by a very different set of ethics. The judge was expected to give each side in a dispute a fair hearing, and to decide it on the merits. If the judge found a personal friend on one side of a lawsuit, that judge was expected to recuse himself or herself—to step aside. A judgeship was a nonpartisan office, and a judge was not allowed to be a member of a political party, or even to endorse a candidate for partisan office.

This would be a difficult adjustment for John Swainson. He understood that he had to resign from his post as Democratic national committeeman, but he had not thrown away that card file with 12,000 names and addresses. Later, in March 1968, as Robert Kennedy was gearing up to challenge Lyndon Johnson for the Democratic presidential nomination (and before Johnson withdrew), Swainson was in contact with Kennedy aide William Geohegan, and sent him a detailed breakdown of the probable makeup of the Michigan delegation to the upcoming Democratic Convention, "ascertained by a few well-placed telephone calls." On the same date he turned down an invitation from New Jersey governor Richard Hughes to join the National Citizens Committee for Johnson, pointing out that judicial ethics prohibited partisan political activity, but adding, "I must confess that my personal feelings toward the present administration are to say the least mixed, and for this reason I am not prepared to commit even my name at this time."[51]

In May Swainson acted as master of ceremonies a huge rally for Robert Kennedy in downtown Detroit. This act may not have violated the letter of the judicial ethics rules banning partisan activity, but it skated close to the edge.

Swainson enjoyed his work as a trial judge, as he said,

because every day was a new challenge. Certainly the case load was adequate to keep you busy. We tried mainly automobile negligence matters although we had jurisdiction over divorce matters and ancillary matters, had a criminal docket . . . a family relations docket . . . , and it was just an enjoyable experience. . . . If you talk about power, straight power, obviously as a trial judge, you have the power on a one on one basis to determine a man's life, his estate, all kinds of things. As a Governor, you are the head of the state, so to speak, but you're in a position of making proposals, and the legislature dispenses what is finally done, and then you're given an opportunity to endorse that or to veto that, but for raw, naked power, there is nothing like a sitting trial judge. And so I enjoyed that very much, and I just was . . . in the idiom of today, "a happy camper."[52]

Life on the bench brought new opportunities for camaraderie. Thomas Brennan, who served with Swainson on the Wayne circuit, and later the Michigan Supreme Court, remembered that Swainson "sort of became the focal point for the judges socializing, and occasionally a bunch of us judges would go down to his office after work, and he had a bottle there and would pour a little shot of whiskey or whatever. And we'd all sit around and have a nip and talk."[53]

There was also an active social life. With two dozen judges serving staggered terms, there were always several incumbents preparing for the next election, and this meant fund-raising receptions nearly every week. Attorneys and bail bondsmen paid to attend these receptions, and at times sponsored receptions of their own. Allen Zemmol witnessed this subculture: "Bail bondsmen tried to become friendly with the circuit and recorders court judges in Wayne County, because they are always worried about forfeitures and they need adjournments if [their client] is a no-show. So bondsmen really did try to engage themselves with the judges." In other words, if a criminal defendant was free on bond and failed to appear for a scheduled court proceeding, the judge had complete discretion either to declare the bond forfeited—which would cost the bail bondsman—or to grant a continuance to give the defendant another chance to appear in court.

Zemmol also noticed that one bail bondsman, Harvey Wish, began to be of help to Swainson.

You've got to understand something. Although John appeared to get around very well, he really did need help from people. . . . He had to be dependent. He was like walking on stilts. If he lifted a heavy object or went any kind of long distance, it started to have its effect. And he would do those things, but at great pain. And if there was somebody around him who could help him, it was extremely important. And Harvey sort of wormed his way into that situation. To be helpful to him. But [John] really needed [the help]. And . . . [Wish] could be engaging.[54]

Swainson's friend David Sparrow, agreed:

That was just again a part of John's personality. There were a lot of hangers-on; he wasn't going to be rude to or even turn them away. He should have, a lot of them, perhaps, or at least not let them have the appearance of influence . . . but if they wanted to say, "John's my friend," he wasn't going to say, "No, I'm not your friend."[55]

The Swainsons' oldest son, Steve, graduated from the Leelanau School for Boys and moved back in with the family at Lafayette Towers. He embraced the new youth culture beginning to flourish in Detroit. He began by experimenting with marijuana, but soon graduated to harder drugs. He would disappear for days. Swainson related to Thomas Brennan that he had gone looking for his son

> many times in the seedier parts of town. And on this particular occasion he found him in some kind of a flop house, in Detroit, sleeping on some kind of a dirty old blanket . . . and with an overgrown beard, filthy and long hair . . . and I could tell how deeply [John] had been affected. So then he took Steve home and they cleaned him up and so on and so forth. And as soon as he had gotten a good meal and got a good night's sleep, he was gone again.

The Swainsons sought help for their son, but nothing worked. Eventually, Brennan recalled, they were advised, by a drug recovery organization,

> Don't be an enabler, don't take him in, don't clean him up. Don't do anything. The only way he's going to get out of this thing, he's going to have to be self-motivated. So you have to stop being a resource for him to get money and to get sort of back on his feet because he didn't want to get back on his feet. He just wants to be pumped up with more money so that he can go back to the same lifestyle. And I remember how difficult that was for John to have to treat his son that way. It was just not his instinct. He was a very compassionate man.[56]

Steve enlisted in the marines and went through basic training, but the pull of drugs was stronger than anything the marines could offer. It is not clear whether he went AWOL, but he was given a general discharge for medical reasons.[57]

In 1967 Steve was arrested, in Port Huron, for selling marijuana. He pled guilty to possession and was put on probation.

Like many families faced with a drug-addicted child, the Swainsons were dismayed with the law's harshness toward addicts and the lack of help available to them. Swainson was strongly motivated to do something about it. He founded Narcotics Addiction Rehabilitation Coordinating Organization (NARCO), a nonprofit corporation dedicated to promoting drug education, treatment, and law reform, which ultimately secured United Foundation funding and set up a drug treatment center in a former hospital.[58] He never hid his son's drug problem, and for the rest of his life he actively advocated development of better drug treatment facilities and law reform.

In 1969 George Romney resigned as governor to accept a cabinet position in the Nixon administration. Romney's successor as governor was Swainson's old State Senate colleague William Milliken, whom Swainson liked and admired. In September 1969 he accepted an invitation from Milliken to serve on a special advisory committee on drug dependence and abuse. He told Milliken, "Present treatment, as indicated by the increased rate of drug usage and dependency, has not been effective, and innovative methods of treatment must be explored. A prison uniform is not going to help them . . . [and] a hospital bed is not needed."

Swainson continued to seek out amputees. In 1968 he learned that Pat Clark, an eighteen-year-old, was in intensive care in Lansing following the loss of his left leg in a train accident. He wrote to the boy, telling him of his loss of both legs at age nineteen:

> At first I felt that my life was over because, like you, I had been active in athletics. Far from being over, I subsequently learned that your life is anything you want it to be, no matter what disability you suffer. . . . Your own determination is your only limitation and from what I have been informed, you have plenty of determination. If I can ever be of any help to you, please do not hesitate to contact me.

A few days later Swainson received a letter from a priest, Father Eugene Henley, who had met Pat Clark while serving as chaplain at St. Lawrence Hospital. He told Swainson that the young man "happily showed me your letter and picture in a double frame on his bedside table. This 18-year-old boy was almost in tears of joy and full of courage for the future because of your gesture. He seemed so much more full of confidence for the future. . . . Please know that your kindness will never be forgotten by Pat—nor me."[59]

CHAPTER ELEVEN

The Supreme Court

IN 1969 THE FAMILY MOVED OUT OF LAFAYETTE TOWERS. ALICE AND THE CHILDREN moved to the farm the Swainsons had bought in 1964, outside the village of Manchester, in Washtenaw County. John visited them on weekends, but during the week he bunked with Alice's uncle, who lived within Wayne County. It was obviously a temporary arrangement.

To anyone paying attention, it would have been clear that John Swainson was not planning to continue as a Wayne County circuit judge much longer. State law required a circuit judge to reside within his Circuit. In Swainson's case, this meant he had to live within Wayne County.

Although Swainson liked the circuit court, he had begun to grow restless as he entered the sixth year of his term. He later told Roger Lane, "After five years, there is a great deal of sameness about the types of matters that you are hearing. You can see that sometimes the law has not kept pace with the actuality of events."[1]

John Swainson had decided to run for the Michigan Supreme Court.

Since at least the mid-nineteenth century all judicial offices in Michigan have been filled by popular election, with candidates running on the nonpartisan ballot. If an incumbent dies or resigns in the midst of his or her term of office, the governor appoints a successor, but if that successor wants to continue in office, he or she must run against all comers in the next general election.

To obtain a spot on the general election ballot, a candidate for judicial office— even an incumbent—must run in the August primary election that precedes the November general election. However, there is one, peculiar, exception. There is no primary election for the office of justice of the Michigan Supreme Court.

To appear on the general election ballot for the nonpartisan office of justice of the Supreme Court, a candidate must be nominated by a state political party convention.[2]

This arrangement has tended to favor the nomination of candidates who have previously served in statewide partisan office; they have the advantage of being well-known names, thus electable. They also have the advantage of having a record of service to the party or its major constituencies, thus having access to large blocs of convention delegates. One result has been the nomination and election of many former state attorneys general and governors to the Supreme Court.

As the Michigan Democratic Party prepared to assemble for its semiannual August convention (held during general election years) in Grand Rapids, two Supreme Court seats, both held by Republicans, were up for election. John R. Dethmers (a former attorney general who had been on the court twenty-five years) had announced he was seeking reelection, so he would be on the ballot. Harry Kelly (a former governor, in poor health) had decided to retire, and the Republican state convention would nominate Edward Piggins, a former Detroit police commissioner, to seek his seat.

G. Mennen Williams, back in Michigan after serving as U.S. ambassador to the Philippines, had announced his intention to run for the Supreme Court, and his nomination was essentially locked up before the delegates assembled on Saturday, August 22, 1970, at the aging Pantlind Hotel in downtown Grand Rapids.

The other nomination was in play, and there was heated competition for it. The main contenders were Swainson, Court of Appeals chief judge (and former lieutenant governor) T. John Lesinski and Detroit Recorders judge Robert Evans.

Michigan Democratic leaders traditionally tried to create statewide tickets "balanced" both geographically and ethnically. Lesinski was counting on the convention to put at least one Polish name on the ticket, to keep the loyalty of the large Detroit-area Polish population. Evans was counting on the convention to do exactly the same thing to keep the loyalty of the African American population.

Swainson had no major ethnic constituency, but he had considerable other strengths. The first was statewide name recognition from his terms as governor and lieutenant governor. The second was considerable sympathy for his personal and political courage. And the third was long-standing ties with organized labor, which sent more delegates to a state Democratic convention than any other identifiable bloc.

Swainson ventured up to Lesinski's hospitality suite and asked the portly Judge, "Ted, why don't you and I get together for a talk?" Lesinski replied, "Sure, John, I'll talk with you tomorrow—at the Morton House." This sarcastic reference was observed by a reporter, as was the reaction: "Swainson's face turned wooden and he muttered a farewell and turned on his heel."[3] Lesinski still had not forgotten the Morton House coup.

In the end, Lesinski was not a factor. He finished well behind Swainson. The surprise was that Robert Evans came very close to winning the nomination. But the labor delegates came through, and John Swainson got a spot on the ballot.

In the November general election Swainson led all candidates for the Supreme Court, receiving 1,264,746 votes to G. Mennen Williams's 1,018,790. The Republican nominees (incumbent John Dethmers and former Detroit police commissioner Edward Piggins) each received less than 900,000 votes. Supreme Court candidates, as usual, received far less attention—and far fewer votes—than the statewide candidates for partisan office. Phillip Hart, the Democrats' leading vote-getter, was reelected to the U.S. Senate with 1,744,716 votes, and Frank Kelley was reelected as attorney general with 1,644,348. In fact the Democrats swept all state offices with the sole exception of governor. Republican William Milliken, George Romney's lieutenant governor, who had inherited the governorship when Romney left to become Richard Nixon's secretary of Housing and Urban Development, narrowly escaped defeat with 1,339,047 votes to Democratic challenger Sander Levin's 1,294,638.

On January 1, 1971, at the State Capitol John Swainson and G. Mennen Williams stood and took their new oaths of office for eight-year terms as justices of the Supreme Court of Michigan. They thus joined five incumbent justices with broad experience and diverse backgrounds.

Thomas Matthew Kavanagh, sixty-one, had grown up in the small town of Carson City and had served two terms as Michigan's Democratic attorney general before being elected to the court in 1957. Short and broad-faced, the pug-nosed Kavanagh was a pillar of the Knights of Columbus. He had served as chief justice from 1964 to 1966, and his colleagues would elect him chief again in 1971. He was known as a stern, tough taskmaster on the court.

In 1962, believing that Justice Paul Adams had reneged on a pledge to support him for election as chief justice, Kavanagh retaliated by campaigning for

Adams's Republican opponent, Michael O'Hara, who defeated Adams (Adams won election back to the court in 1964).[4]

Thomas Giles Kavanagh, fifty-three, son of a Depression-era state Democratic Party leader, had practiced law in the Detroit area before being elected to the then-new Michigan Court of Appeals in 1964. In 1968 the Democratic Party nominated him for the Supreme Court, and he was elected. Court staff often referred to him as "Thomas the Good," in contrast to Thomas Matthew Kavanagh's appellation of "Thomas the Mighty." Politically liberal, tall and bespectacled, with a gentle mien, he did his best to be a congenial colleague to all of his fellow justices.

Thomas E. Brennan, forty-one, had risen through the judicial system with remarkable speed. Born and educated in Detroit, he became active in Republican politics and ran, unsuccessfully, for the State Legislature while still in his twenties. He was elected to the Detroit Common Pleas Court at the age of thirty-two. Two years later, Governor George Romney appointed him to the Wayne County Circuit Court, where one of his colleagues was John Swainson. In 1966, with Romney's encouragement, Brennan sought and won the Republican nomination for the Supreme Court and was elected in an upset at age thirty-seven. Tall, dignified, and an eloquent speaker, Brennan had an independent—some said maverick—cast of mind and was outspoken in dissents to what he saw as the folly of his liberal colleagues on the court. He also had a dry sense of humor. He and Swainson had gotten along well as colleagues in the Wayne County Circuit Court.

Paul Adams, sixty-two, hailed from Sault Ste. Marie in the Upper Peninsula, where he had become politically active and served as mayor. He had befriended G. Mennen Williams when they both attended the University of Michigan Law School in the 1930s. As governor, Williams appointed Adams to fill the vacant office of Michigan attorney general in 1957. After Adams was elected to that office on his own, John Swainson became governor and appointed Adams to fill a vacancy on the Supreme Court in 1961. Adams had lost the ensuing election, but ran again, this time successfully, in 1964.

Eugene Black, seventy-one, was proudly different. A native of Port Huron, he had been admitted to the bar in 1925 without graduating from a law school, instead having prepared for the bar exam by "reading law" in the office of a former circuit judge. He had been elected attorney general of Michigan in 1945 as a Republican, but did not seek reelection. Instead he sought and received appointment to a vacant circuit judgeship from Democratic governor G. Mennen Williams. In 1955 he was elected to the Supreme Court as a Democrat. Brilliant, tart-tongued, and provocative, Black was physically imposing and nearly came to blows with colleagues more than once. His seventeen years of service on the Supreme Court generated more colorful stories and rumors than that of any other justice.[5]

The Michigan Supreme Court is the court of last resort for all criminal and civil cases decided by the lower state courts, including district, probate, and circuit trial courts. Virtually all appeals from the decisions of these trial courts go first to the Michigan Court of Appeals. In practice, therefore, most Supreme Court cases are appeals from decisions of the Court of Appeals.

With few exceptions, the Supreme Court is under no duty to accept or decide any case. Because of this, the first step in any appeal from a Court of Appeals decision is to convince the Supreme Court to accept the case for argument. Lawyers attempt to convince the Supreme Court to accept their appeals by filing an initial Application for Leave to Appeal, which lays out the facts of the case, the lower court's decision, and legal arguments on why the decision should be reversed.

The Supreme Court employs experienced staff attorneys, known as commissioners, to review the applications for leave to appeal (as well as the briefs filed in opposition by the lawyers for the opposing party). The commissioners write detailed summaries and recommendations on whether leave should be granted.

As a practical matter, the court can grant leave to appeal in only a fraction of the cases for which an application is filed; to grant an application is to commit the court to hear oral argument by the parties' lawyers and to issue a written opinion.

The members of the court meet to vote on applications for leave (and miscellaneous other issues, such as proposed court rules) at regularly scheduled "administrative conferences," held in Lansing once a week, except during weeks when oral arguments are being heard.[6]

For one week each month from October to May (except for the month of February), the court meets in Lansing to hear arguments on the cases in which it has granted leave to appeal. Typically, there are three days of oral argument, usually the second Tuesday, Wednesday, and Thursday of the month.[7] Immediately after oral argument, the justices meet in "opinion conference." At this meeting the justices informally discuss the issues raised by the appeal, and when it is clear that a majority of the justices are agreed, one member of that majority is selected at random to draft the majority opinion.[8]

Like their elected colleagues in the executive and legislative branches, the members of the Supreme Court who served with Swainson came from diverse cities and townships throughout Michigan. Unlike those colleagues, however, the justices did not find it necessary to establish second residences in Lansing. Instead, the state arranged for the rental of a local office in the vicinity of the justice's home, and each justice did most of the work at that office. Each justice also had an office at the Supreme Court in Lansing, but that office was usually occupied by the justice only a week or so per month, during the court's regular conferences. Swainson chose a local office at the University of Michigan Law School in Ann Arbor, a forty-minute drive from his farm outside Manchester.

Each justice was allotted the right to hire a law clerk, whose main duty was researching and drafting the opinions assigned to that justice (the independently wealthy G. Mennen Williams hired a second law clerk, paying the salary out of his own personal funds). Swainson's law clerk worked out of the Ann Arbor office, going to Lansing three or four days a month, when Swainson was at the court for opinion or administrative conferences.

Swainson's professional and political habits did not change when he became a justice. He continued to be an early riser, arriving at the Ann Arbor office between 7:00 and 7:30 A.M. most days. He was frequently on the phone to his friends and political cronies, and usually went out for lunch.

John Swainson was, indisputably, handsome, intelligent, and charming. Until his resignation from the Supreme Court in 1975, he was nearly always in a position of political power or public office, and widely viewed as having an even more powerful future. His name and picture were frequently in the newspapers and on television. He had a compelling and admirable life story. Under the circumstances it is not at all surprising that many women were drawn to him.

When he served in the legislature, he lived away from his family. As governor he traveled the state frequently, and as a Supreme Court justice, he spent significant periods away from home, in meetings with his fellow justices and giving speeches throughout the state. If, on occasion, he was tempted, there was no external force restraining him; he was not expected home for dinner.

He was not aggressive; he didn't need to be. He was more often the pursued than the pursuer. And he had purely platonic friendships with many female colleagues.

He was not a secretive man; virtually everyone who knew him, including his family, was aware that he had extramarital relationships from time to time.[9] Yet at the same time, he never put his wife in a humiliating position. There was no public scandal.

Ultimately, he always went home. And Alice let him in. They had built a life together, had endured difficult times; they had a record. They worked it out.

There is no evidence that his extramarital behavior ever affected any decision he made as a public official.

Ascending to the Supreme Court brought no change in John Swainson's fundamental character. No request for his help went unanswered. His first law clerk, Gene Farber, remembered, "He would write letters to colleges for kids. He would always say yes to requests for references by job applicants."

No sooner had he taken office than he was writing to the U.S. Board of Parole at the request of the seventy-four-year-old former Detroit mayor Louis Miriani, imprisoned for tax evasion. "I am well acquainted with Mr. Miriani and the details and circumstances surrounding his case. . . . in my considered judgment [he] is deserving of early parole consideration," Swainson wrote.[10] Miriani did not receive early parole, but with the benefit of time off for good behavior he served only nine months of a one-year sentence.

Swainson's empathy for the unfortunate and his thorough knowledge of government enabled him to continue in the role of a one-man social services agency, as attested by Michigan Department of Social Services director Bernard Houston's December 1972 letter to a Mrs. Nora Valentine of Detroit: "The Hon. John Swainson has shared your concern with us regarding your need for Winter clothing and bed linens. . . . It appears that your grant should have been increased by $7.50. We sincerely hope that this will help you to purchase the needed clothing and bed linens."[11]

He continued to seek out amputees, sending them letters and visiting when he could. On learning of a twenty-two-year-old former high school track star who was about to undergo amputation of a leg, Swainson wrote the young man:

> I know from personal experience that this is a most traumatic time for you. You see, when I was 19, both of my legs were amputated and I am sure like you, I felt the future to be very uncertain. The truth of the matter, however, is that you can accomplish just about anything you are determined to do . . . your future depends on your own mental attitude and effort. . . . If there is ever anything I can do to be of assistance to you, please do not hesitate to contact me.[12]

Farber saw Swainson "go to visit kids in the hospital—amputees. He would casually mention it to me, not to anyone else. Never to the press."[13]

Swainson's second law clerk, Victor Adamo, also remembered that Swainson "was going out quite a bit to hospitals, to people who had lost their legs, showing them that he had recovered."[14]

When he was assigned to author an opinion, Swainson would immediately outline to his law clerk what he considered the main issues. Ronald Carlson (Swainson's third law clerk) recalled a typical instance:

> There was a worker's compensation case. He said that the issue was whether or not a heart attack could be work-related. "And I want you to research this thoroughly, keeping in mind that workers compensation is remedial social legislation and we have consistently interpreted the law as being designed to aid the workers."
>
> And then I would do a draft. Then he would edit it. He might say, "I'd like you to do more research on this point" or "I'd like some more case law on that point." He would want the cases that you cited attached, or at least the headnotes. So he would get another draft and he would edit. And it would get to the point where it was time to circulate it [to the other justices]. After it circulated there would be subsequent drafts, after the [other justices'] comments.
>
> The majority of the time he was an editor. He emphasized policy considerations; his philosophy about Supreme Court opinions was that the proper audience for a Supreme Court opinion was trial judges. Having been a Wayne Circuit judge, he really felt that appellate opinions historically had spent a lot of time on the esoteric or intellectual analysis without providing solid direction for trial courts, without providing some kind of test for the evidence that a judge could use to do the kind of job that the Supreme Court was trying to achieve.[15]

Victor Adamo described Swainson's judicial philosophy this way:

> It would be wrong to say that he didn't care about the law. He did care about the law, but he was not interested in being the next Cardozo or Brandeis [U.S. Supreme Court justices known for their scholarly analysis]. He was more interested in looking at it from the executive level: "This is the policy that I think should apply here. Now let's get it done." He didn't care about the footnotes.[16]

A colleague on the Supreme Court, Thomas Brennan, saw Swainson as

> thoughtful. He would stress his point. You know, he wasn't a pushover for an argument, but on the other hand I always felt that he listened. I didn't feel he was doctrinaire. He was a liberal, no question about that. I didn't agree with him on a lot of things . . . in many, many instances . . . we disagreed, but he was never

disagreeable and we'd joke a little bit about our differences, kid each other about our political philosophies and things like that.[17]

The justices communicated with each other constantly by memo, in person, and through their law clerks, each justice attempting to gain a majority for his proposed opinion in a case. Brennan said, "All the members of the Court would be trying to persuade each other to vote in a certain way. That is what we did for a living."[18] In one case Swainson and Williams negotiated, through their respective law clerks, over the placement of a comma.[19]

During his nearly five years on the Supreme Court, Swainson authored sixty opinions for the court (i.e., opinions signed by a majority of the participating justices) and ten dissents. His written opinions were models of brevity and clarity. Unlike some (e.g., Eugene Black), he had no literary pretension; unlike others (e.g., G. Mennen Williams and Charles Levin), he eschewed long, scholarly analyses of past opinions. According to his law clerk Ronald Carlson, "He felt that opinions should be clear, concise, brief as possible, instructive to the bench and bar, and the esoteric issues could be included but not to the detriment of the actual practice of law."[20]

His judicial philosophy was not difficult to discern.

Of his majority opinions, twenty-one ruled on criminal appeals. Five of them reversed the conviction and granted the defendant outright discharge, ending the prosecution. Thirteen opinions reversed the conviction but remanded the case for a new trial. Three left the defendant's conviction undisturbed. Three of Swainson's dissenting opinions were in criminal appeals, and in each he wrote for reversal and remand for new trial.[21]

If these numbers seem weighted against the prosecution, it is well to remember that the era found state appellate courts in process of implementing the U.S. Supreme Court's recent revolution in criminal law. In a series of historic decisions (exemplified by the famous *Miranda* case),[22] the U.S. Supreme Court had declared the rights of criminal defendants under the U.S. Constitution, and the state courts had no choice but to implement them.

It should also be recalled that the twenty-one criminal case opinions were *majority* decisions. They expressed the judgment of the judicial mainstream, at least in Michigan.

On the rights of employees (counting workers compensation, unemployment compensation, and collective bargaining appeals in this category), Swainson authored seven majority opinions and two dissents. Seven of these nine opinions sided with the employees.[23]

In personal injury cases (including automobile negligence, medical malpractice, products liability, uninsured motorist and "dram shop" appeals), Swainson authored twelve majority opinions and one dissent. One of these cases involved two distinct issues, and Swainson sided with the plaintiff on one and the defendant on the other. Of the remaining twelve cases, he sided with the plaintiff on nine.[24]

A solid Democratic majority dominated the 1971–74 Michigan Supreme Court, and its members were not afraid to overrule old precedents they regarded as unfair. Swainson was certainly an active member of that majority. Among the sixty majority opinions he wrote, five stand out as resolving major public issues and pushing Michigan jurisprudence in significant new directions.

• *People v. Jondreau,* 384 Mich. 539 (1971)

The court overruled a 1930 precedent and held that a 1854 treaty between the United States and the Chippewa Indian Tribe preempted state fish and games laws.

The *Jondreau* decision sparked a series of disputes over the fishing rights of Native Americans that went on for years, until the tribes and the state reached a settlement in a federal lawsuit.

• *Detroit Police Officers Association v. City of Detroit,* 385 Mich. 519 (1971)

The court considered whether a city could force police officers to reside within its boundaries.

The 1967 Detroit riot had accelerated white flight from the city, further eroding an already-depleted tax base and further changing the racial composition of the city's population; African Americans now composed about 40 percent of its residents, and the student population of the Detroit Public Schools had a large black majority. But the Detroit Police Department was still largely white.

White officers began moving to the suburbs, driving back in to the city to report for duty. The city's leaders needed police officers to be available on short notice, and they wanted off-duty police officers to stay within the city as a deterrent to crime. The Detroit Common Council (the city's legislative body) enacted an ordinance requiring all Detroit police officers to reside within the city. The police union, the Detroit Police Officers Association filed suit, asserting that the ordinance denied police officers equal protection of the laws.

Mennen Williams was assigned to write the opinion, but Swainson disagreed with Williams's conclusions, and Swainson persuaded five other justices to join him in what became the majority opinion, upholding the validity of the ordinance.

• *People v. Sinclair*, 387 Mich. 91 (1972)

John Sinclair was a musician, artist, and counterculture leader who vociferously advocated the legalization of marijuana and opposed the war in Vietnam. At a time of generational conflict, the bearded, long-haired Sinclair was a polarizing figure. Many college and high school students admired him. Many of their parents detested him.

Detroit police undercover officers hung out at Sinclair's studio for months, doing errands and asking Sinclair for marijuana. They later testified that he finally gave them two marijuana cigarettes.

Convicted of possession of two joints, Sinclair was sentenced to nine and a half to ten years in prison (it was his third marijuana offense). He appealed.

In the lead opinion, Swainson engaged in a lengthy analysis of the history of scientific evaluations of marijuana *vis à vis* the so-called hard drugs and concluded that the weight of modern scientific opinion compelled the conclusion that marijuana was improperly classified as a "narcotic," violating the Equal Protection Clause of the U.S. Constitution. The court reversed Sinclair's conviction.

• *Young v. Detroit City Clerk*, 389 Mich. 333 (1973)

Coleman Young was a state senator from Detroit, former labor activist, and a friend of John Swainson. In 1969 he had wanted to run for mayor of Detroit, but the city clerk refused to accept his petitions on the ground that a provision of the Michigan Constitution prohibited a sitting member of the legislature from running for any other office. Young sued, and the Michigan Supreme Court affirmed the city clerk's ruling.

In 1973 Young decided to try again. He filed petitions with the city clerk, who again declined to accept them. Young then sued the city clerk, requesting that the circuit court order the clerk to put Young's name on the ballot. Unsurprisingly, the trial court decided the case in favor of the clerk. There was really no choice; after all, the circuit judge was bound by the Supreme Court's 1969 decision and the law had not changed.

Writing for the majority, Swainson ruled that the constitutional provision in question (which originated in the early nineteenth century) was intended to prevent members of the State Legislature from creating new state offices and then running for them. The Supreme Court's 1969 decision had assumed that a mayoralty was a state office, because the office, like all local offices, was created by the State Legislature. Swainson wrote that the proper inquiry was not who created the office, but rather whether the powers exercised by the official were primarily state or local.

Swainson ruled that the office of mayor was primarily local in character, and thus a state legislator was not prohibited from running.

Coleman Young was both a personal friend and political ally of John Swainson. It was and is beyond dispute that the mayor of Detroit can influence a considerable bloc of votes in a statewide election, should he or she so choose, and Swainson was certainly aware of this. If ever there was a case in which he used his judicial office to help a friend, *Young v. City Clerk* was it.

Incidentally, Coleman Young won the 1973 election, becoming Detroit's first African American mayor, and went on to serve for twenty stormy, colorful, and significant years.

• *People v. Turner*, 390 *Mich.* 7 (1973)

Two undercover officers pretended to befriend Thomas Turner. They asked him, repeatedly, to procure heroin for them, but he always refused. Finally, one of the officers told Turner a made-up story that his girlfriend was a heroin addict, and that she was about to break up with him if he could not get her some heroin. Turner replied that heroin was "bad stuff," but he knew an addict and would try to get some heroin from him. The undercover officer gave Turner money and Turner returned with a small quantity of heroin.

Turner, who had no prior adult criminal record, was arrested and convicted of both sale and possession of heroin. The Court of Appeals reversed the conviction for sale, but affirmed the conviction for possession.

The Michigan Supreme Court granted leave on the issue of whether Turner's contact with the heroin was sufficient to constitute "possession" under the law. However, in the course of hearing arguments and discussing the facts, several of the Justices decided that what the case really presented was a vehicle to determine the Michigan law on entrapment.

The question in an entrapment case is whether the agents of law enforcement merely provided the defendant with an *opportunity* to commit a crime, or whether the actively *persuaded* him to commit it. In many cases this is not an easy question to resolve, and both the Federal and State courts have created various tests, or yardsticks, to aid them in making this determination. Two competing approaches eventually emerged. Under the so-called "subjective" test, the Court looked at both the actions of the police and the defendant's propensities: was he "predisposed" to commit the crime, or was he "otherwise innocent"? Under the "objective" test, the Court focused exclusively on the conduct of the law enforcement agents, making no attempt to discern the defendant's criminal propensities.

Joined by Justices T. M. Kavanagh, T. G. Kavanagh and Levin, with Williams concurring in a separate opinion, Swainson adopted the objective test as the Michigan standard for entrapment. The Court reversed Turner's conviction and discharged him from criminal liability.

Swainson wrote:

"The use of the subjective test leads to a battle of semantics at trial over who said what first—the defendant concerned about admitting any evidence of "predisposition" and the undercover agent afraid that stating the wrong phrase at the wrong time will lead to a finding of entrapment. It fails to focus on the real concern in these cases—whether the actions of the police were so reprehensible under the circumstances, that the Court should refuse, as a matter of public policy, to permit a conviction to stand."

● ● ●

As the end of their terms approached in 1972, Paul Adams and Eugene Black announced their retirements. At the 1972 general election Adams was succeeded by Mary Coleman, who became Michigan's first female Supreme Court justice. A Battle Creek probate judge, Coleman was nominated by the Republican Party. Black's successor was Charles Levin, a scholarly Court of Appeals judge. Although Levin was a member of a prominent Democratic political family, he had failed to win the Democratic Party nomination for the Supreme Court. He thereupon created his own political party to get a place on the ballot, and beat both major parties' candidates in the general election.[25]

At the end of 1973 Thomas Brennan resigned to devote full-time efforts to creation of a law school in Lansing. To replace him, Republican governor William Milliken appointed Court of Appeals judge John Fitzgerald, the son of a former Michigan governor.

These personnel changes did not make a large difference in the court's political composition. T. Giles Kavanagh, T. Matthew Kavanagh, Swainson, and Williams continued as a solid liberal Democratic bloc. Black, a maverick Republican turned maverick Democrat, and Adams, a reliable Democrat, were replaced by a Republican and an independent with Democratic roots. Brennan was replaced by a moderate fellow Republican.

In addition, T. Giles Kavanagh, Charles Levin, and John Fitzgerald had all served on the Michigan Court of Appeals, and they brought that court's collegial and nonpartisan traditions with them.

By all accounts, the affable John Swainson got along well with all of them.

There came a day in the spring of 1975 when all justices assembled in the court's conference room for the regular monthly administrative conference. Chief Justice T. Giles Kavanagh had been seen in his office, but he did not appear for the meeting. The others waited, chatting idly. After forty-five minutes, they began to speculate about what was keeping him. At some point John Swainson left the conference room, perhaps summoned by Kavanagh.

Finally, nearly an hour late, Kavanagh entered and took his seat at the head of the table. He was visibly agitated. The others stopped their conversations and waited for Kavanagh to gather himself. Finally, he said, "I have some very sad and serious news." The chief justice then explained that he had just learned that the FBI was investigating the allegation that Justice John Swainson had accepted a bribe to secure the reversal of the burglary conviction of John Whalen.[26]

PART 2

THE FALL

CHAPTER TWELVE

The Burglary

THE TOWN OF ADRIAN NESTLES IN THE SOUTHEAST CORNER OF THE MITTEN OF Michigan's Lower Peninsula. Like many southern Michigan towns, it was settled in the early 1800s. By the late twentieth century many such towns in Michigan had disappeared or become bedroom communities serving nearby cities. But Adrian was too far away from major population centers to become a bedroom community. Instead, it remained a reasonably self-sufficient regional center of 20,000-plus, more spread out geographically and offering more commerce than many other towns of its size. On its outskirts sit two colleges: Adrian College, a private school of 1,000 students, and Sienna Heights University, also private, with about 1,300 students.

Adrian's downtown business district consists mainly of nineteenth-Century two- and three-story buildings, along with the occasional modern addition. As befits a regional center of commerce, its local retailers take in revenues produced by the surrounding rich farm country as well as by local manufacturers.

In 1969 one such retailer was Roberts Jewelers, on Main Street downtown. Next to the jewelry store was Monroe Shoe Repair, and across the street was a bar, the Club 109.

On the evening of Thursday, March 20, 1969, a construction worker named

Russell Doan sat near the large front window of the Club 109, enjoying a beer. It was about six o'clock and still daylight.[1] As Doan gazed idly out the window, he noticed a large, cream-colored car pull up and park across the street. Three men got out. One of them opened the trunk and took out a suitcase. Then they opened the front door of Monroe Shoe Repair and walked in. Doan assumed they were leather goods salesmen.

In fact, Monroe Shoe Repair was closed. The owner, Henry Monroe, had done some work that afternoon, then left, locking the front door on his way out. The three men had used a hand-fabricated key to open that door.[2]

They then went down the stairs at the back of the store into the basement. There they took a hammer, wrecking bar, and drill out of the suitcase. With the earth outside absorbing any sounds, they punched their way through the basement wall into the adjoining basement. Then they walked up the stairs to the main floor of Roberts Jewelry. Right in front of them, in the rear of the store, was the safe.

The three had brought not only a drill but an acetylene torch, with a cutting tip. Working diligently, they were inside the safe within an hour. They began taking velvet-lined boxes out of the safe, opening them and throwing the contents into a bucket. It looked to be a good haul.

Then they heard a noise. It sounded like someone was pounding on a wall nearby. Puzzled, they froze. There it was again. Then a pause, then they heard it again, but louder.

Charles Monroe, brother of Henry Monroe, had been working at the shoe business fifteen years. On March 20 he had left the store at 1:00 P.M. But he had some work to do, so he returned after dinner, around seven o'clock. He turned his key in the lock and felt the usual movement of the latch, but the door would not open. He kept trying and it would not budge. Finally, he realized that the door had been bolted from the inside. This was not uncommon; whenever either of the brothers was repairing shoes after normal business hours, he bolted the door. It was the only entrance to the store, and only he and Henry had keys. Charles recalled that Henry had said something about coming back in that night.

Obviously, Henry was inside. But for some reason he could not hear Charles's knocking at the door. So Charles made a fist and banged on the door, then waited for Henry to appear. Still no response. Now Charles was becoming alarmed. What if Henry was in there, ill? What if he had suffered a heart attack?

Charles reared back and rammed the door with his shoulder, hoping to jolt the bolt loose. He tried it again, with no effect. Then he saw movement inside.

At last! Henry must have heard him. But who was that with Henry? Three men were coming toward the door from the back of the store. As he was taking this fact in, they arrived at the door, unbolted it, and ran out, right past him. And none of them was Henry.

Charles entered the store. A light was on in the rear, and he went toward it. Nobody else was inside. Then he saw that the basement light was on. Cautiously, he tiptoed down the stairs. There he saw a suitcase on the floor, next to a fresh hole in the wall. There was also a torch and a tank, and various tools lying on the floor. And black jewelry boxes.

There was no telephone in the store, so Charles ran down the street to the police station.

Meanwhile, fourteen-year-old Maurice Evans was riding his bike on the sidewalk across the street from the shoe store, on his way to purchase a kite at a nearby store. He saw a group of men come out of the shoe store and head down the sidewalk at a fast clip, carrying something. They got into a white Lincoln, which headed south.

Michigan State Police troopers Joseph Lipinski and Michael McDaniel were policing the scene of an accident when the call came over their radio to assist at a blockade point on U.S. 223 at the Ohio State line, to stop a large white car, possibly a Cadillac.[3] That was only a mile away. They jumped into their dark blue State Police cruiser and took off. A minute later, as they were approaching U.S. 223, they saw a large white car speed by, heading south on the two-lane road.

They turned onto U.S. 223 and gunned it. Ahead of them was the Lincoln, and ahead of the Lincoln was a Chevrolet Corvette. The troopers activated the red "gumball" flasher atop their cruiser. The Corvette and the Lincoln slowed, as if to pull off onto the shoulder. Seeing their targets complying, the troopers also slowed down, whereupon the Lincoln accelerated, passed the Corvette, and took off. Lipinski and McDaniel gunned it again, and raced down the highway in pursuit.

The troopers caught up just as the group of three cars crossed the border into Ohio. They passed the Corvette, which was not going fast, and went after the Lincoln. When it became apparent that the Lincoln could not escape, the driver slowed, then pulled it onto the shoulder and stopped. The Corvette, catching up, also pulled onto the shoulder and stopped behind the police cruiser.

Lipinski headed for the Lincoln while McDaniel took the Corvette. McDaniel questioned the Corvette's driver briefly, ascertained that he had nothing to do with the burglary, and sent him on his way. Meanwhile, as Lipinski was approaching the Lincoln, the driver got out and approached *him,* effectively blocking his way. Seeing this, McDaniel walked past them to the passenger side and shined his flashlight into the vehicle.

Inside McDaniel could see two figures crouched down, as though asleep. Directing the beam around the interior, he then saw several felt-lined boxes, a bucket and loose jewelry lying on the rear floor.

McDaniel unholstered his .38 and rapped on the car window. Both of the figures inside popped up. McDaniel ordered them to keep their hands in sight and to step out of the car, slowly. Seeing another police vehicle arriving, they complied. The troopers then arrested the driver and two passengers without incident. After more police cars arrived, the prisoners were taken to the Lenawee County Jail, identified and booked on charges of burglary.

All three resided in Metropolitan Detroit.

The driver of the Lincoln, Christopher Glumb, thirty-two, was the principal planner of the crime. He had been in and out of prison since 1956, for two convictions on uttering and publishing (i.e., check forgery), auto theft, and a 1965 concealed weapon charge.

Bucyrus "Bucky" Wolf, twenty-nine, the front seat passenger, was the "muscle" of the group. His record included past prison terms for breaking and entering in 1957, unlawful use of a motor vehicle in 1961, and armed robbery in 1963. In fact, Wolf had been discharged from parole supervision only a month earlier.

The other passenger, John Whalen, was twenty-four years old. At twenty-one he had served a nine-month sentence in federal prison for theft of an interstate shipment. No sooner was he out than he went to state prison for larceny in a building, in 1967. He, too, had been released on parole not long before the Adrian burglary.

It was not a particularly difficult case for Lenawee County prosecuting attorney Harvey Koselka to put together, and trial was scheduled for the fall of 1969. All three defendants were granted release on bond pending trial.

In June Bucky Wolf failed to appear at a preliminary hearing. The court ordered his bond forfeited and issued a bench warrant for his arrest, but he had disappeared. The court then canceled the bonds of Glumb and Whalen, who were arrested and placed in the Lenawee County Jail to await their trial.[4]

In late 1969 the trial of Glumb and Whalen began at the beautifully preserved nineteenth-century county courthouse in Adrian, but the judge declared a mistrial when he learned that the owner of Roberts Jewelry had spoken with a juror.⁵ The trial was rescheduled for October 1970.

Sometime after midnight on March 15, 1970, Christopher Glumb took out a hacksaw blade that had been smuggled into the jail. He sawed through the bars of his cell, climbed up to a catwalk, sawed through the bars on a window, and jumped to the ground, where a car was waiting. He, too, disappeared.

John Whalen went to trial as the lone defendant.

The evidence against him was overwhelming. Not only had he been arrested in the white Lincoln with the proceeds of the burglary, but a Detroit welding supplies salesman testified that he had sold Whalen an acetylene tank and cutting tip the day before the burglary. Whalen did not testify. The jury found him guilty of burglary and larceny (technically, the breaking into the building with intent to steal was burglary; the actual taking of the jewelry was larceny). Whalen's bond was revoked and he was kept at the jail, awaiting sentencing by Lenawee County Circuit judge Rex Martrin.

That was not all. In April the U.S. attorney had placed a federal detainer on Whalen and Glumb on charges of interstate transportation of stolen goods.⁶ This meant that federal agents would be waiting to arrest them the moment they were released from state custody. The federals were not particularly interested in the interstate shipment charges. They wanted the two men held while they investigated a much larger crime: Glumb had set up a counterfeiting operation and was moving bogus U.S. currency around the country. Whalen was helping him.

And even that was not all John Whalen faced. At the time of the Adrian burglary Whalen still had been on parole from his 1967 larceny conviction. The Michigan Department of Corrections had released him from prison before he served his maximum sentence. They could revoke that parole and bring him back to serve out the remainder of that sentence. And if they "flopped" him (the term that cons use for parole revocation), he would have to serve out the balance of his 1967 sentence before he could begin serving his new sentence.

The Department of Corrections charged Whalen with parole violation, and he was returned to the State Prison of Southern Michigan at Jackson, to await a hearing.

To the Michigan Attorney General's Office, the parole revocation hearing looked like a slam dunk. The only issue would be whether Whalen had committed a crime while on parole, which he clearly had. It seemed like a good opportunity to provide some trial experience for a young attorney who had recently joined the legal staff.

So they sent me.

I had gone to work for the attorney general right after passing the bar, less than two years earlier. I had tried a few appeals and assisted other attorneys at trials, but had never conducted an actual trial on my own. I would be presenting evidence and cross-examining witnesses for the first time.

I drove down to the prison and was admitted through the front gate, then passed through several interior gates to the building where the hearing was to be held.

The hearing room was not large. There was a table for each attorney and one for the Parole Board's hearing officer. The witnesses waiting to testify sat in chairs against the walls. Whalen sat with his lawyer.

Whalen wasn't what I expected. He was soft-spoken and slender, about five feet, seven inches tall, with very dark eyes and jet-black hair. His face was handsome, almost refined. He was represented by Nick Arvan, an experienced criminal lawyer from Detroit, with a moderate resemblance to the comic Allen King. Arvan had a confident manner and a smooth, but unctuous way of using his deep voice. It was all a little intimidating, but I wasn't worried; I didn't see any defense he could possibly have.

I called my witnesses, who testified to the facts of the crime and the capture of Whalen and his cohorts, with the loot, as they fled. When they finished, I rested our case.

Arvan called Whalen and had him sworn. But then, before he questioned Whalen, he made a bizarre request: he asked that all members of the Detroit Police Department be ordered to leave the hearing room. He stated that he had certain matters that must be discussed, but not in their presence. I objected. Arvan then asked for a sort of "sidebar" conference with me and the hearing officer, out of earshot of everyone else. This I could not object to.

At the sidebar, Arvan said that his client had certain testimony to offer, but if it got back to the wrong people, it could get him killed. He asserted that there were known to be leaks in the Detroit Police Department. I had not anticipated anything like this. I said all right, I will withdraw my objection.

The Detroit cops left the room and Whalen then testified. He said that he had been working with the FBI, keeping them informed about the activities of his own associates. Whalen said that Bucky Wolf had been driving the car with Whalen and Glumb as passengers, when Wolf suddenly revealed that they were going to Adrian to rob a jewelry store. At that point, Whalen said, he could neither inform the FBI nor back out without being suspected as a snitch, so he went along.

Arvan then called an FBI agent to the stand. The agent verified that Whalen had an ongoing relationship with the FBI.

As I recall it, the hearing officer took the case under advisement (eventually, he ruled that we had proved that Whalen had violated his parole). I hung around for a while, chatting with the various law enforcement people. In the corners of the room, several of them whispered to me that Whalen was living the most dangerous life imaginable. He had become a professional snitch, ratting out people to avoid serving his own sentences.[7]

It was the classic slippery slope; to avoid prison time, you give the cops information on your associates who are involved in organized crime. It is just a matter of time before they find out. When they do find out, they and their friends will come looking for you. If you are in prison, you won't be hard to find.

I walked out through the heavy metal doors, drove back to Lansing, and forgot about it.

If John Whalen had any remaining doubts about what his colleagues knew about him as a snitch, those doubts vanished October 20, 1970. That morning a passerby found a body in a vacant lot in Shelby Township, near Detroit. It was Nick Arvan. He had been executed with a shot through the head.

They knew.

After jumping bond, Wolf was later arrested in California on federal charges, convicted and sentenced to federal prison.

In April federal agents investigating the counterfeiting ring found Christopher Glumb in Dallas, Texas. They sent him back to Michigan to await his state and federal trials. He was temporarily housed in the Wayne County (Detroit) Jail, the state's largest.

Glumb, whose IQ was reported to be 158—in the "genius" range—then planned and led the largest escape in the history of the Wayne County Jail (seven inmates got out with him), on June 26, 1971.[8] He remained free five months, until he was arrested in Cincinnati, again by federal agents investigating the counterfeiting operation. This time Glumb was caught with $500,000 in counterfeit U.S. cash.

Facing numerous federal charges, Glumb agreed to a plea bargain that resolved counterfeiting cases in Ohio, Illinois and Texas, and in 1972 was sentenced to thirty years in federal prison.[9]

Knowing that Glumb and Wolf would be in federal prison longer than any sentence they could have received for the Adrian burglary, the Lenawee County prosecuting attorney dropped the charges against them. Glumb was paroled from the Leavenworth Federal Prison in 1990. Wolf died in California in 2004. Neither Wolf nor Glumb served even a day in prison for the Adrian burglary.

All this was well publicized. What went unreported at the time was that Whalen was also charged for his participation in the counterfeiting operation. However, the initial charges against him were dropped at the same time Glumb pleaded guilty.[10] This was hardly a coincidence.

The *Detroit News* later reported that "a confidential police file shows that Whalen's testimony to federal authorities was responsible for Glumb's conviction. Although Whalen's role in that case was never publicized, police sources say a five-year probated sentence [i.e., no incarceration] for conspiracy . . . that appears on his criminal record stems from his cooperation with federal authorities."[11] In other words, the counterfeiting conviction would be on his record, but Whalen would serve no time for it, and would not even have to report to a probation officer. It was a "sentence" in name only. Anyone with experience of the criminal justice system would infer that Whalen had done something to earn it.[12]

Whalen had reduced his exposure considerably, but he still had to deal with two problems. The short-term challenge was the Michigan circuit court's standard practice of sending a convicted defendant to prison immediately after sentencing. Although a convicted defendant had a right to appeal his conviction to the Michigan Court of Appeals (and virtually all convicted felons did appeal), an appeal did not stay execution of the sentence. Normally, a defendant was transported to the Department of Corrections as soon after sentencing as transport could be arranged.

In December Judge Rex Martin sentenced John Whalen to seven to ten years in prison for the Adrian burglary and three to four years for the larceny. The two sentences were to be served concurrently.

But shortly after Judge Martin sentenced Whalen, Prosecutor Koselka received a phone call:

> T. John Lesinski, who was chief [judge] of the Michigan Court of Appeals, telephoned me. . . . The purpose of the call was to arrange to get John Whalen out on bail and our conversations were in essence that he was cooperating with police agencies in Wayne County [where Detroit is located] to get other criminals

and they would like to have him released on bond. . . . Judge Lesinski told me to take care of it.[13]

Koselka thought this request "was most unusual. That's why I recall so well, first time I had ever talked to an appellate judge, let alone Chief Judge of the Court of Appeals."

The call was strange for another reason. Only one Detroit-area law enforcement agency had called Koselka about Whalen, and did not say he was cooperating. The agency said he was a professional burglar and urged the prosecutor to get him the longest sentence he could.

But Judge Lesinski had made it clear that he was not merely recommending that Whalen be released on bond. "He told me," Koselka said, "to take care of it."

The prosecutor believed that he had little choice. He went to the sitting Lenawee circuit judge and advised him that the People had no objection to the granting of Whalen's motion for bond reduction and release pending appeal of his conviction. The judge signed the order.

Within days the Court of Appeals issued its own order: "Having been apprised of the action of the Honorable Rex B. Martin, Judge of the Lenawee County Circuit Court, granting bail and reducing the amount from . . . $75,000 to . . . $50,000 . . . therefore, it is ordered . . . that the action of Judge Martin . . . be and the same is hereby approved."

The wording of this order created the appearance that the Court of Appeals was merely confirming the action taken by Judge Martin in his wisdom. That was an illusion.

John Whalen, facing seven to ten years in prison plus the remainder of his paroled 1967 sentence, was released on $50,000 bond December 21, 1970.

Now he had breathing space to figure out a solution to his remaining, long-term challenge: to avoid ever going back into prison at all.

CHAPTER THIRTEEN

The Strike Force

IN THE UNITED STATES THERE ARE FIFTY-ONE CRIMINAL JUSTICE SYSTEMS. THE federal system operates under its own statutes and rules, and so does each state. But they all have certain features in common, most of which are mandated by the U.S. Constitution.

Anyone arrested for an alleged crime is entitled to be arraigned without undue delay; in Michigan the time limit is forty-eight hours after arrest in most cases.

The arraignment process is fundamental to the American criminal justice system. The judge explains the defendant's legal rights, supervises the reading of the formal charges against the defendant, ensures that the defendant understands the charges, and then sets bail—the terms under which the defendant can be released from custody pending trial.

In cases where the charges are relatively minor and the defendant has substantial community ties (family, a steady job, home ownership), the defendant will be released "on his own recognizance," meaning he simply promises to appear at all scheduled court proceedings in his case. In cases of the most serious charges—such as premeditated murder—the court may deny bail entirely, remanding the defendant to jail to await trial.

Most felony cases fall in between these extremes; for these the court sets a "cash or surety" bond. The court specifies an amount of money that it will require before it will release the defendant. The defendant has the choice of either posting the amount in cash or presenting the court with a bonding company's promise to pay that amount, should the defendant fail to appear at a scheduled court proceeding.

The average criminal defendant is not wealthy; in order to post a cash bond of, say, $25,000, most defendants would have to sell nearly everything they own (and at fire sale prices). Few, therefore, post cash bail. Instead, they seek a surety bond. For that they must turn to a bail bond agent.

A surety bail bond is, technically, an insurance policy, and the bail bond agent is, technically, an insurance agent, licensed by the state, as are all insurance agents. But the bail bondsman specializes in one type of insurance, known formally as an "appearance bond." In return for a premium (usually 10 percent of the bond amount), the bonding company guarantees the court that the defendant will appear at all court proceedings and if he or she fails to appear, the bonding company guarantees the court that the full amount of the bond will be paid. It is not at all unusual for a bail agent to require that the defendant (or the defendant's family) put up the equity in one or more homes as collateral. Then, if the defendant fails to appear ("jumps bond"), the agent can seize the properties and sell them to get back the cash the agent has to pay to the court. If the agent fails to pay the full amount, the bonding company must pay it. Then the bonding company will go after the bail bondsman for the full amount.

The bail bond agent gets a separate fee for taking this risk and for working as the intermediary who brought together the defendant and the bonding company.

A bail bond agent's nightmare is that a defendant to whom the agent has sold a large bond will flee. If that happens and the defendant cannot be found, the bail bondsman is on the hook for the full amount of the bond. The bondsman may seize the collateral, but that costs time and money, including hefty attorney fees. The preferred option is to produce the client. That is why the law authorizes bail bond agents to arrest their own clients.

Harvey Wish had a bail bond agency in downtown Detroit. One of his clients was John Whalen.

Vincent Piersante, who ran the Detroit Police Department's criminal intelligence section and later served as chief of detectives, described Harvey Wish as "notorious in Detroit as a fixer. That was his main forte, although he was a bondsman . . . taking care of cases, you know, getting them dumped, and he had a large acquaintanceship among Detroit police officers."[1]

According to Whalen, in December 1970 Wish said that he had paid $1,000 to Judge T. John Lesinski of the Court of Appeals to get Whalen's bond continued after his conviction of the Adrian burglary.[2] Wish wanted that money reimbursed, immediately. Whalen handed it over.

According to Whalen, Wish said he could "guarantee" a reversal of the conviction in the Court of Appeals for $10,000 to $20,000.[3] But Whalen's attorney told him his chances for a successful appeal looked good, so Whalen decided there was no need to spend this extra sum on top of his already large attorney fees.

Then, on May 31, 1972, the Court of Appeals issued its opinion. The three-judge panel affirmed the conviction.

After the Court of Appeals affirmance, Whalen fired his attorney and hired Neil Fink, one of Michigan's most prominent criminal lawyers. Fink's first move was to file an Application for Leave to Appeal in the Michigan Supreme Court on June 20, 1972.

Unlike the Court of Appeals, the Supreme Court was under no compulsion to accept or decide any particular case. It was therefore first necessary to convince the court to accept Whalen's appeal of the Court of Appeals decision. The means of attempting this was the Application for Leave to Appeal. If the Supreme Court denied leave to appeal, the Court of Appeals decision affirming Whalen's conviction would stand. If the Supreme Court granted leave, then the court would schedule arguments and briefing by the attorneys, and Whalen could at least hope for a favorable outcome. Also—and this was no small consideration—if the Supreme Court granted leave, there was a decent chance that Whalen's bond pending appeal would be continued during the twelve to eighteen months it would take for the Supreme Court to hear the arguments and issue a decision, and he could stay on the street during the entire period.

The Supreme Court was inundated with petitions for leave to appeal, hundreds of them each year. Yet it could decide only a relative handful of cases. For the three calendar years 1970, 1971 and 1972, the court received an average of 310 applications for leave per year for criminal appeals, but issued an average of just thirty-five opinions in criminal cases, a rate of just over 11 percent.[4] The odds of Whalen's case being accepted were not good.

Harvey Wish had reason to be nervous. Whalen's two partners, Glumb and Wolf, had respectively escaped from jail and jumped bond. Whalen had not run, pinning his hopes on appealing his conviction to the Michigan Court of Appeals. But now that hope was gone. Even worse, now that he had lost in the Court of Appeals there was a substantial chance that his bond would be canceled. To Wish, it would be natural to wonder whether Whalen was considering jumping bond and disappearing.

Wish did not know it, but Whalen wasn't going anywhere. He had placed his fate in the hands of the federal government, and there was no turning back. But it was imperative that no word of his cooperation leak out. So Whalen left Harvey Wish in the dark. Only months earlier he had helped the Secret Service get the information they needed to find and arrest Christopher Glumb in Cincinnati, in return for a promise to help him get a light sentence on his own counterfeiting charges.[5] Glumb, confronted with overwhelming evidence against him, would plead guilty to counterfeiting and be sentenced to thirty years in a federal prison.[6] As Whalen's reward, the U.S. Justice Department would voluntarily dismiss one counterfeiting charge against him and endorse a sentence of five years nonreporting probation on the other. Now, Whalen and the feds were even-up. But that still left him facing seven to ten years for the Adrian burglary. And now that he had given Glumb to the feds, Whalen was more certain than ever that if he went to state prison, he "would not last through lunch hour."[7] As Vince Piersante put it, "He gave the information to the FBI for a number of . . . reasons: One, to prevent more prosecutions of him; and two, to protect his life, because he had run out the string by then as an informant."[8]

And then Harvey Wish presented Whalen's deliverance.

A few days before Fink filed the Application for Leave to Appeal to the Supreme Court, Wish and Whalen had a talk in Wish's office. According to Whalen, "He told me it wasn't too late, and if I still wanted to do some business, he had some friends up in the Supreme Court that could guarantee a dismissal."[9]

Whether this claim was true Whalen could have no idea. But this wily survivor saw Wish's offer as a lifeline of another kind. He took it to the FBI and offered to help them get evidence of corruption on the Supreme Court. In return he wanted only one thing: a pass on the Adrian sentence.

Special Agent Ed Schley, who was to become Whalen's main FBI contact during the Swainson investigation, began meeting with Whalen "almost on a day-to-day basis," and the Adrian sentence "was a constant topic of conversation, almost every time we met."[10]

The FBI was interested from day one. Whalen's information had proved to be reliable and valuable in the counterfeiting cases. Possible corruption on the state's highest court was a once-in-a-career opportunity for any FBI agent. Schley and his boss, Norm Simon, decided that the case merited the commitment of substantial resources. They also agreed that the investigation would have to be very closely held, very secret. In fact, its existence would not be revealed to any Michigan authorities at all.

The U.S. Justice Department had sent groups of prosecutors into major cities to act as "strike forces" against local organized crime groups. The Detroit Strike Force was headed by Assistant U.S. Attorney Lawrence Leff. Whalen and Glumb were part of organized crime. Their gang was a northern offshoot of the "Dixie Mafia."[11] Whalen was believed to be the top "commercial" burglar in metropolitan Detroit. He stole large quantities of easily resalable goods—such as home electronics and cigarettes—then sold them to fences for a fraction of the normal wholesale price. This was why the strike force had been handling him, and they decided to keep control of this new investigation.

Whalen's testimony alone, they knew, would not be enough to convict a Supreme Court justice. They needed more objective evidence; they needed Harvey Wish on tape.

The first step was to get Whalen's agreement to wear a body transmitter, which would transmit the sounds of his meetings with Wish to a nearby agent with a tape recorder. He readily agreed, on condition that the feds give their word that he would never serve the Adrian sentence. They gave their word.

They tried it out on August 8, 1972. Special Agent Ed Diem strapped the microphone and transmitter to Whalen's abdomen and Whalen drove to Wish's office. Diem sat in a car outside, recording the transmission from the body mike.

Whalen prompted Wish about putting in the fix at the Supreme Court, but most of Wish's answers were unintelligible on the recording. In response to Whalen's offer of counterfeit money or bonds (presumably stolen), Wish said that Whalen would have to produce cash, and if the court did not act favorably, Whalen would get his money back.[12]

A month later, on September 9, the Supreme Court denied Whalen leave to appeal. Neil Fink immediately began drafting a motion for reconsideration, asking the Court to take a second look at the issues he had raised about Whalen's trial. He filed the motion on September 25. It was the last thin straw between Whalen and prison.

On September 28, three days after Fink had filed his motion for reconsideration, Whalen went to Wish's office. Wish told Whalen that he had passed the word that the motion was filed, and "my man called me because I thought you said there was a letter [i.e., the motion] coming in for a rehearing. There is supposed to be. Well, he hasn't seen it yet."[13] The strike force later subpoenaed the telephone records of both Swainson and Wish, and found a call from Swainson's phone to Wish's number on this date.[14]

On October 6 they met again, and Wish told Whalen, "I just talked to him [Wish's contact at the Supreme Court]. I read it. He says, well, I'm going to present it . . . in other words I said it will be presented to the Michigan Supreme Court on Monday, October 17."[15] But, according to Wish, Swainson still had not seen the motion for reconsideration, "and he said read it to me and I read it to him . . . not the whole thing, just—and he'll look at it you know."[16] The subpoenaed telephone records later confirmed a call from Swainson's phone to Wish on October 18.

Neither Whalen nor Wish yet knew it, but that same day the chief justice, Thomas Matthew Kavanagh, had signed an order denying the motion for reconsideration. Under the Supreme Court's practices, a motion for reconsideration did not go before the full court for decision, so Swainson himself was unaware of this order.[17]

On October 18 Whalen again visited Wish, who called Swainson at his home and asked, "What is the good word, if any? Oh, is it on the agenda? It is. And uh, they're gonna discuss it tomorrow, and then I can—well, I'm gonna be out of town tomorrow. You'll leave a message at the office? I certainly will appreciate it!"

After hanging up, Wish told Whalen, "Coming up tomorrow—he had it up there in front of them yesterday, you know, and everybody had a copy of the whatever and he said they just couldn't get to it. But it will be up tomorrow. He will call my office."[18]

Swainson did call Wish's office. On October 20 Wish told Whalen, "This is the message he [Swainson] left here yesterday. It is done. An order granting leave to appeal will be entered today."[19] But four more days went by and Whalen's attorney Neil Fink had received no word of any new order from the Supreme Court. The Lenawee County authorities were inquiring when Whalen planned to turn himself in to begin serving his sentence. On the twenty-fourth, an increasingly frantic Whalen went to see Wish again.

Wish reassured him, "He [Swainson] said they had that meeting on Thursday, they had five judges pass it, and he says and now this guy's gonna have a good year on the street . . . it'll be a good year before the Supreme Court hears it."[20] Whalen thought this meant the Supreme Court had decided to continue his bond, but Wish corrected him; the court had only decided to grant leave to appeal. They had not reviewed the bond situation. Swainson had simply meant that he assumed the decision to grant leave to appeal would result in a continuation of bond, whenever the court got around to it.

Wish had one other bit of news. The terms of the deal were different from those he had previously understood. The leave to appeal would cost $10,000, payable immediately. Reversal of the conviction would cost a separate $20,000.[21]

On the same day that the FBI was recording this conversation, the Supreme Court clerk entered the court's decision on the books as an official order. Reversing its previous denial, the Supreme Court had granted John Whalen leave to appeal.

Whalen still had to wait to find out about his bond. With leave granted, the prosecutor could no longer simply require Whalen to turn himself in and begin serving his sentence. A court would have to make a decision, one way or the other. On December 22 Whalen received an early Christmas gift. The Michigan Supreme Court ordered his bond continued.

The strike force instructed Whalen to make cash payments to Wish, but they did not offer to put up the money. Whalen, already strapped from paying nearly $40,000 to attorneys,[22] was left to his own devices. He put together a team and pulled a series of burglaries, fenced the loot and paid Wish in installments.[23] FBI agents never expressed any curiosity about the source of these funds, but they recorded the serial numbers of his bills, then followed Whalen to various bars and hotels and watched him hand envelopes to Wish. On one occasion Wish took out the money and counted it openly on the table at a restaurant.[24]

It is difficult to say what the agents hoped to accomplish in these surveillances. They never attempted to search either Wish's or Swainson's office or home, and never found any evidence that any of Whalen's money ended up in Swainson's hands.

On three occasions Wish mentioned to Whalen that he was expecting to meet with Swainson. As soon as they heard this, the strike force sent groups of agents to follow Wish or Swainson so they could observe the meeting. On September 16, 1972, they followed Wish to Manchester, then watched from a corn field as Swainson and Wish careened around Swainson's farm on a dune buggy. Then Wish took several boxes out of his car trunk and carried them into Swainson's garage.[25] On October 13 they watched as Swainson drove up to Wish's office, stayed less than five minutes, and came out carrying what appeared to be a wrapped picture or painting.[26] In October 1973 agents followed Swainson as he drove to Schweitzer's Restaurant in downtown Detroit, then watched Wish and Swainson have lunch. After lunch, they watched as a parking lot attendant transferred a large box from Wish's car to Swainson's. The box bore the label of a television manufacturer.[27]

Ultimately, the strike force interpreted these events as the delivery of gifts. On August 8 they had heard Wish tell Whalen that Swainson wanted a TV set. Wish had made other, vague references to $400 for a painting and $42 for embroidered jackets.

The Supreme Court scheduled the oral argument in Whalen's appeal for October 3, 1973. The attorneys had to draft their briefs well ahead of that date, so that the briefs could be printed in the special booklet-sized format required by the court, and distributed to each justice.

Whalen's brief made two principal arguments for reversal of the conviction. The first was that the police had violated his constitutional right to be free from unreasonable, warrantless searches. Fink asserted that the police were in process of setting up a roadblock to stop *all* vehicles on southbound U.S. 223, when they happened to see the burglars' car speed by. In stopping that vehicle, they had no probable cause to believe its occupants had committed a crime. Further, after they stopped the car, they had no right to "search" it by shining a flashlight into the interior, where they saw the proceeds of the burglary.

If the Supreme Court agreed with this argument, it would reverse the conviction and order all evidence resulting from the vehicle stop suppressed, which would amount to the "dismissal" Whalen hoped for; without that evidence there would be no case.

The second argument critiqued the trial itself.[28]

Whalen had called as alibi witnesses two women—a Mrs. Cone and Mrs. Reese—who claimed he was with them at the time of the burglary. Mrs. Cone had gone through a bitter divorce in which her husband was represented by Harvey Koselka, now the Lenawee County prosecutor. In his cross-examination of Mrs. Cone, Koselka asked whether it was true that she had shared a bed with Mrs. Reese, and whether the divorce was granted "because of your sexual preference."[29] Fink asserted that this cross-examination question had no bearing on the witness's credibility, but was designed only to inflame the jury's prejudices.

If the Supreme Court agreed with this argument, it would still reverse the conviction but the court would remand the case back to Lenawee County for a new trial, since other the evidence against Whalen would still be admissible and the error could be cured in a second trial.

On October 3 the attorneys filed into the Supreme Court's new chamber on the seventh floor of the recently built, seven-story Law Building in Lansing's downtown Capital complex. There Neil Fink and prosecutor Harvey Koselka were given thirty minutes each to make their arguments. The court also heard arguments in several other cases, then adjourned. By tradition the justices gave no hint of which way they were leaning and no indication when a decision would be made, but most decisions were issued within seven months of the oral argument, many within two months.

On December 18 the court released its decision. Writing for a unanimous court (including two new members, Mary Coleman and Charles Levin), Chief Justice Thomas Matthew Kavanagh addressed each of Neil Fink's issues.

The court ruled that under U.S. Supreme Court decisions construing the Fourth Amendment, police officers could stop and briefly detain a moving vehicle if they had a reasonable suspicion that the vehicle had been involved in a crime.

> We find that the stop of this vehicle was justified and reasonable under all the circumstances. The car fit the general description given the police of the getaway vehicle. The driver was dark complected and wearing a tan jacket, also fitting the description. The car was stopped shortly after the robbery had occurred, on a highway frequently used by criminals in that area for purposes of fleeing to another state. . . . Under these circumstances a brief stop of the vehicle for purposes of identification was the appropriate thing to do and that most reasonable in light of the facts known to the officer at the time.[30]

Moreover, once they stopped the car, the police officers had the right to use a flashlight to look through the vehicle's windows into its interior:

> In *United States v Booker*, 461 F.2d 990, 992 (CA 6, 1972) the Court ruled that "[s] since it would not constitute a search for the officer to observe objects in plain view in the automobile in daylight, it ought not to constitute a search for him to flash a light in the car as he was walking past it in the night season.[31]

The evidence observed and seized by the police was therefore admissible against Whalen. He would not get his "dismissal."

But then the court turned to its review of the prosecutor's conduct at Whalen's trial:

The defendant's defense at trial was alibi. He did not take the stand and testify in his own behalf. However, he presented two alibi witnesses, Mrs. Reese and Mrs. Cone, who testified to the effect that the defendant was present at a lounge, the Orbit Inn, at the time of the burglary.

In his cross-examination of Mrs. Cone, the prosecutor asked if she had ever shared a bed with Mrs. Reese, inferring a possible lesbian relationship between the two alibi witnesses. Over objection, he continued his cross-examination of this witness with reference to a prior contested divorce action in which he, the prosecutor, had represented Mrs. Reese's husband successfully. During those divorce proceedings the prosecutor had severely grilled both alibi witnesses for a considerable length of time.[32]

The cross-examination by the prosecutor in this case . . . had no legal connection with the question being tried, and the end to which it was obviously directed was utterly indefensible and resulted in an unfair trial. . . . It did no more than put in front of the jury the fact that he, the prosecutor, *personally* felt these witnesses to be of disreputable character and unworthy of belief. The prejudicial effect of such remarks by . . . a quasi-judicial officer is obvious. An objection to this entire line of questioning was raised by defense counsel. It was an abuse of discretion on the part of the trial judge to deny it.[33]

The Supreme Court thus granted John Whalen a new trial.

On January 10, 1974, three weeks after the decision was issued, the FBI recorded its last known wire transmission of Whalen and Wish.

After seventeen months, the meetings had grown less frequent and the vein of significant material—never thick—had petered out. All they had were a couple of possible gifts, Wish's words on tape, telling Whalen there was a bribe, mentioning some inside information about the Supreme Court, and a few instances of Wish's side of phone conversations with Swainson—conversations in which money was never mentioned, nor was there any reference to an effort to affect the outcome.

Worse yet, as things stood, Wish's words on tape were inadmissible in any prosecution of Swainson. They were inadmissible because they were out-of-court statements not under oath and because Swainson could not cross-examine Wish on the statements if Wish declined to testify at the trial.

There were only two methods of making them admissible: the first was to somehow turn Harvey Wish, to make him a cooperating witness and put him on the stand. The second was to develop independent evidence of a conspiracy—completely separate from the wire recordings. Under the law an alleged conspirator's (Wish's) out-of-court statements about the conspiracy were admissible against his alleged co-conspirator (Swainson) if independent evidence of the conspiracy was also presented. To get independent evidence would undoubtedly require interviewing the members of the Supreme Court.

But to pursue either of the two methods, the strike force would have to reveal the existence of the investigation. They reflexively abhorred this prospect.

And so the investigation sputtered along. Later, a source inside the strike force told the *Detroit News*, "We could have moved earlier on this, but we couldn't sell it to the Justice Department in Washington. At the time the Justice Department was in total chaos . . . totally preoccupied with the Nixon matter."[34] Perhaps, but the fact was that they did not have much to sell. And so things languished for a year.

Then, in February 1975, Robert Ozer arrived in Detroit, took over the strike force, and kicked down the doors.

CHAPTER FOURTEEN

The Grand Jury

A ROUND-FACED, CURLY-HAIRED BEAR OF A MAN, ROBERT C. OZER WAS THE SON of a Philadelphia truck driver. Ozer had begun his career fresh out of law school in 1967 in the local prosecutor's office in Baltimore. There he had gone after public officials who took payoffs to allow gambling. After two years he had left for Philadelphia, joining the Federal Strike Force in the local U.S. Attorney's Office. There he led an investigation of bribery and kickbacks in the sale of voting machines. Public officials and executives of the voting machine company were indicted across the country, and all were convicted.

This success won him assignment as the youngest strike force chief in the United States. At twenty-nine he took over the Buffalo, New York, operation. There he initiated an investigation of another voting machine company, which led to more indictments. But after only thirteen months in Buffalo, Ozer resigned. According to a later *Detroit News* profile of Ozer, he had requested a transfer back to the Philadelphia Strike Force, but "members of the office there who had worked with him rebelled at that."[1] He moved back to Philadelphia anyway, and joined a private law firm.

But Ozer found private practice boring after the excitement of prosecution. He stayed with the law firm less than a year and a half. In late 1974 he went back to the U.S. Justice Department in Washington, and worked in the Criminal Division while awaiting an opening to lead another strike force.

Ozer had loved the aggressiveness of the strike forces. He had added his own ingredient—speed. One of his early bosses remembered Ozer comparing notes with another young assistant prosecutor, one who believed in meticulous preparation. "You're wrong," said Ozer. "In this job you have to be like a Panzer division. You have to be like Rommel in Egypt. You have to crash through, keep them off balance."[2]

In the Philadelphia gambling probe Ozer had sat in on interagency meetings with the IRS, Postal Service, and other federal law enforcement authorities. He observed that

> the usual IRS investigatory procedure is very time-consuming. It isn't unusual for them to have a year go by without dramatics. . . . We changed the nature of the investigation. Instead of the drawn-out treatment it would get in the IRS, it got the crash treatment that the Strike Force was set up to deliver. We got every federal agent we could lay hands on, and we moved the case very quickly into the grand jury. We had results in two months.[3]

Ozer loved grand juries. There he could question a witness under oath while the witness's attorney had to wait outside. "The point is to not let him relax . . . but to keep him off balance." Ozer called this "prosecution by terrorism."[4]

Nearly all of Ozer's experience as a prosecutor involved corruption and bribery, usually by organized crime. That was the pattern he had found and that was the pattern he had come to expect.

In early 1975 Lawrence Leff decided to leave the Detroit Strike Force. Ozer arrived as his replacement on February 5.

As we will see, Ozer's handling of the Swainson case was to embroil him in more controversies, but he would continue to lead the Detroit Strike Force through the first stages of the investigation into the disappearance of Jimmy Hoffa. Then, on July 16, 1976, U.S. Attorney Phillip Van Dam (Ralph Guy's successor) publicly fired him, citing "personality conflicts."

After leaving the strike force in 1976, Ozer would continue his peripatetic life. He went back to the Maryland Attorney General's Office, but then jumped to the staff of the U.S. House Select Committee on Assassinations. He departed before the committee completed its work, moving to Colorado as director of the State's Medicaid Fraud unit. But in 1979 a state judge cited him for criminal

THE GRAND JURY ■ 155

contempt of court for leaking to a reporter the names of persons he expected a grand jury to indict, before the grand jury had even deliberated.[5]

It is not clear whether he was fired or resigned, but by the end of 1979 he had left government service for good. He then opened the first of a series of law offices in Colorado. From time to time he took in partners or merged with other firms, practicing in Denver, Conifer, Evergreen, and finally Colorado Springs. Surprisingly, he represented jail inmates against the government. He represented plaintiffs in personal injury cases. He even represented criminal defendants.

In 1986 the Federal Court for the Colorado District would find that Ozer had filed a frivolous suit on behalf of a group of chiropractors, and formally sanctioned him and the plaintiffs, requiring them to pay the defendants' legal expenses.[6]

But the case that would carve Ozer's name into Colorado jurisprudence forever—it is cited to this day—was one in which his primary role was not advocate, but defendant. As recited by the Supreme Court of Colorado, the basic facts were undisputed:

> In June of 1990, [Robert] Borquez began working as an associate attorney for Ozer & Mullen, P.C. (the Ozer law firm). During his employment with the Ozer law firm, Borquez received three merit raises, the last of which was awarded on February 15, 1992, eleven days prior to his termination.
>
> On February 19, 1992, Borquez, who is homosexual, learned that his partner was diagnosed with Acquired Immune Deficiency Syndrome (AIDS). Borquez' physician advised him that he should be tested for the human immunodeficiency virus (HIV) immediately.
>
> Borquez telephoned Ozer, who was president and shareholder of the law firm, and disclosed these facts, asking that Ozer keep them confidential.
>
> After speaking with Borquez, Ozer telephoned his wife, Renee Ozer [also a shareholder], and told her of Borquez' disclosure. Additionally, Ozer informed the law firm's office manager about Borquez' situation and discussed Borquez' disclosure with two of the law firm's secretaries. On February 21, 1992, Borquez returned to the office and became upset when he learned that everyone in the law firm knew about his situation.
>
> On February 26, 1992, one week after Borquez made his disclosure to Ozer, Borquez was fired. The Ozer law firm asserted that Borquez was terminated due to the law firm's poor financial circumstances.
>
> Borquez filed suit against the Ozer law firm and against Ozer as an individual,

claiming wrongful discharge and invasion of privacy. He cited a Colorado statute
. . . which makes it an unfair and discriminatory labor practice to discharge an
employee based upon the employee's lawful activities outside the workplace.

The jury awarded Borquez $90,000, and Ozer appealed.

In a historic decision the Colorado Supreme Court ruled, for the first time,
that "we now recognize in Colorado a tort claim for invasion of privacy in the
nature of unreasonable publicity given to one's private life."[7]

After Ozer arrived in Detroit in 1975 to take over the strike force, he decided
to take personal charge of the Swainson investigation.[8] He wanted to meet with
Whalen as soon as possible, and a meeting was set up within a week.

Whalen was brought into the office. Ozer walked in and introduced himself.
Then, as he later recalled:

> Whalen . . . said to me that he wanted to get reassurance from the new chief of the
> Strike Force that the previous commitments that had been made to him would be
> honored. [I asked him] what were they and he said "I have been guaranteed that
> I will not do any of the time that I've been sentenced to on my Adrian burglary
> conviction" and I told him he was surely in error and I am quite certain that no
> one could have or would have made that commitment to him and he said, "They
> sure did," and looked over to Special Agent Schley who was seated there and I
> looked at Special Agent Schley and he said, "That's right." I said, "What?" and
> he said, "That's what we promised him."[9] . . . I said, "Well, that's crazy. . . . that
> promise shouldn't have been made. That can't be made and it cannot be kept."[10]

The problem was the dual structure of American government: Whalen had been
convicted of a state crime (burglary) in a state court. Had he been convicted
of a federal crime in a federal court, the Justice Department prosecutors could
have concurred with the defense in a motion for a new trial, or a motion for
resentencing. With both sides in agreement, the federal court would almost
certainly grant their request. But the federal prosecutors had no authority to
petition a *state* court regarding a conviction of a *state* crime or a *state*-imposed
sentence. Only the Lenawee County prosecutor or Michigan attorney general
could do that. But the strike force had hidden the Swainson investigation and
Whalen's cooperation from the State and local authorities. And even when
they learned of it, they had no reason to help Whalen. He had not helped them
solve any cases.

Whalen was angry. He had done substantial work and added to his already substantial risks by wearing the wire. He had made it clear from the beginning that he was doing this work in exchange for the firm promise that he would not have to serve the Adrian burglary sentence. And now, *after* he had done his part, the feds said they couldn't do theirs.

So Whalen refused to cooperate any further. He would not be a witness for them. He would refuse to testify.

In a situation like this, Ozer normally would bring the witness's lawyers in and have him talk to them, but the strike force didn't know if Whalen's lawyers were in on the alleged bribe.

Characteristically, Ozer made up his mind and acted immediately.

"What I did do was decide we would get that question out of the way quickly and I think it was that very day that I issued Grand Jury subpoenas for both attorneys."[11]

Whalen's attorneys, Detroiters Neil Fink and Deday Larene, were shocked to be hauled before the federal grand jury. After questioning them under oath, Ozer was convinced that neither of them had known anything about a bribery scheme.

After the attorneys testified, Ozer sheepishly met with Deday Larene. "I had to, you know, with a great deal of embarrassment explain to Deday . . . that a promise had been made to his client that could not be kept and that . . . I could give him my personal assurance that I would do every conceivable thing . . . to try to persuade (Lenawee County Circuit) Judge Martin to give him a break, but that . . . he knew and I knew that I couldn't guarantee any result."[12]

That was the carrot, such as it was. And here was the stick: "We were going to call John [as a witness] and he could cooperate or he could fight us and get nothing . . . [13] I know that I never spelled it out for him, 'If you don't cooperate, we won't do anything for you. You'll go to Jackson [prison] and get killed.' . . . but that was certainly the import of where he would be."[14]

After discussing his situation with Larene, Whalen realized that he really had no choice. He agreed to testify.

Ozer then made the decision that no one had been willing to make: if the investigation could go forward only at the price of casting aside secrecy, he would cast it aside. On March 21 an FBI agent went to Lansing and interviewed Michigan Supreme Court chief justice Thomas G. Kavanagh. Other agents soon followed, asking the other justices for interviews.

With at least six justices becoming aware of the investigation, it was only a matter of time before the State Capitol press corps would find out. So on April

16 Ralph B. Guy, the U.S. attorney for the Eastern District of Michigan, issued an announcement that the strike force was investigating "an allegation that a $40,000 bribe was paid to Michigan Supreme Court Justice John B. Swainson [and] that the investigation had been underway for two years." The U.S. attorney added that "Swainson had not been called before the Grand Jury and is not expected to be called."[15]

The same day Guy issued his statement, Chief Justice Kavanagh announced that the Supreme Court had retained prominent Chicago attorney Albert Jenner to advise "as to how we might protect the Court itself from the insinuations of such damaging allegations." Jenner had recently served with distinction as minority counsel to the U.S. House Judiciary Committee in its investigation into impeachment charges against President Richard M. Nixon, and his independence was indisputable.

Ozer now unleashed his Panzer attack. He had already brought Harvey Wish before the grand jury.[16] On April 30 Internal Revenue Service agents questioned John Swainson under oath, going into every detail of his personal income and expenses, looking for an unreported five-figure increment. Then, on May 6, Ozer sent Swainson's tax attorney a letter, inviting Swainson to appear before the grand jury.[17] This was, of course, a direct contradiction of the public statement made three weeks earlier by Ozer's nominal boss, U.S. Attorney Guy.

Ozer waited seven days for an answer. None was received, so he subpoenaed John Swainson to appear before the grand jury.

The difference between a prosecutor using the police and a prosecutor using a grand jury is the difference between resources and power. The police certainly have resources. They possess forensic expertise. They know how to interview suspects and process a crime scene. They can put boots on the ground to canvass a neighborhood for witnesses. But neither the police nor the prosecutor has any legal authority to force a witness to appear for an interview, put the witness under oath, or punish the witness for refusing to answer questions. The grand jury has the power to do all of these things. Acting for the grand jury, the prosecutor can subpoena a witness to appear, under penalty of contempt of court. Once the witness is present, the prosecutor can place him or her under oath. The witness must appear in the grand jury room alone, without an attorney (although the witness is allowed to leave the room to consult an attorney). The witness must testify unless he or she utters the magic words, "I decline to answer on the grounds that the answer may tend to incriminate me." Even then, the prosecutor can grant the witness immunity from having testimony used against him or her. If the witness still refuses to answer, the prosecutor can request a finding of contempt of court—which is nearly always granted—and put the witness in jail for the rest of the grand jury's term.[18] John Swainson's appearance before the grand jury was scheduled for May 19—only a month after U.S. Attorney Guy had announced the investigation. The justice needed an attorney, and quickly. He spoke with his old friend Dave Sparrow. Sparrow was a successful attorney, and he would do anything he could to help, but he did not believe that he had the background to represent Swainson in this situation. Sparrow did, however, have a friend who might be suitable: Konrad Kohl. The two had met as law students and, by coincidence, had married on the same day and honeymooned in the same place, beginning a long friendship as each developed his practice in the Detroit area.[19] Kohl had developed a reputation as a tough and aggressive litigator in civil damage cases.

Kohl was not in politics, nor was he a criminal lawyer. But Swainson did not want a criminal lawyer. He told his Supreme Court law clerk, Ron Carlson, that "hiring a criminal defense attorney [would be] admitting that he had done something criminal and was just trying to . . . get off. He actually hired Connie Kohl *because* he was a civil attorney."[20] At Sparrow's suggestion, Swainson called Kohl, and they met, alone, for lunch. Swainson liked Kohl's aggressive approach; he would need a Patton to counter Ozer's Panzer attacks, and Kohl seemed fearless. Swainson retained him on the spot.

Shortly before 10:00 A.M. on Monday, May 19, 1975, John Swainson appeared at the Federal Building in downtown Detroit, accompanied by Kohl and Sparrow. They were intercepted by a cortege of print and television reporters, shouting questions. Swainson, described by the *Detroit News* as "unsmiling and serious," paused to make a brief statement.

He said, "I have refrained from commenting on this matter to this point because of the ethical standards demanded of a member of the judiciary and of a lawyer. Even after all that has transpired in recent days, I do not believe it would serve any purpose for me to engage in public arguments or debate on this matter, and therefore I decline any further comment."[21] Then, he, Kohl and Sparrow entered the building. They first went to the grand jury room on the fourth floor. Finding that the grand jury was not ready yet, they took the elevator to Ozer's ninth-floor office. In a few minutes, Ozer escorted Swainson back to the grand jury room and entered with him. The doors closed behind them. Kohl, Sparrow, and the public were barred, and John Swainson was sworn.

As he took the oath, Swainson knew that Ozer was investigating an alleged bribe to him in the Whalen case, but he knew little more than that. Neither he nor his attorney knew that FBI agents had recorded Whalen's meetings with Harvey Wish, and Wish's side of some phone calls to Swainson. They had no idea that FBI agents had followed and photographed him with Wish on two occasions.

Nor could Swainson know how little admissible evidence the strike force actually had. Ozer's plan was to get additional evidence through admissions from Swainson. Ozer had prepared very specific questions about particular meetings and conversations that the FBI agents had observed or recorded. If Swainson acknowledged that they had taken place, Ozer would have his admissible evidence.

If, on the other hand, Swainson denied that a particular meeting or conversation had occurred, Ozer could charge him with perjury and then present the FBI agents' testimony in court to show that Swainson's denials were false. This was what some attorneys call a "perjury trap."

Realistically, the only way Swainson could have prepared for what he was about to face would have been to keep a diary of every phone conversation and personal encounter he had experienced for the past two and a half years.

Ozer began with a series of general questions, designed to establish that Swainson was aware of the Whalen case and was acquainted with Harvey Wish. Swainson readily acknowledged these facts. Then, Ozer threw in a specific question:

QUESTION: Do you recall in September 1972 discussing the case in any way whatsoever with Harvey Wish?
ANSWER: I do not.
QUESTION: Do you recall in September 1972 having Harvey Wish visit your home?
ANSWER: I do not recall that, you know.

Ozer returned to general discussion of the Supreme Court's deliberations in granting Whalen leave to appeal. Then:

QUESTION: Now focusing on this time period of August up until October 6, 1972, did you have any occasion to meet with Harvey Wish during that period of time?
ANSWER: I really don't have any specific recollection and it could very well be true. I have had a casual relationship with Harvey Wish for a number of years. I have had telephone conversations with him. I have discussed with him at times the bail bond system that we have in the state of Michigan. I

have discussed personal involvement that my son had in the narcotics area with him. (TR 1325)

QUESTION: During this period I have asked you to direct your attention to, namely October 1 to October 6, 1972, did Harvey Wish visit you at your home?

ANSWER: He was at my home. I don't know specifically that it would be in that time but it could very well be.

QUESTION: Did he during this period of time, August 1 to October 6, 1972, make any gifts of any kind to you?

ANSWER: He did not.

QUESTION: Did he make any purchases for you?

ANSWER: Yes, I think we have discussed one of them. Well, it wasn't a purchase. It was having some embroidery done on some little nylon jackets.

QUESTION: Anything else?

ANSWER: There has been, throughout the time that I have been aware of this case, a box being mentioned. Now whether this is the time frame or not, I do not know, but I do know what is being talked about in that regard.

QUESTION: What?

ANSWER: Apparently there was purchased, I know there was purchased a wall hanging at Hudson's, J. L. Hudson's, and it was on my behalf and he picked it up for me and I paid him for it.

QUESTION: How much money?

ANSWER: To the best of my recollection, something like $135.

QUESTION: Where did you pick it up?

ANSWER: I think right in front of the Detroit police station or the parking lot across from the police station, to the best of my recollection.

• • •

QUESTION: Aside from the wall hanging and the embroidery of the jackets, and you also mentioned to the Internal Revenue Service that a lunch might have occasionally been paid for by Mr. Wish. Were there any other gifts from Mr. Wish?

ANSWER: There were not. (TR 1329)

Now Ozer became very specific:

QUESTION: On October 6, 1972 did you have occasion to speak on the telephone with Harvey wish, concerning the Whalen appeal?

ANSWER: I have no recollection of ever talking to Mr. Wish about the appeal.

October 6, 1972? I have talked to Mr. Whalen and on the phone but I don't recall talking to him about the appeal.

QUESTION: You just said you talked to Mr. Whalen on the phone, I assume you meant to Mr. Wish?

ANSWER: Yes, I'm sorry, I did mean to Mr. Wish. I don't know Mr. Whalen.

QUESTION: Again, Justice Swainson, and you used the term you don't recall. I want the record to be clear whether you feel there is any, you know, doubt or uncertainty in your mind, whether you had occasion to speak with Wish about the Whalen appeal while it was being considered by the Supreme Court.

ANSWER: I have no recollection of that, Mr. Ozer, at all. (TR 1329)

• • •

QUESTION: Well, specifically did you have occasion on October 19, 1972 to telephone Harvey Wish at his office and leave a message for him to the effect that the court is entering a—or granting leave to appeal in the Whalen case?

ANSWER: I have no recollection of doing that at all, sir. (TR 1339)

• • •

QUESTION: What I am asking you is, when you say you don't recall the specific incidents that I'm directing your attention to them, is that terminology to you meaning that you do not believe that it happened or you do not believe that Harvey wish brought you parcels in September, you do not believe you went to his office and picked up a package on October 13th, and you did not go to the office and pick up a parcel on October 19, is that what you're saying?

ANSWER: I am saying, I have no recollection of this. I mean that exactly. It might have been those jackets. It wouldn't seem possible. It might have been that wall hanging. It could well have been. I could have made a call. I can't imagine myself telling him something like this unless I was asked. I don't know.

QUESTION: Then, if Mr. Wish had asked you about the Whalen case you would tell him that the court had in conference decided to enter an order granting leave to appeal?

ANSWER: If he had asked me something like that, I probably would have said it. (TR 1340–41)

• • •

QUESTION: On October 6, 1972, did you return a telephone call to Mr. Wish at his office and did he on that occasion read to you a portion of the pending application for leave to appeal?

ANSWER: October 6, 1972?

QUESTION: Yes.

ANSWER: I have no idea that that happened, Mr. Ozer. (TR 1352)

And finally, Ozer came to the television set:

QUESTION: Did you have occasion before the opinion was signed, specifically on October 15, 1973, to receive a television set from Harvey wish?

ANSWER: I did not. (TR 1355)

Ozer had previously brought Schweitzer's parking lot attendant Melvin Holloway before the grand jury. Holloway had testified that on October 15, 1973, while Swainson and Wish were having lunch in the restaurant, he had transferred a large box, printed with a television manufacturer's logo, from Wish's car to Swainson's, and Swainson had tipped him a dollar when he came out of the restaurant. Ozer had the court reporter read Holloway's testimony to Swainson. He then resumed the questioning:

QUESTION: Will you please explain that incident, Justice Swainson?

ANSWER: I can't explain that incident, Mr. Ozer. I have no recollection of it at all.

QUESTION: Did it occur?

ANSWER: I am shocked here. That's what I am saying. It did not occur as far as I know. I know a parking lot attendant named Mel.

QUESTION: And is the testimony that you have just heard inaccurate or incorrect in any way?

ANSWER: As far as I am concerned, it's inaccurate, Mr. Ozer. (TR 1360)

Ozer had previously brought FBI Special Agent Ed Diem before the grand jury. Diem had testified that he was present at Schweitzer's October 15, and he had observed Holloway placing a large box in the back seat of Swainson's car. Diem then saw Swainson come out of the restaurant, ask Holloway, "Did you make that exchange?" and tip Holloway a dollar before driving off.

Ozer had the court reporter read Diem's testimony to Swainson, then asked,

"Justice Swainson, having further refreshed your recollection by the testimony of Special Agent Diem, can you explain the incident?"

Swainson answered, "I cannot." (TR 1364)

Shortly after this exchange, Swainson's testimony ended.[22] He had been on the stand one and one-half hours, plus two recesses to consult his attorneys. Drained, he left the building with Kohl and Sparrow. But that was not the end of it.

Swainson had been ill-prepared for Ozer's specific questions. He and Kohl were aware that Ozer now might charge Swainson with perjury for the justice's denials of any memory of the events Ozer described. But it might be possible to forestall such charges. In 1970 the Congress had enacted a new statute governing prosecution of perjuries committed before grand juries. Part of that statute (18 U.S.C.A. § 1623(d)) provided:

> Where, in the same continuous court or grand jury proceeding in which a declaration is made, the person making the declaration admits such declaration to be false, such admission shall bar prosecution under this section if, at the time the admission is made, the declaration has not substantially affected the proceeding, or it has not become manifest that such falsity has been or will be exposed.

So, during the next twenty-four hours Swainson, his attorneys, and his staff pored over his appointment calendars for 1973.[23] His law clerk, Ron Carlson, was in Swainson's Ann Arbor office. Swainson and Kohl were in the Lansing office (i.e., the Supreme Court chambers), and the justice was on the phone to Carlson, who recalled:

> I remember they scrambled around, pulling phone records and trying to reconstruct things. . . . Kohl was with him . . . I remember a discussion about that, the hubbub of it. John said, "[Ozer] asked me about all these dates and I have no idea what I was doing on those dates. It wasn't like I went in there [to the grand jury room] with my calendar; I couldn't reconstruct it. We're going to find out. We're going to look at everything. Pull your calendar. I'm having Nancy [his secretary] pull my calendar. We're going to try and figure out why he's asking about those dates."[24]

Alan Zemmol, who never met Ron Carlson, had a similar memory:

I know that he [Swainson] had a recollection that came after the first . . . appearance before the grand jury. I know that we had discussed the television set at a couple of points, and he really didn't remember. I know that we had actually discussed that prior—I think we discussed it prior to his first appearance and he had no recollection.[25] It was in his second appearance and then we discussed it again, I think, and then all of a sudden, "Oh my God, that's what I gave to Tom!" (As Swainson later testified, he had not kept the television set, but had immediately given it to his brother, Tom, who had just come out of the military.) Zemmol didn't remember where this discussion took place, but it was in the evening.[26]

Meri Lou Murray, at that time chair of the Washtenaw County Board of Commissioners and a close Swainson friend, also remembered seeing Swainson at the time of his grand jury appearance: "He was very concerned because he [Ozer] was talking to him about specific phone calls that John truly didn't remember, because it was a number of years beyond the time, and this is a person who obviously had a lot of phone calls."[27]

On May 21—two days after his initial appearance—Swainson returned to the grand jury room. Ozer came right to the point.

QUESTION: I would now direct your attention back to October 15, 1973, the date upon which your attention was directed two days ago and would you please relate to the grand jury any explanation you might have regarding the testimony that was read to you by two other witnesses concerning your activities on that day?

ANSWER: Mr. Ozer and members of the grand jury, I have had an opportunity to consult with my attorney regarding the matters upon which I was questioned two days ago. At that time it was related to me by the then court reporter of the statement of Mr. Melvin Holloway and the statement made by Mr. Edmund Diem, I believe, a special agent with the FBI. I can only say that I do recall the events that they testified to as they testified to them. By that, I simply mean that the box that was transferred to my car was transferred to my car from the car of Harvey Wish.

You asked me further, Mr. Ozer, about the parcel on September 16, 1972 being brought to my home by Mr. Harvey Wish. I indicated at that time that I did not recall that. I have since had a chance to, again, consult with counsel, and a parcel was brought to my house at that time by Mr. Harvey Wish. You also questioned me at that time about a telephone conversation. I believe it was, of October 6, 1972. A phone call was by Mr. Harvey Wish and you indicated that there was a reading of a portion of an application for leave to appeal. That is also correct. I wish to correct my recollection as I stated it two days ago. You indicated at that time on October 13 that there had been a package taken from the office of Harvey Wish. I don't specifically recall it, but it probably is true. You mentioned, again, at a later time of a telephone call on October 19, 1972, wherein I ordered to call the office of Mr. Harvey Wish to inform or leave a message with the secretary that the leave to appeal was granted. That is correct."[28]

The press reported that Swainson was only before the grand jury about five minutes, so he cannot have said much more than the words quoted above.

The statement is peculiar. We know that Ozer's sharp focus on particular dates during his initial appearance had taken Swainson by surprise. We know that after that initial appearance Swainson and his staff devoted considerable effort to reconstructing what he had done or said on those dates. It would seem that the product would be an explanation, perhaps taking the grand jury through the justice's calendar notes and showing how he used them to refresh his recall of events two and a half years in the past. Yet there is not a word about any of this. Instead, the statement comes close to saying, "After talking with my lawyer, I decided to come back and tell the truth."

From Swainson's viewpoint the result of his appearance was the worst of all possible worlds. Ozer got the admissions he wanted—and thus admissible evidence of the meetings and phone calls with Harvey Wish—*and* he got material with which to charge Swainson with perjury. Moreover, Swainson had stubbornly resisted Kohl's urging that he take the Fifth Amendment because it would create the appearance that he had something to hide. Yet after answering Ozer's questions, and consulting with Kohl, he *did* claim the privilege on May 19 and again after making his statement on May 21, and the *Detroit News* headlined its story "Swainson Takes 5th in Grand Jury Probe."[29]

Forty-three days later the grand jury issued an indictment charging John Swainson and Harvey Wish with conspiracy to commit bribery, and charging Swainson with three counts of perjury before the grand jury.[30]

John Swainson, senior fullback, Port Huron Big Reds, poses in his driveway, 1942.

High School senior picture, 1943.

Private Swainson, Fort Benning, Georgia, 1943.

With Aunt Terry in England, 1944. This is believed to be the last photo taken of John Swainson standing on his natural legs.

Outside Percy Jones Hospital, Battle Creek, Michigan, 1945. John Swainson on right. Unidentified soldier on left. The man at the center is believed to be Takaji John Goto, the Nisei warrior whose sacrifice and positive attitude served as a lifelong inspiration to Swainson.

Alice and John, University of North Carolina campus, undated, early 1950s.

Two happy warriors, Detroit, August, 1960, Michigan VFW convention. JFK rarely allowed himself to be photographed wearing a hat, but he made an exception for his fellow vets. G. Mennen Williams, standing, lends his own smile.

Inauguration Day, January 1, 1961, the Governor's Office. *Left to right:* mother Edna Swainson, Alice, brother Thomas Swainson, Governor Swainson, sister Carrol Whitehead, father Carl Swainson.

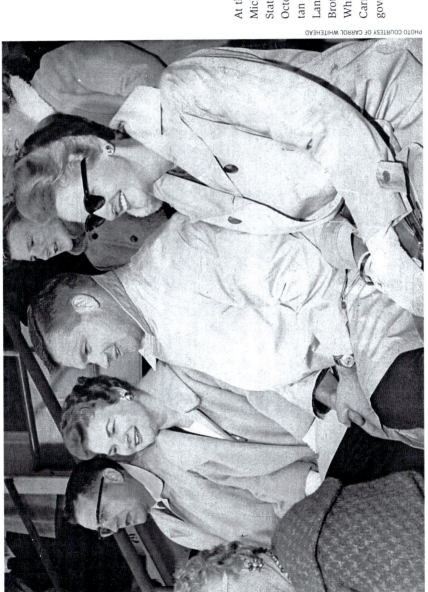

At the annual Michigan-Michigan State football game, October, 1961 Spartan Stadium, East Lansing. *Left to right:* Brother-in-law George Whitehead, sister Carrol Whitehead, the governor, Alice.

Wayne County Circuit bench, 1966. Swainson is standing, third from left. Thomas Brennan is standing, fourth from right.

The justices of the Michigan Supreme Court, 1972. *Standing, left to right:* G. Mennen Williams, T. Giles Kavanagh, Thomas Brennan, John Swainson. *Seated, left to right:* Paul Adams, T. Matthew Kavanagh, Eugene Black.

"The Hustings," the Swainsons' beloved farm near Manchester.

CHAPTER FIFTEEN

The Trial: Prosecution

On Monday, May 20, 1975, the trial of *United States v. Swainson and Wish* commenced at the U.S. Courthouse in downtown Detroit, a squat, gray 1934 neoclassical revival building.

The *Detroit News* observed that Swainson appeared relaxed as proceedings began. His wife and daughter accompanied him into the courtroom.

After most of the Detroit-area federal judges had disqualified themselves (because of their personal acquaintance with Swainson), the U.S. Sixth Circuit Court of Appeals had brought in Carl Rubin, a federal judge based in Cincinnati, Ohio.

Using streamlined procedures that were years ahead of their time, Judge Rubin astonished nearly all observers by selecting a jury of twelve in less than two hours. Seven were women and four were men. All were white.

The prosecution's lead-off witness was T. Giles Kavanagh,[1] who had recently become chief justice of the Michigan Supreme Court. Slender, balding and bespectacled, Kavanagh possessed a gentle, scholarly demeanor that served as cover for his tenacious advocacy of the rights of the underprivileged.

Ozer led him through a detailed explanation of the court's procedure for deciding whether to grant or deny leave to appeal. Kavanagh explained that the court employed three commissioners, lawyers whose job was to winnow the hundreds of petitions for leave that came in. Each petition was assigned to a commissioner, who would make a written recommendation to the justices. Attached to the commissioner's recommendation was a proposed order incorporating that recommendation. Unless a justice filed an objection (called a "hold") by a specified date, that order would be entered as the Supreme Court's decision.

When Whalen's petition for leave had come in, the commissioner had recommended denial, but Kavanagh thought Whalen's appeal raised significant issues, so he filed a hold. Following the court's standard procedure, the matter then was placed on the agenda for the justices' next administrative conference.[2]

At that conference, held on September 5, 1972, Kavanagh failed to persuade even one of his colleagues to grant leave for Whalen to appeal. The clerk then entered the court's official order denying leave.

Soon after the order of denial was entered, Whalen's attorney sent the court his motion for rehearing. There was nothing unusual about this, and the commissioners reviewed the motion. The court's procedure, Kavanagh testified, was that if the commissioners saw no reason to reconsider, they would simply communicate this view to the chief justice (at that time T. Matthew Kavanagh), and he would sign an order denying rehearing. None of the other justices would even be notified of the motion. And that is what happened to Whalen's motion for rehearing.

The court's next administrative conference was scheduled for October 17–18. An agenda was prepared by the chief justice. Any of the justices could request that a matter be placed on the agenda. The Whalen motion for rehearing was not on that agenda.

However, it was not uncommon for the justices to discuss matters that were not on the agenda, and the minutes of the October 17–18 conference show that they discussed the Whalen motion for rehearing, and made a unanimous decision to grant leave to appeal. Kavanagh had no recollection of the discussions,[3] but had "no reason to think that we varied from our usual procedure . . . which would have me be the leader of that discussion and the one that was arguing most vociferously in favor of granting the application for leave."[4]

The minutes of the conference indicated that the granting of leave to appeal was moved by Swainson and seconded by T. Giles Kavanagh.[5] However, Kavanagh testified that it was not unknown for the late chief justice, after consensus had been reached, to ask a colleague to make the motion and another to second it.[6] Later in the trial Justice G. Mennen Williams agreed, testifying, "We are a collegial group and who moves what doesn't make that much difference because we try to get the business done. The Chief Justice will turn to somebody on his left or right and they will respond in order to get the thing moving."[7]

In fact, T. Matthew Kavanagh's handwritten notes of the conference included the notation that Thomas E. Brennan had moved the grant of leave, but the chief justice had then scratched out Brennan's initials and substituted Swainson's. Brennan himself noted that "there are many strikeovers and many corrections in these original notes," and opined that "the Chief Justice simply made a mistake and he corrected it."

Of the six justices who had participated in the administrative conference, one (T. Matthew Kavanagh) died before the trial; four of the remaining five testified.[8] None of these justices had any detailed recollection of the October 1972 administrative conference, and none recalled Swainson making any special effort to persuade them to grant leave to Whalen, either at that conference or on any other occasion. To the extent they recalled anything, it was that T. Giles Kavanagh made that effort.[9]

That was all there was on the grant of leave to appeal. No one could remember who brought it up and no one had any specific memory of anything Swainson might have said, or even whether he actually made the motion.

Kavanagh now turned to the Supreme Court's next action in the Whalen case: Whalen's motion that his bond be continued pending the outcome of his appeal.

As we have seen, the Lenawee Circuit Court had granted Whalen bond pending appeal after Court of Appeals chief judge T. John Lesinski intervened with the prosecutor. The Court of Appeals, unsurprisingly, had affirmed the continuance of bond pending appeal. But after the Court of Appeals had affirmed Whalen's conviction and the Supreme Court denied leave to appeal, it would normally be just a matter of days before bond was revoked. Thus, along with his motion for rehearing, Neil Fink had submitted to the Supreme Court a motion to continue bond.

There is no evidence that the justices considered the motion to continue bond at the October 1972 administrative conference. Unlike the motion for rehearing, it wended its way through normal channels. Sometime in late October or early November a commissioner reviewed the motion and recommended denial. The commissioner attached a proposed order of denial, which would be entered automatically November 17, 1972, unless one or more justices objected.

Kavanagh identified the prosecution's Exhibit 10, a hold memo on the bond denial, filed November 16 by John Swainson. This hold memo had the effect of stopping the entry of the commissioner's proposed order denying bond and placing the issue on the agenda of the Supreme Court's next administrative conference, scheduled for December 21, 1972. Until then John Whalen would remain free.

Unlike the ambiguity about whether it was Swainson who made the motion to grant leave, there is no question that he filed the hold memo to continue Whalen's bond pending appeal. Considered by itself, this fact would appear to identify Swainson as, if not Whalen's chief advocate on the Supreme Court, at least firmly Whalen's advocate.

However, that impression is not supported by what Swainson actually wrote in the hold memo: "Hold for conference. I am not sure I completely understand the charges involved."[10] As Swainson testified later, the hold memo referred to a computer printout of Whalen's record of prior criminal convictions and pending charges, which was attached to the commissioner's memo recommending denial of bond.[11]

Swainson said, "Now, obviously when you set bond or continue bond, you want to know how reliable that person is, what his background is . . . we knew that the man had been on bond and . . . he hadn't run away . . . , but there did appear . . . a duplication of things listed here [on the printout] as to pending cases, and I know when I read it I was somewhat confused."[12]

Swainson's claim of confusion turns out to be not at all implausible; Judge Rubin, prosecutor Ozer, and defense counsel Kohl consumed nearly twenty pages of trial transcript, over what appears to be several hours, in attempting to resolve exactly the same question: how many separate counterfeiting offenses the federal government had charged against Whalen, and the outcomes of those cases. And they had more complete records than Swainson.[13]

Justice Kavanagh ended his testimony with a discussion of the *Tanner* case, a Supreme Court decision on the permissible limits of criminal sentences, which decision he believed ultimately had no effect on the Whalen case.

Ozer next called a small parade of FBI agents. Each described a particular incident.

Special Agent Robert Langford testified that on October 13, 1972, he had set up Whalen with a body mike and then waited outside Wish's office while Whalen went in. He had then observed a car arrive and Swainson emerge from the car and go into Wish's building. After about a minute he saw Swainson come out, carrying a flat package of roughly two by three feet. Swainson got into the car, which was driven by another man, and they drove away.[14]

Langford next testified that he had also followed Wish to Swainson's farm outside Manchester on September 16, 1972, and watched as Swainson and Wish rode an all-terrain vehicle around the farm. Wish then went to his car and took several small boxes into the house.[15]

Special Agent Ed Schley testified that on November 27, 1972, he recorded the serial numbers of $2,500 in currency that Whalen had brought, then followed Whalen to a Holiday Inn in Windsor, Ontario (across the river from Detroit) and sat in the bar, watching as Harvey Wish arrived.[16]

On October 11, 1973, Schley drove to the same Holiday Inn and recorded the serial numbers of $10,000 in a room. Later, he saw Harvey Wish arrive.[17]

Special Agent Margaret Epke was assigned to surveillance in the bar of the Holiday Inn that day, and watched as Whalen handed an envelope to Wish, who then opened the envelope and took out a bundle of currency, which Epke saw him count.[18]

Special Agent Michael Leyden testified that on October 15, 1973, he had followed Swainson as he drove from his University of Michigan office to Schweitzer's Restaurant in downtown Detroit. After waiting a minute, Leyden entered the restaurant and observed Swainson seated at a table with Harvey Wish. After about an hour, Wish left. Swainson stayed behind, chatting with several men at a table in the bar. Then a parking lot attendant came in and handed Swainson his car keys. Leyden heard Swainson ask, "Did you make that exchange alright?" and gave the attendant a dollar.[19]

The prosecutor also called the parking lot attendant, Melvin Holloway. He testified that when Swainson arrived he had told Holloway that another man would be putting a package in his car. Later, a second man arrived (presumably Wish) and asked for Holloway's assistance in putting a large box in Swainson's car. Holloway moved Swainson's car near the other man's car, and the two of them then moved a box into the back seat of Swainson's car. The printing on the box indicated that it contained a television set.[20]

We now come to the prosecution's most significant, and controversial, witness—a witness who never took the oath, sat in the witness chair, or submitted to cross-examination. This was the voice of Harvey Wish, secretly recorded by John Whalen's body microphone.

The tapes of Whalen's conversations with Wish comprised approximately ten hours, of varying intelligibility. The earliest tapes were the poorest, and the quality appears to have improved as the FBI agents and Whalen acquired experience in placing and operating the equipment. Nevertheless, the overall quality was such that the FBI laboriously prepared three successive editions of typed transcripts of these conversations.

All of Wish's statements on the tapes were hearsay. They were nevertheless admissible as evidence against Harvey Wish because self-incriminating statements are an exception to the hearsay rule. The controversy was whether they were admissible as evidence against Swainson.

Under the Sixth Amendment to the U.S. Constitution the defendant in a criminal trial has the absolute right to "confront" (i.e., cross-examine) the witnesses against him. But a witness who is heard only on tape cannot be cross-examined.

Yet Harvey Wish was present in the courtroom. Why couldn't Kohl simply call him as a witness? The answer is that Harvey Wish was also on trial, and under the Fifth Amendment, a defendant in a criminal case has the absolute right not to take the witness stand. To force him to testify at his own trial would be tantamount to forcing him to incriminate himself.

So it would seem that Harvey Wish's unsworn, non-cross-examinable words on tape could not be used as evidence against John Swainson (and without the tapes, the prosecution had no real case).

In pretrial motions Kohl had made exactly this argument. But he lost, because the judge ruled that the tapes fit within a narrow exception to the Sixth Amendment's Confrontation Clause that the U.S. Supreme Court had recognized for well over a century.

The "co-conspirator exception" holds that where there are two alleged co-conspirators, the out-of-court statements of conspirator A can be used as evidence against conspirator B *if* there is independent evidence of the conspiracy (that is, evidence other than conspirator A's out-of-court statements).[21]

Judge Rubin's pretrial ruling was provisional, because it was based (of necessity) only upon the attorneys' predictions on what testimony would be presented at the trial. It was understood that the judge would hear arguments and make his final ruling only after all prosecution witnesses had testified. Then he would be basing his ruling not on attorneys' predictions, but on the witnesses' actual testimony. Of course, by that time the jury would have heard the tapes and it would be virtually impossible for them to forget what they had heard. Therefore, if the judge agreed with the defense that there was no independent evidence of conspiracy, it was presumed that he would either dismiss the bribery charges against Swainson or declare a mistrial.

FBI agent Ed Diem played the tapes for the jury, who thus had to sit through roughly ten hours of often obscene, at times barely intelligible, minutia. A typical Wish-Whalen conversation went like this:

WISH: . . . I'll be here, I don't want you to have any more problems other than your own.

WHALEN: Right, yeh, right.

WISH: . . .

WHALEN: See, ah, if a guy's a partner and he takes a bust I got to stand behind him.

WISH: Fine.

WHALEN: You know.

WISH: But what's the fuck good is it you being a partner if you ain't around.

WHALEN: Right, that's right.

WISH: I'm telling you, and I've told you this a thousand times, you better worry about you. If you don't start worrying about you, you're going to fuck yourself.

WHALEN: Right, right.

WISH: Now if this rehearing comes off, they will hear it—

WHALEN: Yeah right."[22]

As we have seen, the tapes caught Wish on October 6 telling Whalen that Swainson had told Wish that Whalen's motion for rehearing would be presented to the justices on October 17.

On the October 18 tape the jury heard Wish call Swainson at his home and say, "What is the good word, if any? Oh, is it on the agenda? It is. And uh, they're gonna discuss it tomorrow, and then I can—well, I'm gonna be out of town tomorrow. You'll leave a message at the office? I certainly will appreciate it!"

On the October 20 tape Wish told Whalen, "This is the message he [Swainson] left here yesterday. It is done. An order granting leave to appeal will be entered today."

The playing of the tapes consumed three days, from Wednesday to Friday, and the judge sent the jurors home for the weekend.

On Monday the twenty-seventh, the prosecution introduced what the *Detroit News* called their "star witness," John Whalen.

Journalists love a colorful character, and Whalen was certainly that, given his background as a professional thief, but he was hardly a star witness. In fact,

Whalen's credibility was so questionable that Ozer, in his closing argument at the end of the trial, would tell the jury, "There is nothing in this case in which I am going to ask you to take John Whalen's word."[23]

Whalen reiterated much of what the jury had already heard on the tapes, and added some things that they had not heard before. He told the story of Wish calling Judge Lesinski of the Court of Appeals and getting the bond for a bribe of $1,000.[24] He recalled that it was a "a few days" prior to Neil Fink's filing application for leave to appeal that Wish had mentioned that "if I still wanted to do some business, he had some friends up in the Supreme Court that would guarantee a dismissal."[25] Whalen, as we have seen, went to the FBI and reported this conversation.

Whalen remembered being at Wish's office on September 14, 1972, when Wish told him to come up with $400 to pay for a painting that Wish was giving to Swainson. Whalen saw Swainson enter the office, stay only a few minutes, and leave with a package the shape of a painting.[26] Another man, whom Whalen did not recognize, waited for Swainson in the car.

In describing the morphing of the bargain, Whalen said Wish at first told him that the price would be $30,000, to be placed in "escrow," the money to be returned if the Supreme Court did not grant him a "dismissal." However, shortly after the court granted leave to appeal, Wish changed the terms, explaining that the grant of leave to appeal, by itself, would keep Whalen on the street for twelve to eighteen months, and this was worth $10,000. The remaining $20,000 would still be placed in escrow and refunded if Whalen did not get his dismissal at the end of the process.[27]

Whalen made cash payments to Wish of $2,500, $5,000, and $2,500 over a period of a month. On October 3, 1973, the Supreme Court heard the oral arguments of the prosecutor and Whalen's attorney, Neil Fink (under the Supreme Court's practices, it was at this time that the justices first discussed the merits of Whalen's appeal, and the opinion was assigned by blind draw to Thomas Matthew Kavanagh). Whalen testified that two days after oral argument, Wish again changed the terms: "He advised me . . . that the best Justice Swainson can do is to get the case sent back for a new trial, and that will cost me $10,000 instead of $20,000."[28]

However, the FBI had taped the October 5 conversation, and on the tape Wish does not make that statement. What he does say to Whalen is, "What do you want me to say—if the guy says—you know they can send it back—to trial."[29] Ozer's characterization of the conversation, entered on a chart with the judge's approval, was, "Wish asks Whalen what he, Wish, should say if the guy says they could send it back to trial."[30] The difference between Whalen's version and the tape's version is significant. Under Whalen's version, Wish has *already learned* from Swainson that the justices will not grant Whalen a discharge, and the best he can get will be a new trial. But on the tape Wish merely asks Whalen what he wants to do *if it should turn out* that a new trial is the best he can do.

When the Supreme Court granted leave to appeal in a criminal case, if the convicted defendant ended up winning in the Supreme Court, this usually meant that the case was "remanded" back to the lower court for a new trial. In a minority of cases, however, the Supreme Court did not order a new trial but simply reversed the lower court and discharged the defendant from any further criminal liability (this was what Whalen referred to as a "dismissal").

In any event, Whalen left the October 5 meeting with a firm impression that he needed to come up with $10,000 within a week, which led to the following exchange with Ozer:

QUESTION: Well, alright, we might as well face up to this. How did you get the money, Mr. Whalen?
ANSWER: Well, over the weekend me and a few friends of mine went out and committed some burglaries.[31]

Whalen then delivered the $10,000 to Wish at a hotel in Windsor, Ontario, after the FBI recorded the serial numbers.[32]

Ozer's direct examination was finished, and he offered Whalen for cross-examination. Harvey Wish's attorney, Murray Chodak, went first. One of Chodak's major contentions was that Wish had simply made up the bribe story in an effort to con Whalen out of the $20,000, because Whalen refused to pay the premium on his bond. Pursuing this, Chodak asked Whalen if he understood that the premium was 10 percent annually, or $5,000 a year, on his $50,000 appeal bond. Whalen answered:

ANSWER: "A year?"
QUESTION: Yes, an annual premium of ten percent of the bond.
ANSWER: I was getting screwed.
QUESTION: Pardon me?
ANSWER: I was getting screwed on the $5,000 a year. I understood that you paid

the $5,000 once and that is all, but Mr. Wish kept thinking I have got to pay him year after year.[33]

And so, Whalen testified, he stopped paying.[34]

Under cross-examination by Konrad Kohl, Whalen revealed that he himself—not Wish—had originally come up with the figure of $20,000 for a bribe:

> Mr. Wish advised me that if he put a fix in the Court of Appeals, he told me it would be anywhere from $10,000 to $20,000. I felt due to the fact the Supreme Court is a higher court, it would be $20,000, and Mr. Wish came back and told me he talked to Justice Swainson and Justice Swainson said it would be $30,000.[35]

According to Whalen, Wish wanted the money "up front" because "Justice Swainson may have to pass the money around to a few other justices."[36]

As Whalen's testimony was drawing toward its close, Chodak took one last shot at trying to get him to admit that Wish had conned him out of his money, resulting in one of the trial's few bits of comic relief:

QUESTION: Do I understand that your testimony now is, Mr. Whalen, that you had full confidence in Mr. Wish that he would con you?

ANSWER: Not on this case.

QUESTION: But you earlier testified that you thought he was "screwing you," isn't that correct?

ANSWER: Screwing me, right.

QUESTION: Which is, so I understand it, about the same thing.

ANSWER: No, it is not.

QUESTION: It is not?

ANSWER: No, it is not.

QUESTION: Where is a difference?

ANSWER: Yes, there is a difference, a big difference.

QUESTION: Alright, tell me about it.

ANSWER: The big difference is when you know someone is screwing you, in other words, when someone is overcharging you for an automobile, like if I got a 1968 Ford and the Blue Book says Fords are only worth $1,200 and you try to sell it to me for $1,900, you are trying to screw me.

QUESTION: That isn't conning you, though?

ANSWER: No, it is not. Conning me is when you don't have no Ford at all and you are trying to get $1,900. (laughter)[37]

By the time Whalen stepped down it was Tuesday, October 28, and the trial was well into its seventh day. Ozer then called Neil Fink (Whalen's attorney), Joanne Whalen (Whalen's wife), and Harold Hoag (Clerk of the Michigan Supreme Court), each for brief testimony. Fink identified several documents that had been mailed to him by the Supreme Court in the course of Whalen's appeal. Joanne Whalen recalled that on October 19, 1972, Harvey Wish had called from New York and left a message for her husband, to the effect that the Michigan Supreme Court had agreed to hear his appeal. Hoag described the court's internal procedures leading up to the mailing out of an official order.

This concluded the prosecution's evidence on the bribery charge. It only remained for Ozer to present his evidence on the perjury counts.

The indictment against Swainson charged him with three counts of perjury. The first count charged that he lied when he denied that he had received a television set from Harvey Wish on October 13, 1973. The second count charged that he lied when he denied any recollection of having called Harvey Wish on October 6, 1972, and hearing Wish read a portion of Whalen's application for leave to appeal. The third count charged that he lied when he denied having any recollection of calling Wish on October 19, 1972 and leaving a message that the Supreme Court had decided to grant leave to appeal.

Ozer and Kohl, in conference with the judge, agreed to submit a nearly complete transcript of Swainson's May 19 and May 21 appearances before the grand jury. Swainson's assertions of his Fifth Amendment privilege would be excised, but essentially all of his substantive testimony would be read to the jury. Ozer then read Swainson's grand jury testimony to the jury.

With that, the prosecution rested.

CHAPTER SIXTEEN

The Trial: Defense

WITH THE GOVERNMENT'S EVIDENCE COMPLETED, THE TIME WAS APPROPRIATE FOR each defendant to move for directed verdicts of acquittal on several of the counts. In such a motion the defendant asks the judge to take the decision out of the jury's hands based on the argument that the prosecution has presented all of its evidence and no rational jury could find the defendant guilty based on that evidence.

The most significant of these motions was Kohl's renewal of his pretrial argument that there was no "independent" evidence of a conspiracy outside of the tapes, and therefore the tapes did not fit within the "co-conspirator" exception to the Confrontation Clause. "I am suggesting to the Court that in the first instance there would have to be some reasonable evidence to go to the jury that Justice Swainson did get this matter before the [Supreme] Court at their October, 1972 administrative conference, and there is not a scintilla of evidence in support of the view that he did get the matter before the Court."[1]

Kohl continued, "What evidence—absent the tapes—is there that in fact this alleged conspiratorial conduct did exist so as to cause Justice Swainson to vote in favor of granting leave to appeal to Whalen?"[2]

It was then Ozer's turn. He came right to the point, stating that he would give the Judge "a run-through of the evidence, putting aside completely the content of the tapes." First there was John Whalen.

> Now, John Whalen certainly could have testified were there no tapes in the case at all. . . . Whalen could have testified that . . . he paid $20,000, and what did he get? He got his case heard and reversed.
>
> Now, all the evidence of the communications between Justice Swainson and Harvey Wish that Justice Swainson has admitted to before the grand jury on May 21, 1972 [sic; the actual date was May 21, 1975] would certainly be admissible against Justice Swainson, which would show that as of sometime prior to October 17–18 and specifically October 6, 1972 Justice Swainson at least was discussing this case with Harvey Wish . . . and then on October 17–18 Justice Swainson made the motion . . . [to grant leave to appeal] and it would be for a jury, of course, to decide whether that means he, in fact, brought it to the Court and whether there has been some explanation as to why he brought it to the Court.[3]

After a brief recess to consider the arguments, the Judge denied Kohl's motion, without explanation. The tapes of Harvey Wish talking to John Whalen would be admissible evidence against John Swainson.

The prosecution having completed its case, and the judge having denied Swainson's motion for acquittal, the defense now called its witnesses. Kohl went first.

Before the trial the defense had listed thirty-two prominent persons who were to be called as what is popularly known as "character witnesses." But under the law a character witness does not testify about the defendant's character; rather, the character witness testifies about the defendant's reputation for truthfulness. As the trial neared, it became apparent that any such witness would be subject to cross-examination regarding Swainson's lack of truthfulness in one area of his life: his extramarital relationships. The character witnesses were quietly dropped.[4]

Four of the first five defense witnesses were justices of the Michigan Supreme Court.

Justices Thomas E. Brennan and G. Mennen Williams had served on the Supreme Court at the time of the October 1972 administrative conference in which the Supreme Court granted leave to appeal in Whalen's case, and Williams was still a justice. Mary Coleman and Charles Levin had joined the Supreme Court at the beginning of 1973 and had participated in the decision to reverse Whalen's conviction.

Coleman and Levin testified that John Swainson had never attempted to influence them on the Whalen decision, and that they had each signed T. Matthew Kavanagh's opinion because they agreed with it.

G. Mennen Williams testified that even after going over the records he had no independent recollection of the October 1972 administrative conference at which the justices decided to grant leave to appeal. In fact, he had no recollection of anything about the Whalen case prior to the circulation of Kavanagh's proposed opinion. When asked if Swainson had ever offered him money in exchange for his vote, Williams—the scion of a wealthy family—answered, "No, that would be preposterous!"[5]

Thomas E. Brennan, tall, handsome, and loquacious, had left the court in 1974 to found a law school in Lansing. When asked whether Swainson had attempted to influence his vote in the Whalen case, Brennan's answer was, characteristically, aggressive and original:

> Well, I would guess that he did. I would guess that all the members of the Court would be trying to persuade each other to vote in a certain way. That is what we did for a living. We are all in the process of trying to persuade each other to our particular point of view with respect to the cases that were before us, and in most of those instances during those bleak years in 1973 when I was the sole Republican on the Court, they were all trying to persuade me.[6]

But, he said, Swainson had never come to him privately or tried to exert any undue influence on him regarding the Whalen case.[7]

On cross-examination, Ozer asked Brennan, "Now, if in fact Justice Swainson had been requested by bondsman Harvey Wish . . . to do what he could to have that leave to appeal granted, would it be your understanding that the duties and functions of a justice of the Supreme Court would have required that such a communication be reported to the other members of the Court who were then considering the motion?" Brennan answered, "No, I don't think so."

Ozer, who obviously did not know Brennan, could not let it go. In obvious disbelief at Brennan's answer, he changed the question slightly and put it to Brennan again. Brennan, clearly annoyed, set him straight:

> Now my answer was if somebody asked him to do something about a leave to appeal, I don't think that there would be any need for him to mention it to the Court at all. As a matter of fact, I would be very surprised if he would even

remember it. It was not at all uncommon if you go to a bar association gathering, to run into some lawyer that would get you aside and try to talk about his case, and everybody on the bench has been exposed to the kind of inappropriate things that citizens or lawyers or other people think is proper to raise with a judge, but the fact that some request or some communication had been addressed to a judge is just a thing that you pay no attention to.[8]

With the justices' testimony completed, Kohl could feel that he had cast serious doubt on the prosecution's theory that Swainson had somehow been the moving force that caused the Supreme Court to accept Whalen's appeal and then to reverse the conviction.

Not one justice remembered Swainson doing anything on Whalen's behalf. The only evidence of even a minor act was the notation in the minutes that Swainson had made the motion to grant leave at the administrative conference in October 1972, and even this evidence was hazy.

Now Kohl moved to demolish Ozer's allegation that Wish had given Swainson a television set and Swainson had lied to cover it up.

David Auer, a mortgage banker, had been a supporter of Swainson's for the past decade, and the two of them had spent many happy hours together in a duck blind at Auer's hunting club. One night Auer's seventeen-year-old daughter had been arrested for public intoxication. Not having been involved in anything like this before, Auer called Swainson for help. Swainson learned that the daughter's case was before city of Troy municipal judge David Bolle. He called Judge Bolle, whom he had never met.

Judge Bolle recalled that Swainson had introduced himself and asked if Bolle had the case. Bolle checked his docket and matched the girl's name with a charge of violating a Troy municipal ordinance against public intoxication. Swainson then "suggested that he knew the family . . . and suggested that she was a good kid, she had no prior record, and would I simply keep that in mind if and when she appeared in front of me."[9] Swainson did not ask Bolle to dismiss the case.

Bolle testified that he had never spoken with Swainson before or after this phone call. When the seventeen-year-old girl appeared before him, he found that she had no prior record, just as Swainson had told him. Bolle placed her on six months probation with the understanding that if she got in no further trouble and reported faithfully to the probation officer, the case would be dismissed. Over objections, Judge Bolle testified that this was exactly what he would have done in the case, if Swainson had never called him.[10] Bolle also acknowledged that he was still practicing as an attorney (municipal judge was a part-time position), and that one or more of his cases could conceivably end up before the Michigan Supreme Court.[11]

At some point after this incident, Auer and Swainson went hunting together again. While sitting together in a duck blind, Auer recalled, "We were talking about different types of color television sets, and he expressed an interest in one type . . . and I said I would like to buy it for him and give it to him as a gift, and he said that is not necessary."[12]

But Auer decided to do it anyway. He asked John Kalkanian (an old friend and the vice president of Auer's company) to see if he could find the kind of television set that Swainson had mentioned, and to buy it for him at a discount if possible. This Kalkanian did, buying the television set from Piedmont Jewelry in Detroit.[13]

Kalkanian had gone to high school with Harvey Wish, and they were still friends, living in the same neighborhood. Shortly after he had picked up the television set Kalkanian ran into Wish. He knew that Wish and Swainson were acquainted, and asked Wish for directions to Swainson's house. Wish told Kalkanian that he was going to see Swainson shortly, and would be happy to deliver the television set to him, so Kalkanian gave the set to Harvey Wish.[14]

Kohl then called several Supreme Court employees for brief testimony about the Whalen case.

Robert Dean had served as law clerk to the late chief justice T. Matthew Kavanagh. He testified that he had drafted the Whalen opinion for Kavanagh, and Kavanagh had adopted it with only a few changes in phrasing. Swainson had never had any contact with him on the subject of the opinion.[15]

Eleanor Coleman had served as T. Matthew Kavanagh's secretary. She testified that he would prepare the agenda for the monthly administrative conference, and she would then type it and circulate copies to all of the justices a week in advance. During the following week. Kavanagh would advise her of the matters he wished to be added as "non-agenda" items. He had done so in preparation for the October 1972 administrative conference, telling her to add a number of matters, including the Whalen case.[16] She had no knowledge of whether he had added any particular item on his own or at someone else's request.[17]

Marcel Greenia had served as the senior commissioner of the Supreme Court at the time of the application for leave to appeal in the Whalen case. He testified that the Whalen case's last-minute inclusion in the October administrative conference might have been the result of a question about whether Whalen's sentence was affected by the Supreme Court's prior decision in the *Tanner* case, which redesigned the permissible limits of the minimum sentence under Michigan's indeterminate sentencing law.

Then Kohl called his last witness: John Swainson.

Swainson moved to the witness chair with his rolling walk. He had faced German shelling in the war. He had plunged into the 1960 primary and general elections with the odds against him. But no previous moment in his life had offered consequences such as he faced now, and much would depend on how he conducted himself on the stand.

The Detroit *Free Press* reported that "dressed in a charcoal black suit, white shirt and black tie, Swainson sat in the witness chair with his legs crossed . . . and occasionally stroked his legs at about the place where they join his artificial limbs."[18]

Kohl began by taking the justice through a brief description of his career, then asked him to describe his relationship with Harvey Wish.

> I believe I met Harvey Wish in the Wayne County Circuit Court. I knew him as a bondsman. . . . I have known him casually since . . . '66 or '67.
>
> We also had a problem in our family, Alice and I, with our son . . . in the drug culture I guess is the way I would have to express it. . . . I was very concerned as to what was happening . . . with the youngsters that were being arrested . . . and the harshness of the sentences . . . I know I spoke to him on occasion in that regard.[19]

Turning to the Whalen case, Kohl asked whether Swainson had ever been offered a bribe or been asked to influence the outcome of the case. Swainson answered, "I was not."[20]

Now Kohl came to the issue of Swainson's testimony before the grand jury, and the perjury charges.

Swainson testified that during his first grand jury appearance, he had been asked about the specific dates of October 6 and October 19, 1972, and "I was very hard put to recall any specific actions of mine on that particular date or the other date."

Then, perhaps betraying his lack of criminal trial experience, Kohl made what appears to be a major tactical blunder. He asked, "Have you since then and have you with me reviewed additional information . . . including the telephone logs that have been introduced in this case?"

Swainson answered that he had, and that he was now satisfied that he must have spoken with Wish on the two dates.

The problem with this question and answer was that it was irrelevant to the perjury charges.

While arguing against the defense motions for directed verdict of acquittal, Ozer had summed up his strongest argument on the perjury charges in one sentence:

> If Justice Swainson had a clear recollection on May 21 without qualification, [a jury could conclude] that he, in fact, had a recollection on May 19 and *there is nothing dramatic that would have caused his recollection to become clear on May 21* but was in some way unclear on May 19.[21]

In other words, the essence of the perjury charge was that on May 19 Swainson had said he had no memory of the events, but two days later he admitted that the events had occurred, and he had offered no explanation for this change in his testimony. In the absence of any explanation from Swainson, Ozer posited that there could be only one explanation: on May 19 Swainson had lied. Then, after learning that the FBI had evidence of the events, on May 21 he came clean.

But, instead of asking Swainson what had caused him to change his testimony between May 19, 1975, and May 21, 1975, Kohl asked what Swainson had learned between May 19 and the *current* date. Thus, the only explanation available to the jury remained Ozer's.

Kohl led Swainson through his other contacts with Wish. Swainson testified that after Wish had expressed interest in Whalen's application for leave to appeal, "I probably said 'I will let you know what the Court does as far as granting leave or not granting leave,' and probably did so call him up and say that leave to appeal had been granted in that matter."[22]

As to whether he had made the motion to grant leave, Swainson had no recollection, but his memory of T. Matthew Kavanagh's habits as chief justice was in accordance with that of the other justices who had testified: "When he felt the discussion had reached the point where some consensus had been arrived at, he would say, 'All right, John, you make the motion. T. G., you second it. All in favor,' and record it unless somebody strongly objected saying I don't want to be reported as having made the motion."[23]

After further discussion of the Supreme Court's procedures, Kohl brought

Swainson back to the subject of perjury, specifically the television set. This time, Kohl asked exactly the right question:

QUESTION: When you appeared before the Grand Jury, you stated that you did not the first time recall this television incident. . . . And then you did come back and say you did recall that there was such an incident. Can you explain that?

But Swainson did not explain it. He gave a meandering answer that reiterated his shock at hearing the testimony of parking lot attendant Melvin Holloway and FBI agent Ed Diem, read to him on May 19 at the Grand Jury room. And when he returned to the Grand Jury Room two days later, "I said I received the TV set. I had no recollection, but they read it off saying I received it, there were boxes transferred, but I had no idea—"

Kohl interrupted his answer with another question:

QUESTION: At that time did you in any way relate a television set to anything involved in the Whalen case?
ANSWER: That completely left my mind. As it was related, it was done in the parking lot at noon at Schweitzer's and I wasn't even out there, and I certainly did not relate it in any shape or manner.

In his answer Swainson kept emphasizing that when he was first asked about TV set incident in front of the grand jury (on May 19, 1975), he simply had no memory of it. Then, in testifying about his second grand jury appearance (on May 21, 1975) he seemed to be saying that he had agreed that the TV set had been transferred to his car, even though he *still* had no memory of it. But that was not what he had testified on May 21; he had said then, "*I do recall* the events that they [Holloway and Diem] testified to" (emphasis added).

Was he now simply referring again to the state of his memory on May 19, prefatory to an explanation of what happened May 21? We don't know, because Kohl cut him off, asked the judge for a recess, and never returned to the subject. Instead, when he resumed his direct examination of Swainson he moved on to David Auer's frantic call and Swainson's recollection of his own call to Judge Bolle; which was essentially the same as Bolle's testimony. And with that, Kohl ended his direct examination of John Swainson.

Now Ozer got his chance to cross-examine Swainson. He began with Wish's September 16, 1972, visit to the farm, and the FBI agent's observation of Wish taking several packages into the house. Swainson, who had had time to think about it, explained that the packages probably were the four jackets that he had given Wish to get embroidered with campaign slogans for a friend who was running for local office. Even now, he had no specific recollection of the incident.[24]

Ozer turned to Wish's telephone call of September 16, 1972. Swainson repeated again that he did not recall *any* discussion of the Whalen case with Wish.[25] Ozer put it to Swainson that in his second appearance before the grand jury he had said that he now remembered that call. Swainson corrected him, saying that he had merely concluded, from the available evidence, that there must have been such a call; the same was true of October 19, 1972, message left for Wish: "I was trying to avoid perjury and, under any conditions, they were probably made. That is my testimony."[26]

Ozer turned aggressive:

QUESTION: And until you learned you had, in fact, been under surveillance during the period that you were questioned about that day, you had no desire or intention to correct your testimony, did you?"

Swainson remained unrattled:

ANSWER: If you refer back to . . . the May 19 transcript, I think I said it as clearly as I could at that time . . ."If he asked me something like that, I probably would have said it."[27]

Ozer now moved to Swainson's brief October 13, 1972, visit to Wish's office. Swainson still had no recollection of the visit, but now surmised that this must be the occasion when he had picked up a wall hanging that he had ordered from Hudson's. He had paid Wish for the wall hanging, about $135.00. He had asked Wish to pick it up because "it is difficult for me to park a car in a parking lot downtown and walk over to Hudson's and upstairs and carry something down because of my physical disability."[28]

Next Ozer zeroed in on the message that Harvey Wish had told Whalen Swainson left for him on October 19, 1972, telling him that the Supreme Court had decided to grant leave. Once again, Swainson did not deny it: "Apparently I did. I do not have any specific recollection, but I cannot deny that I did so."[29]

Ozer asked when Swainson had first found out that the Whalen case was going to be "on the agenda" for the October 17 administrative conference.

Swainson answered, "Probably at the conference of October 17. I wouldn't have seen the non-agenda items until that day." Ozer thought that this list had been attached to the agenda, which the justices received a week in advance. Swainson corrected him: "No, it isn't attached to the agenda . . . the Chief Justice hasn't revealed to any of us what is on the non-agenda list. We go through the agenda first, and then . . . that is where the non-agenda items or non-agenda list comes into being."

Swainson further explained that if a justice wanted an item discussed at an administrative meeting, he or she would bring it up "by sending a memo to your colleagues, saying . . . I have asked the Chief Justice to place it on the agenda," not by trying to get it on the nonagenda list. Further, Swainson pointed to the testimony of Eleanor Coleman, the secretary to the late chief justice, that she did not prepare the nonagenda list until the night before or the morning of the October 17 meeting. Therefore, no one could have known on October 6 that the Whalen case was going to be "presented to the Court" on the seventeenth, as Wish had told Whalen.[30] Swainson surmised that he may have told Wish that the justices' next meeting was scheduled for October 17, and implied Wish had either assumed or fabricated the idea that the court would take up Whalen's case at that meeting.

Finally, Ozer returned to the television set. Swainson did not remember when he and Wish had agreed to meet at Schweitzer's Restaurant, but he assumed that it was done on short notice. As to the TV, "It just came. It wasn't requested or solicited or something like that."[31] When Ozer asked Swainson whether he actually recalled the occasion, Swainson answered, "Vaguely, vaguely."[32] He admitted that it was an unusual occurrence for a TV set to be placed in his car, and conceded that Wish must have told him in advance that he had a package for Swainson, and on whose behalf he was delivering it, but he could recall no foreknowledge that the package was to be a television set.[33]

Ozer had finished. Kohl had no redirect for Swainson, who stepped down from the witness chair and resumed his seat at the defense table. Kohl had no further witnesses. The judge then recessed for lunch.

After lunch everyone reassembled and the jury was brought back in. It was Harvey Wish's turn. But when the judge requested Murray Chodak proceed, he stunned the courtroom: "No, your Honor. Defendant Harvey Wish rests." The judge then turned to Ozer and asked whether the government wished to present any rebuttal evidence. Ozer said he had none. Thus ended the presentation of evidence.

CHAPTER SEVENTEEN

The Trial: Verdict

JUDGE RUBIN IMMEDIATELY BROUGHT ALL COUNSEL INTO HIS CHAMBERS. HE KNEW that they would need to discuss proposed instructions to the jury, but he was thinking beyond that: "Gentlemen . . . on the one hand we can complete our conference, start final argument, and charge [i.e., instruct the jury] this afternoon and let the jury go out to dinner and start deliberating this evening, or we can do nothing this afternoon and allow them to deliberate tomorrow morning. Now one of the questions this turns upon is what sort of time you gentlemen are considering for final argument."[1]

The standard order for closing argument was for the prosecution to go first (because the prosecution bears the burden of proof), then the defense, and finally a brief rebuttal argument by the prosecution. Ozer requested ninety minutes for his initial argument and thirty minutes for his rebuttal. The judge summarily rejected this request as far too much time. Kohl then volunteered, "I did not plan on more than half an hour in argument." Chodak chimed in that he, too, would easily finish within a half hour. Ozer then proposed that his initial argument be limited to one hour, with a fifteen-minute rebuttal after the defense concluded their two thirty-minute closings. Judge Rubin accepted this proposal.[2]

The prosecution had presented a huge amount of evidence; their witnesses' testimony consumed 1,136 pages of the trial transcript, to only 307 pages for defense witnesses (these figures include direct testimony, cross-examination, and redirect). Yet Kohl, perhaps anticipating what the judge would order anyway, had voluntarily locked himself into a time limit of thirty minutes total for his entire argument to the jury.

Judge Rubin had made it clear more than once that he would go to great lengths to avoid either wasting or extending the time of the sequestered jury. He was ever mindful of the burden placed upon the jurors by this trial. Now he determined that the closing arguments would proceed without delay, and the jury would begin deliberations the same evening, after a break for dinner.

Some time after 3:00 P.M., Ozer rose and faced the jurors.

He began by praising the defendant:

John Swainson is a man of very considerable reputation, I am sure a man whose name has been known to you all in your private lives. He has served his country well and has suffered grievously in doing so, and he is entitled to every benefit of the law and every reasonable doubt.

From the standpoint of the United States, however, . . . the allegation is that the highest court in the state . . . has been compromised and that a person, John Whalen, has been able to get a result from that court not because of the merits of his case [but] because he paid money.[3]

There are many cases where the case turns upon conflicting testimony. Someone is accused of robbing a bank and the bank teller says 'that is the man. I would know him anywhere.' And the man says, 'it is not me.'

In this case . . . the evidence presented from the two sides is not conflicting . . . you will not have to make up your minds as to can you believe this witness or can you believe that witness, the one exception being the testimony of the Defendant John Swainson.[4]

This was true only in the narrow technical sense that Harvey Wish was not a "witness." In reality, the whole case turned almost entirely on whether his recorded words were to be believed. But the fact that Wish was also on trial meant that the attorneys were prohibited from mentioning the fact that Wish had not actually testified.

Because the witness testimony had ended suddenly and the judge insisted on giving the jury the case immediately, the attorneys had little time to prepare their closings. But Ozer had obviously at least outlined his presentation long before. It was coherent, logical, and integrated. And at times it was inaccurate, stating as facts what Ozer had expected the evidence to show, rather than what it actually showed.

> We start out by knowing that Whalen was told that even though the [Supreme] Court has turned down his case and decided not to hear it, if you pay money they will hear it. You also know that the Court did hear it . . . From there we move ahead to decide why did the Court hear it.[5]

Ozer then made what at first blush would appear to be a startling concession: "There is no part of the evidence in which I ask you to rely on John Whalen's word to convict either defendant."[6] Actually, it was not a concession at all. Almost everything that Whalen had testified to was either on the recordings or verified by other witnesses. What Ozer was really doing was anticipating that the defense lawyers would attack Whalen's credibility; he was inoculating his case.

Ozer told the jurors:

> In that October 6 conversation, you will recall Harvey Wish had been told it will be presented to the Supreme Court on October 17. No one knew that at that point except Harvey Wish. . . . There are no other Justices who knew it. The Chief Justice didn't even know it . . . as of October 10 when the Chief Justice put out the agenda [for the October 17 administrative conference], he didn't know that the Whalen case was going to be brought up, or he would have put it on the agenda.[7]

On October 17 Wish told Whalen that he had not been able to reach Justice Swainson, but "yesterday he said he was going to try to get it on the agenda for today."[8] And, indeed, the next day Swainson makes the motion to grant leave. And Swainson "admitted that it was he who is talking to Harvey Wish on the 16th. . . . In the meantime, John Swainson when asked to explain these things, says I just don't know. I never had any interest in the Whalen case."[9]

"On October 24, again tape recorded, Wish says his man says they will continue the bond."

But Wish had not said this. In fact, he had corrected Whalen's assumption that the Supreme Court had agreed to continue his bond, saying, "The bond they're not interested in."[10]

On November 17 [sic], though, . . . the Commissioner . . . recommended denial because Whalen had a long record. . . . and an order [denying bond] will be entered November 17 unless some Justice does something to stop it.

On November 16 . . . John Swainson sends in a holding memo and keeps that order from going through . . . because as of November 16, the first $10,000 had not been paid.[11]

On November 17 Swainson called back Harvey Wish and ten days later the last payment of money was made, and that money was photocopied by the FBI. . . . You have heard the telephone calls, and you have heard John Swainson on the witness stand admit that it was he that Harvey Wish was making these arrangements with, but he says I don't remember any of them. He says . . . I don't remember any of these calls. Since the government has proved I made them, I will admit I made them so I can't be prosecuted for perjury, but I don't remember anything beyond that.[12]

This was another stretch—Swainson did not admit to any "arrangements" with Wish.

"[A]lmost a year later, . . . on October 3, 1973 the case was argued before the Supreme Court. . . . Two days later Harvey Wish tells John Whalen that the guy wants to know what if he can only send it back for a new trial? . . . Now Wish says you will only have to pay $10,000 if all they can do is send it back for a new trial."[13] This was inaccurate. The FBI transcript had Wish saying, "Hey, I don't know that you can get anything. What the, you know, I can't all I'm doin' is tellin' you got nothin' unless you got—That's why I ask you, what do you want me to say—if the guy says—you know they can send it back—to trial."[14]

On October 11 the FBI counted the money [$10,000] and sat there while Whalen passed the money to Harvey Wish. . . . They now know if Wish had just been paid, he is probably going to meet Swainson because they are in this together. They put a surveillance on them. Sure enough, on October 15, 1973 the two of them get together. . . . When [Swainson] got into his car, surprise of surprises. There was a television set on the back seat.[15]

And now Ozer segued into his perjury argument: "He will admit only that which the other witnesses can testify to. Melvin Holloway, he told him there is a package you can put in the car, so he admits he was told there would be a package."

John Swainson lied to the Grand Jury. When he thought the Grand Jury knew nothing, he told them nothing. When he thought the Grand Jury knew about the telephone calls, he admitted about the telephone calls. . . . [W]hy, four days after the money is paid, is John Swainson meeting with Harvey Wish?

He can give you no explanation. Again, his memory is a complete blank.[16]

. . . only after he heard for the first time in 1975 that the FBI was out there, it is not just John Whalen who you have to dispute, it is not only Melvin Holloway, the parking lot attendant, but an FBI agent was there and he saw it. Only after that happened did he [Swainson] come back two days later and say all right, that incident on the 15th, it happened. The telephone call on October 6, it was me. The telephone call on October 19, yes I did it. Those packages on September 16 my house [sic], yes, they came.

Now you ask him, explain why. What were the packages the 16th?

"He says I don't know. I don't remember." But Swainson had testified that he thought they were the embroidered jackets.

"Well, what happened in the call on the 6th?"

"I don't know. I don't really remember there was a call, but just so that I don't commit perjury, I will admit there was one."

"Well, the call on the 19th, why did you make it?"

"I don't know. I just don't remember it. I had no interest in the Whalen case."[17]

And now Ozer came to what must have been a long-planned conclusion:

You are now in a position of ordinary people from ordinary walks of life being able to do justice to an exalted person, to a powerful person, to a person who doesn't care about the law, doesn't care about his obligations as a judicial officer and doesn't care about his oath to testify truthfully before the Grand Jury, and now you have heard it all and you can do the justice that must be done. Thank you.[18]

Ozer returned to the prosecution table and sat down. The judge turned toward the defense table and asked who wished to go first. Kohl rose and replied, "With your permission, I will proceed."

Kohl moved to the podium and faced the jury. "We are not asking for your sympathy," he said. "We are asking you to judge this case on the facts and the facts alone." He then began to review what he called "some amazing things." The first amazing thing was that "with their 27 recorded conversations . . .

not one recording is made where Wish received money from Whalen, and in particular any discussion that obviously would have occurred . . . that it was to be used to bribe John B. Swainson."[19] While this critique might sting the FBI, it is difficult to see what it would accomplish with the jury; there were plenty of witnesses to Whalen handing Wish the money, and plenty of recordings of Wish telling Whalen what the money was for.

Next Kohl pointed out that federal law allowed the FBI to seek a court's permission to install a wiretap on Swainson's telephones, but they had never sought such an order.[20] Again, this was a fair shot at the FBI, but by itself it had nothing to do with whether the evidence presented by the government proved John Swainson's guilt.

As he moved to his next argument, Kohl's scorn for the FBI was palpable:

> Ladies and gentlemen, here we have a situation in 1972 where allegedly they have got the goods on John Swainson. . . . The claim is that Swainson is going to influence the Court, . . . that Swainson did influence the Court . . . [A]s a matter of simple common sense, what is the easiest way to find out whether he did? You go to the people who allegedly he did it with. In other words, the Chief Justice at the time, who was T. Matthew Kavanagh. . . . He prepares the agenda, . . . he prepares the non-agenda items, and all they had to do . . . is go to T. Matthew Kavanagh . . . and say . . . in People versus Whalen, leave to appeal was granted. Did John Swainson talk to you? Did he ask you to put it on the agenda?[21]

Yet the FBI had never interviewed T. Matthew Kavanagh. He had died April 19, 1975, and the grand jury indicted Swainson three months later.

Kohl turned to the lunch at Schweitzer's Restaurant:

> Now they are specifically tailing him [Swainson] because of this alleged money from Whalen to Wish. So, now they have got three agents outside of Schweitzer's Restaurant and inside of Schweitzer's Restaurant waiting for the payoff, and the serial numbers are recorded, and they are waiting for Wish to slip the envelope to Swainson, and there they are and that is all they needed, and when that happened they had him cold, but it never happened. It just plain didn't happen.[22]

The indictment charged that Swainson had received a television set from Wish two months before the Supreme Court issued its decision in the Whalen case, and this was supposed to influence him. "Well, what a myth that turned out to be. There was no relationship whatever between this Whalen case and John Swainson."

Here Kohl mentioned the perjury charges, briefly: "He goes into the jury room and what is on his mind? This allegation that he received a bribe, and they say did you receive a television set from Harvey Wish, and the simple fact of the case is no, he did not receive a television set from Harvey Wish. He received a television set from David Auer back in 1973, and yes . . . Harvey Wish as a courtesy delivered the set."[23]

Kohl pointed out that Wish's main concern was Whalen's bond. Both of Whalen's co-defendants had fled. He needed information from the Supreme Court to keep ahead of the situation.

> I can understand why Mr. Wish would be awful concerned with whether Whalen might run too, and undoubtedly on October 6 there is this one-minute conversation where Wish reads from the application for leave to appeal. It is a matter of common sense. If John Swainson was involved in some conspiracy with this rehearing application . . . already on file, why would Wish have to read from the application?
>
> Then we get to this date of October 16 . . . and you heard one side of that conversation . . . and Wish says have you had a chance to look into that rehearing situation? . . . If John Swainson was interested in that Whalen case, he would have known not only that the rehearing application was filed [eleven days earlier], but that it had already been rejected by T. Matthew Kavanagh and an order of the Court had gone out . . . and the answer was no, but I will look into it. Why? Because if a motion for rehearing had been filed, then the next conference of the Court which was already scheduled for October 17 would be the time when the Whalen rehearing would be before the Court. Does that show John Swainson's involvement in a . . . conspiracy on the 16th? He asks have you had a chance to look into it? Swainson says no.[24]

Kohl now turned to the perplexing question of why Chief Justice T. Matthew Kavanagh had placed the Whalen case on his nonagenda list for the court's October 17, 1972, administrative conference. Ozer had speculated that Swainson must have made a private request to Kavanagh. Kohl posed a different theory.

Earlier in 1972 the Supreme Court had issued a decision in *People v. Tanner*. The *Tanner* decision placed new limits on the discretion of trial judges in determining minimum sentences, and any criminal defendant whose sentence was outside those limits would be entitled to resentencing, if he or she had appealed after *Tanner's* effective date. But there was a question about what date that was. At its September 5 conference the Supreme Court had been unable to decide whether a group of eighteen cases—currently on appeal to the Supreme Court—were covered by the *Tanner* precedent. The justices had voted to put off decision on those eighteen cases until the October 17 conference. Yet when the agenda for the October 17 conference was printed, the eighteen *Tanner* cases were not on it.

This would seem to imply that the chief justice had decided to postpone consideration of those cases for another meeting. But there was a subtle problem; one of the eighteen cases was *People v. Whalen,* and the Supreme Court had *already* denied leave in the Whalen case (and the chief justice had now denied Whalen's motion for rehearing), for reasons having nothing to do with *Tanner.* But this denial would also, inadvertently, eliminate Whalen's case from consideration as one of the eighteen *Tanner* cases.

"To make a long story short," said Kohl, "the Court goofed because they shouldn't have decided on the Whalen case until the next administrative conference . . . which was scheduled for October 17. . . . T. Matthew Kavanagh himself had denied the rehearing and obviously in preparing his agenda . . . he put Whalen back on the agenda [sic—actually the nonagenda list] on the 17th so that the full court could review it."[25]

Finally, his allotted time running out, Kohl addressed the perjury charges:

> Three years later he comes in before the Grand Jury and they say to him did you have a telephone call of October 6 and he says I don't recall any conversation. A one-minute conversation he is supposed to remember . . . where obviously he said to Wish, tell the lawyer he has got to file a motion for rehearing.
>
> He is asked about October 17 . . . He says if Harvey Wish called me, I might have told him. I don't recall. . . . If they had called him before the Grand Jury in 1972 or 1973 even, he might have very well said yes, I do recall a conversation.
>
> Yes, he did come back in and he did not want to face perjury charges, and obviously they had specific dates and he said then, it must have occurred . . .
>
> You have seen the man. You have heard the man. You judge the man, you and you alone, each one of you.
>
> I have no more time. I ask you to return the verdict of not guilty, because he is not guilty, and only you can make that decision.[26]

With that, Kohl returned to the defense table and sat down.

It was late afternoon and the jury had been listening to argument for one and a half hours. The judge declared a brief recess to let the jury members stretch their legs and use the restrooms. At 4:35 everyone reassembled, and the judge said, "Mr. Chodak, you may proceed."

Chodak had presented no witnesses. The only evidence he could comment on was the government's. So the first thing he did was attack Whalen, "the government's big witness" as "a thief, a liar, a criminal . . . he lied on the stand, and he admitted he lied."[27] Chodak did not seem to realize that Ozer had inoculated his case against just such an attack.

After lambasting Whalen for several minutes, Chodak turned to the core issue, which was whether Wish had gotten the money from Whalen for the purpose of bribing Swainson (as he told Whalen), or just to protect his bond.

Here Chodak had a small problem, of his own making. He wanted to direct the jury's attention to certain facts, but those facts were not in evidence, and he had not called any witnesses to put them in evidence. In the closing argument an attorney may make factual reference only to evidence (testimony and exhibits) introduced in the trial. He may argue about the meaning of the evidence. He may argue what inferences should be drawn from the evidence. He may argue that certain of the evidence should be accorded no weight. But he cannot describe or refer to any facts not in evidence; to do so would be to testify.

That did not stop Chodak.

"Now I want to stop for one moment and explain something to you," he said. "The thought may occur to you why didn't Mr. Wish get off the bond? To get off a bond is a very difficult procedure. You must take the person physically . . . to the judge and ask that you be taken off the bond, and at the judge's discretion he decides whether or not that bondsman is relieved from that liability. . . . If Mr. Wish had asked to have the bond canceled and the judge refused . . . , what kind of problems would he [Wish] then have had with Mr. Whalen and, if you will recall, Mr. Whalen was a very unstable man."[28]

Then, said Chodak, to make things even worse, Whalen decided that Wish's charging an annual premium for his bond was "screwing" him. "Mr. Wish was stuck with him and couldn't collect the bond money, and so as a result of this, one day he is approached by Whalen who says do something for me on this appeal, and I am not saying Wish was right in doing this . . . , I am not saying he was right or wrong in involving John Swainson's name in this, but he did it."[29]

To say that Wish was "approached by Whalen who says do something for me on this appeal" was a stretch. The only evidence describing Wish's first conversation about the Supreme Court was Whalen's testimony: "I told him we went to the Court of Appeals and it was turned down. He told me it wasn't too late, and if I still wanted to do some business, he had some friends up in the Supreme Court that would guarantee a dismissal."[30] This testimony, though self-serving, suggests that it was Wish, not Whalen, who broached the subject of "doing something . . . on the appeal."

Chodak once again attacked Whalen, "a man that hasn't filed an income tax return since 1970. . . . He also claimed that he paid on his bond. I said did you get receipts? He said sometimes I did and sometimes I didn't [this was, indeed, Whalen's testimony]. They didn't put this in evidence. He didn't have any receipts because he hadn't paid."[31]

Chodak wound to his conclusion by questioning the government's motives:

In 1972, [FBI agent Ed Diem] said, we didn't want anyone to know about this . . . ongoing investigation because of Justice Swainson's political power. I said what power did he have in 1972 that he could have handled this case or done something about it, that he didn't have in 1975? They couldn't answer that because they didn't really know what it was all about. I suspect . . . that there is a lot more involved than what this case is about. This is an election year, and I think that is why we are here today, but I don't want to waste time going into that.[32]

Chodak finished with another attack on Whalen's credibility

Justice Swainson and Harvey Wish should not be punished for a crime they didn't commit specifically on the basis of the word of a liar, a thief and a criminal. . . . I ask you, ladies and gentlemen, to take Mr. Wish in your hands, and Justice Swainson, and find them innocent of all charges because you believe they are innocent.[33]

The prosecution, as bearer of the burden of proof, got the last word. Ozer reminded the jurors of his previous inoculation of Whalen's testimony:

I told you in the beginning and I told you in the end, . . . this case had been presented to you with a commitment by the government that we do not ask you to convict anybody on the word of John Whalen, not entirely. He was brought in so that you could see him and . . . see that the government was not hiding

any of [the evidence] from you, but when Mr. Chodak condemns and castigates
. . . John Whalen, who was it that was dealing with John Whalen? . . . Who was
saying I will help you John, you come up with the money and I will keep you
out. That wasn't the FBI. That wasn't me . . . That was Harvey Wish.[34]

Ozer then reminded the jury that the government was not accusing Swainson
of spreading money to the other justices, but "John Swainson said he would do
his best. He did do his best . . . John Swainson is the man who moved for the
leave to appeal . . . He moved for bail, and no one else felt vehemently opposed,
and it was granted."

And finally, he returned to the perjury charge:

If Justice Swainson had merely said look, this television set from Harvey Wish,
no I don't think so, being confused in his mind. . . . but as long as he thought
that he could just say Mel is lying, Grand Jury, that man is lying . . . It is not me.
It is the parking lot attendant, Mel. . . . Only when he heard that the FBI was
there . . . for the first time, did he think how much do I now have to admit . . .
and then he came back and made the admission, limited admission regarding his
conversation on the 6th, but he said I don't remember what. I left a message on
the 19th, but I don't remember why. I got a television set on the 15th, but I don't
know what the meeting was about. I got a package on the 16th of September, but
I don't know what they were and I don't know why I got them.[35]

The closing arguments were at an end. Without a break, Judge Rubin began
instructing the jurors on the applicable law. By the end of this lecture (which
consumed thirty-one pages of trial transcript) the jurors must have been woozy,
but the judge sent them to the jury room to begin deliberations. It was a little
before 6:00 P.M. At some point the judge gave everyone a dinner break, and at
8:30 the jurors sent out a note asking to end their work day. The judge granted
their request, ordering them to resume deliberations the next day (Friday) at
9:00 A.M.

On Friday the jury asked to hear several of the wire tapes, which request
was granted. They put in a full day of deliberation without sending any other
communications to the court.

On Saturday they resumed, and deliberated into the afternoon again without
communicating to the court. This provoked some anxious moments among the
attorneys, who speculated on whether the jurors were deadlocked. But at 4:00

P.M. the jury sent out a note with several questions. They wanted to know if Harvey Wish had appeared before the grand jury. In fact he had appeared, but had immediately invoked the Fifth Amendment and answered no questions, which the jury could not be told without prejudicing his right to a fair trial.

They also asked, "Is a bondsman able to cancel a bond if the person fails to pay an annual premium?" This was significant. First, it showed that they understood Chodak's argument—that Wish needed Whalen's money to protect his bond. Second, it showed that they understood the difference between argument and testimony, and that Chodak's narrative about the difficulty of Wish getting off Whalen's bond was not evidence, and it underlined the importance of Chodak's failure to present any evidence on this point. The judge simply ruled that "this involves questions of law, which the Court is not prepared to answer."[36]

The jury ended a full day of deliberations without reaching a verdict, and the judge sent them back to their hotel with instructions to resume at 1:00 P.M. Sunday.

As they resumed their work Sunday, the seven women and five men had been sequestered in the dreary downtown Detroit Howard Johnson Motor Inn, away from their families and friends, thirteen nights. They had to be weary. Yet their diligence never flagged, which they proved by sending out several more questions seeking clarifications of the law that applied to this case.

Finally, at about 7:00 P.M., after twenty-two hours of deliberation, they sent out a note announcing that they had reached a verdict. As the word reached those waiting in the courtroom, and those in the corridors, the yawning tedium of the long wait metamorphosed into tension.

After all interested parties were present in the courtroom, a U.S. marshal led the jury in and they were seated in the jury box. In response to Judge Rubin's inquiry, the jury foreman replied that they had reached a unanimous verdict on each defendant. The foreman then handed the verdict to the U.S. marshal, and the judge requested that Swainson and Wish stand for the reading of the verdict. They pushed back their chairs and rose.

The clerk then read the verdict:

"We the jury herein unanimously find Defendant John B. Swainson guilty as charged in Counts 4, 5 and 6 of the indictment and not guilty as charged in Count 9 of the indictment." The jury thus found Swainson guilty on all three counts of perjury and not guilty of conspiracy to accept a bribe.

"We the jury herein unanimously find Defendant Harvey Wish guilty as charged in Count 9 of the indictment and not guilty as charged in Count 1 of the indictment." Harvey Wish was thus found guilty of conspiracy to bribe and not guilty of making an interstate telephone call in furtherance of bribery.

According to the Detroit Free Press, Swainson and Wish "remained almost expressionless" as the verdicts were announced.[37]

Alice came forward and took Swainson's arm. Their daughter Kristina, in the first row of the spectator section, burst into tears. Swainson calmly walked over and put his arms around her, then took her out into the corridor, talking to her calmly all the while.[38]

The judge thanked the jury profusely for the sacrifices they had made, complimenting them on an "outstanding job," and discharged them. U.S. marshals led them out of the building and back to the Howard Johnson Motor Inn, so they could retrieve their personal possessions. When reporters approached several of them, they replied that all jurors had agreed that none would comment.

Both Swainson and Wish had been free on minimal $5,000 personal bonds. Ozer could have asked the court to increase their bonds or even jail them to await sentencing, but when the judge asked for his position, Ozer said, "I make no request for modification." Both defendants thus remained free on bond pending sentencing, which was delayed.

Judge Rubin declared the trial adjourned. Swainson and Wish had no public comment, so reporters gathered around a smiling Ozer. He did not disappoint them. Describing the jury's decision as "a compromise verdict," Ozer said, "If the jurors thought Swainson was really innocent of conspiracy, they would have acquitted him on all counts. A jury is unwilling to convict such an exalted figure like Swainson without conclusive evidence like they see on TV or the movies."[39]

CHAPTER EIGHTEEN

The Trial Reconsidered

JOHN SWAINSON WAS CONVICTED OF THREE COUNTS OF PERJURY. HE APPEALED HIS conviction, unsuccessfully, to the U.S. Court of Appeals and the U.S. Supreme Court declined to accept the case. Thus, the verdict is final. But nothing precludes us from examining the evidence—all the evidence we can find—and reaching our own historical verdict.

• *Did John Swainson receive a fair trial?*
He himself addressed this question. In July 1977, while appearing before a panel of the State Bar of Michigan that was considering his disbarment, Swainson said that, while he did not agree with the jury's verdict, he believed that he had received a fair trial.[1] Ten years later, in an interview with *Detroit News* political columnist George Weeks, Swainson's view had not changed. He said, "Although I felt [members of the jury] were misled by the prosecutor, as a judge I knew there has never been a perfect trial, and I could not say that I was denied a fair trial, and a review by an appellate court."[2]

I have read most sections of the nearly 2,000-page trial transcript more than once, and each section at least once. Although the transcript is public record, and anyone can read it, it is not easy to access. I therefore feel a keen responsibility to describe the trial fairly—"judiciously," if you will. And, of course, my reading is informed by my own background, which includes fifteen years as a trial judge.

I would describe Judge Rubin's day-to-day conduct of the trial as even-handed. He had three very aggressive attorneys before him, and he (properly) kept a tight rein on all of them. At various times he admonished each of them.

The judge's routine rulings on such issues as the admissibility of evidence show no obvious bias. Each attorney lost his fair share (Chodak lost more often than Ozer or Kohl, but Chodak tended to take extreme positions and, unlike the other two, he would sometimes defy the judge's ruling, trying to pursue a line of questioning that the judge had already ruled improper).

After the prosecution had rested, Judge Rubin granted some of the defendants' motions to dismiss particular charges, ruling that the prosecution had failed to produce any evidence in support of those charges. Others he let stand.

Probably the single most important issue the judge had to decide was whether to allow the jury to hear the Whalen-Wish tapes, knowing that if Wish chose not to testify, Swainson would be denied the right to confront the single most damaging witness against him. As we have seen, under the "co-conspirator exception" this decision turned upon whether there was "independent evidence of a conspiracy" between Wish and Swainson—that is, evidence other than the tapes themselves.

Judge Rubin ruled that the tapes could be used as evidence against Swainson. He did not explain his ruling,[3] but we can assume that he agreed with Ozer's arguments that the phone calls and meetings between Swainson and Wish (which Swainson admitted to the grand jury), in which the Whalen case was discussed, and what appeared at the time to be gifts, plus the fact that the Supreme Court did grant leave and then reverse Whalen's conviction, constituted independent evidence of conspiracy.

This ruling was consistent with what appears to me to be Judge Rubin's judicial philosophy: where there was a close question about whether to put a factual issue before the jury, he'd trust the jury. This view is not at all uncommon among trial judges, and implies no bias for or against one side or the other. Although I may not agree with the ruling, I cannot say that it was utterly without any rational basis at the time it was made.

And perhaps my quarrel is not so much with Judge Rubin as with the co-conspirator exception itself. Those who promulgated it never anticipated a situation in which a person—Harvey Wish—would say that he was a member of a conspiracy, if in fact he wasn't.

So, in general John Swainson received a fair trial.

There is, however, one aspect of the Swainson trial that I find a bit disturbing, and which may have affected the result. It arose from Judge Rubin's decision to sequester the jury. Because of the intense publicity surrounding the case, U.S. marshals escorted the jurors to a motel each night. They were allowed no contact with their families or friends while the trial went on.

This was a judge who was very concerned with the well-being of his jurors, which he made clear on numerous occasions, repeatedly reminding the attorneys that they must not waste the jurors' time. And as the trial consumed more and more of the jurors' time, Judge Rubin's concern grew. This could not help but put pressure on both sides to speed things up. But since the defense could not start their presentation until the prosecution's presentation was finished, most of this pressure fell upon the defense.

In every trial the prosecution goes first. They have the burden of proof, and it is not at all unusual for the prosecution's case to consume the majority of the trial. But the proportion in this case was exceptional: the prosecution's case used nearly six and a half days, creating 1,183 pages of transcript. Of course, part of the prosecution's time was actually used by the defense, cross-examining the prosecution's witnesses, but that is beside the point, which is this: when the time came for the defendants to present their proofs, the jury had been sitting, and sequestered, for nine days.

The defense case therefore used only a little over a day, creating 306 transcript pages. Kohl's presentation began at 10:45 A.M. on Wednesday, October 29. His last witness (John Swainson) finished his testimony at noon the next day.[4]

But even that was not the worst result.

After Swainson concluded his testimony on October 29, the court recessed for lunch. At 1:40 P.M. the attorneys met with the judge in his chambers to discuss the procedures for closing arguments. It was and is customary for the prosecutor to present his closing argument first, then the defense, and finally the prosecutor again (since the prosecutor goes first, the defense has heard the prosecutor's argument and thus has the opportunity to comment upon it. But the prosecutor cannot comment upon the defense argument before he or she has heard it; therefore, the prosecutor is given a brief second opportunity to speak; this is known as the "rebuttal." The question was what time limits would apply.

Ozer asked for ninety minutes for his first closing and thirty minutes for his second, or rebuttal, closing. Considering the quantity of testimony the jury had heard, this was not an unreasonable request. But the judge would not hear of it. He said, "I am not going to allow two hours for the government under any circumstances at any time."5

Ozer was in a difficult position. No attorney ever wants to argue with a judge, and yet Ozer needed a longer time limit. So, he tiptoed back and forth with Judge Rubin for a few minutes, trying to get the judge to commit to more time, fruitlessly. Kohl and Chodak said nothing, undoubtedly enjoying Ozer's discomfort.

But then, apparently sensing a tactical opportunity, Kohl jumped in. He said, "Your Honor, the time I use does, of course, depend to some degree on the length and nature of the government's argument, but frankly I did not plan on more than half an hour." The judge turned to Chodak, and asked, "What about you?" Chodak, who had presented no witnesses, said "A half hour will be fine. I don't think I could hold out any longer than that."

This increased the pressure on Ozer, who reluctantly agreed to one hour for his initial closing and fifteen minutes for his rebuttal, wrapped around a half hour for each defendant.

But what had Kohl achieved with his interjection? Ozer had a total of seventy-five minutes to explain the evidence to the jury. Kohl had just thirty minutes to rebut Ozer's arguments and to explain away six and a half days of prosecution testimony. It was analogous to a general, before a battle, agreeing with the enemy general, "If you reduce your forces to two and a half divisions, I'll reduce my forces to one division."

The result was foreseeable. Too late, Kohl realized that he had insufficient time to adequately address all of the charges against his client. After addressing the jury on the bribery charges for twenty-five minutes, Kohl asked, "Your Honor, how much time do I have left?" The judge told him, "About five minutes." Kohl then said, "Ladies and gentlemen, there are so many things I would like to discuss with you, but I just don't have the time to do it."

The judge said, "Mr. Kohl, I will give you an additional five minutes."6

Kohl thanked the judge, and continued arguing the bribery charge. Then, his newly extended deadline fast approaching, Kohl finally got to the three counts of perjury. He spent approximately two and a half minutes on these charges,7 then said, "I have no more time. I ask you to return the verdict of not guilty, because he is not guilty, and only you can make that decision."

As we have seen, the jury acquitted John Swainson of bribery conspiracy, but they found him guilty on three counts of perjury. Konrad Kohl's closing argument was not ineffective; it was simply incomplete.

• *Did John Swainson deliberately lie to the grand jury?*

Ozer's argument that Swainson lied to the grand jury was essentially this: On May 19 Swainson told the grand jury that he had no recollection of the television set, the October 6 phone call with Wish, the October 19 phone call with Wish, or Wish bringing any packages to his house. Only after he was confronted with the testimony of others, establishing that these things happened, did he come back on May 21 and admit what he could not deny, that they did happen. Therefore, Swainson's May 19 grand jury testimony of no recall was a deliberate lie.

This sounds like a powerful argument, but it rests upon an unspoken assumption: when a witness says he has no memory of a particular event, but then—only after being confronted with the testimony of other witnesses—acknowledges that the event happened, this is inconsistent with innocence, and therefore the witness's initial denial of any recall must have been a deliberate lie.

But the assumption is untrue. People forget past events all the time, and then acknowledge them when reminded by others who were present.

Swainson's attorney, Konrad Kohl, barely addressed this in his own closing argument.

But there is other evidence, which the jury never heard.

Meri Lou Murray and Ronald Carlson each had contact with Swainson at the time of his appearance before the grand jury. Murray (chair of the Washtenaw County Board of Commissioners and a close Swainson friend) remembered that

> [Swainson] was very concerned because . . . [Ozer] was talking to him about specific phone calls that John truly didn't remember, because it was a number of years beyond the time [i.e., beyond the time the phone calls had taken place], and this is a person who obviously had a lot of phone calls, obviously talked to a lot of people. . . . But he truly did not remember some of the things they were talking about. I don't remember the timing on that but I do remember it was specifically at the time he was going [to the grand jury], because he was just concerned because he just did not remember.[8]

Carlson, Swainson's law clerk, received a phone call from Swainson after the first appearance before the grand jury.

> I remember they scrambled around, pulling phone records and trying to reconstruct things. Kohl was with him. I wasn't there, but I remember discussion about that; I remember sort of the hubbub of it with John. He said "[Ozer] asked me

about all these dates and I had no idea what I was doing on those dates. You know, it wasn't like I went in there with my calendar or anything. I couldn't reconstruct it, so we're going to find out, you know, we're going to look at everything. Pull your calendar. I'm having Nancy pull my calendar, we're going to try and figure out why he asked about those dates." That's how I remember it.[9]

Although Carlson and Murray later became acquainted, they have not had any contact for many years (Carlson estimates their last contact as 1988 or 1989), yet both describe essentially the same story of John Swainson, after his first grand jury appearance, desperately trying to reconstruct events which truly had vanished from his memory.

A prosecutor might argue that Swainson simply made self-serving statements and put on an act for his friends. But his only conceivable motive for putting on an act would be to set up Murray and Carlson to be defense witnesses at his trial. Yet Swainson did not call either of them as a witness. In fact, he did not even put their names on his list of potential witnesses given to the judge before the trial.[10]

Is it plausible that a judge would forget the things that Swainson said he forgot? The question is not easy to answer; most people remember an event or conversation only if it seemed important at the time it occurred. But this leads to a circular result. If Harvey Wish was bribing Swainson, their conversations and meetings on that subject would have been significant to Swainson, and he would likely have remembered them, and had good reason to lie about it. But if Wish was not bribing him, then a two-minute phone conversation regarding one of dozens of cases then before the Supreme Court would be insignificant, as would Wish bringing a package into Swainson's house.

However, the delivery of the television set is different. Here, we know what really happened, from two witnesses with no reason to lie. The testimony of David Auer and John Kalkanian establishes beyond a doubt that Harvey Wish simply delivered an unsought gift from Auer. The incident involved no criminal wrongdoing by anyone.

The point is that Swainson had no reason to lie about the television set—he had no reason to hide the truth, and everything to lose by lying. He knew that Ozer was setting a perjury trap. To deliberately lie about it under oath would make no sense. But if Swainson simply forgot about the television set, then his answers make perfect sense.

In addition to the circumstantial evidence, there is *direct* evidence that

Swainson did not remember the television set. His friend and law partner, Alan Zemmol, helped Swainson's and Wish's attorneys prepare their clients for their grand jury appearances.

> I very clearly remember meeting with John and Wish and Chodak at Chodak's house in Huntington Woods. Both John and Wish were perplexed about the IRS questions regarding a TV set. I said, "This TV shows up in a lot of questions. *Somebody* thinks it's important. . . . The [FBI] surveillance report and IRS audit both referred to a TV set. It shows up in a couple of different places. What do you know about a television set?" And everybody said, "What do you mean?"
>
> The issue of where [the television set] came from, he didn't remember. And that was before the grand jury [appearance]. He really had no recollection . . .
>
> I know that we . . . actually discussed that prior . . . to his first [grand jury] appearance and he had no recollection. It was [prior to] his second appearance . . . [that] we discussed it again, I think, and then all of a sudden, "Oh my God, that's what I gave to Tom!" I don't remember where this took place but it was in the evening.
>
> . . . He never used it. It never was in his house. That's why he didn't remember it. He gave it to his brother Tom, who had just come out of the service. But they [Swainson's family] had two or three television sets at that time and there was really no need for it, so he gave it to his brother Tom.[11]

We return to the question, is it plausible that a judge would forget something that turns out to have been significant?

After he retired, former chief justice T. Giles Kavanagh related this story:

> Mr. Ozer and one other agent came over to my office in the Lafayette Building and asked me if I had ever gone to the office of . . . I think it was Chucky Goldfarb, a bondsman, with John Swainson, and I couldn't remember . . . I had in the back of my mind for some dumb reason that the Goldfarb office which used to be . . . near Recorder's Court, had been transferred. I thought they had moved their offices. . . . I didn't know Chucky Goldfarb at that time from Adam . . . , and I don't know why I had the notion that his office had been moved out of downtown Detroit out into near Northland someplace.

This interview would have occurred early, at a time when Ozer still harbored suspicions that other members of the Supreme Court might be involved in bribery.

When they asked me the question, I said, "No, I was never at Chucky Goldfarb's office." [They asked,] "You don't remember going there with John Swainson?" "No."

Well, Dave Doumochel [Kavanagh's former law clerk, who went on to work for the U.S. Justice Department] told me many years later that the FBI or this task force had pictures of me at Chucky Goldfarb's office with John Swainson. What had happened . . . John and I had decided we were going to go out to lunch together and so he said, "I've got a picture that is coming from the J. L. Hudson Company, and I've got to pick it up. Do you mind going by . . ." and so and so, I forget who it was [it was, of course, Harvey Wish], was going to pick it up for him. [Swainson said] "and I've got to pick it up there, and we'll go to lunch then."[12]

So I drove. We went over, and as it turned out later, it was Chucky Goldfarb's office. John went in and got his painting which he said was from the J. L. Hudson Company . . . and we went to lunch and I promptly forgot all about it. I attached no significance to that at all.[13]

Finally, consider this: When former Supreme Court justices John Fitzgerald and Mary Coleman were interviewed for the Michigan Supreme Court Historical Society Oral History Project, they both recalled that they first learned of the bribery allegation against Swainson at a meeting that took place *after* the death of former chief justice T. Matthew Kavanagh.

But that cannot be true. Since they learned of the bribery allegation for the first time at the meeting, this meeting had to have taken place before the bribery allegation first appeared in the press, which it did on April 17, 1975. T. Matthew Kavanagh died two days later, on April 19, 1975.

Were the two justices lying in their interviews? Of course not; they simply forgot.

• *Did John Swainson conspire to commit bribery?*

The jury found Swainson not guilty of conspiracy to accept a bribe, and we might conclude that this was the end of it. However, after the trial Robert Ozer implied that he thought the jury had believed that Swainson may have accepted a bribe, but that the prosecution had failed to prove it beyond a reasonable doubt. Since the court of history is already in session, let us examine this charge.

According to Whalen's testimony (which is all we have on the subject), Wish's first mention of a bribe to a Supreme Court justice occurred "a few days before" Whalen's attorney filed his application for leave to appeal on June 20, 1972. At this point, according to Whalen, Wish said he could "guarantee a dismissal."[14]

The question before us is this: Assuming that Whalen was telling the truth and Wish actually said this to him, was Wish merely passing on an offer from Swainson, or was Wish making it up?

What would it take to "guarantee a dismissal"?

It would require that

- Swainson knew in June 1972 that he could get at least three other votes (besides his own) to grant leave, and
- Swainson knew that he then could get at least three other votes to reverse, and
- Swainson knew that he also could get at least three other votes to discharge the defendant, rather than remand for a new trial.

Yet at the time of the "guaranteed dismissal" promise, Whalen's attorneys had not even filed their application for leave to appeal. Nobody at the Supreme Court knew anything about the facts of Whalen's case, or the law pertaining to it. To guarantee a dismissal at that time, Swainson would have to have three other justices' commitments that they would—literally—vote at his command.

Moreover, assuming that the court were to grant leave, the case could not be argued and decided until 1973. Eugene Black had already announced that he would retire at the end of 1972, and Paul Adams would have to decide whether to run for reelection to retain his seat (in fact, he retired too). Therefore, the only votes that Swainson could—even in theory—"guarantee" were the two Kavanaghs, Thomas Brennan and Williams. Williams, the proud long-time governor and scion of a skincare products empire,[15] was independently wealthy. Brennan, then the lone Republican on the court, was not sympathetic to the rights of criminal defendants. In fact, when the court later voted to continue Whalen's bond pending the outcome of his appeal, Brennan dissented. Clearly, he was not voting at Swainson's command. It is therefore vanishingly improbable that the "guaranteed dismissal" offer was made by Swainson. It must have been concocted, either by Wish or by Whalen himself.

As we have seen, on October 20, 1972, the justices voted to grant Whalen leave to appeal.

On October 24 Wish and Whalen met, and this time their conversation was recorded by Whalen's body microphone. We no longer have to rely on Whalen's word that the conversation took place.

At this meeting Wish told Whalen that there has been a "misunderstanding." The agreement was not one price for one result, but two prices for two results: "10 for getting, you know, the hearing; 20 if he got you off. . . . And that'll bring it to 30. And if he gets it dismissed, give him the 30."[16]

Just as in the first conversation, the promised result is a "dismissal." There is no acknowledgment of the difference between reversal with discharge (which could be called a dismissal) and reversal with remand for new trial (which is not a dismissal by any stretch of the imagination).

Consider also that the granting of a discharge with a reversal was relatively rare, even in that liberal Court. In calendar 1971, for example, the court issued opinions reversing twenty-two criminal convictions. Of the twenty-two reversals, seventeen were accompanied by remands. In only five of the reversals did the Supreme Court reverse *and* discharge the defendant.

Swainson was arguably the Court's most liberal justice. Yet of his own twenty-four written opinions in criminal appeals, he ruled for discharge only five times. If Swainson *was* accepting a bribe offer, he had to know that "dismissal" was something he could not promise. But Wish would not know that.

On November 16, 1972, Swainson filed a "hold" memo to bring the question of continuing Whalen's bond before the other justices.[17] Without that hold memo, the court's clerk would have, automatically, issued an order revoking Whalen's bond.

Continuation of his bond was extremely important to Whalen, who believed that his life depended on staying out on the street. If Swainson had told Wish that he was attempting to get Whalen's bond continued, Wish would have relayed this to Whalen—it would have reinforced the desired impression that Swainson was doing Wish's bidding. Whalen certainly would have remembered it; he would have told the FBI, and he would have testified to it at the trial.

But there was no such testimony.

Wish never told Whalen about the bond continuation hold memo, because Swainson never told Wish.

Ozer argued to the jury that Swainson had agreed to use his "best efforts" on behalf of Whalen at the Supreme Court.[18] But with the single exception of the bond continuation, there was no evidence that Swainson ever made *any* efforts to advance Whalen's cause in the Supreme Court. Five justices testified at the trial; none of them remembered being approached by him about the case; none even remembered him arguing in Whalen's favor at their conferences.

Objectively, we must consider one other theory: that Swainson accepted the money and let Wish believe what he wanted to believe; in other words, that Swainson conned Wish. Then, if the Supreme Court were to deny Whalen's appeal, Swainson could either keep the money anyway, saying he had done his best, or refund it to Wish. However, there are two good reasons for doubting that this happened.

Some time before Swainson's grand jury appearance (the exact dates are unknown), agents of the Internal Revenue Service conducted a full audit of Swainson's finances, including questioning him under oath. Such audits typically require the targeted person to produce all income and expenditure records, and to document sufficient income to explain all of his expenditures. As we have seen, Ozer liked to use IRS investigators; they had investigative tools and techniques that nobody else had, and could discover things that other investigators could not.[19]

A bribe of $20,000 would have represented a 40 percent increase over Swainson's income from his salary as a Supreme Court justice. That would have been difficult to hide. If the IRS had found evidence of unreported income from bribe money, there is no doubt that they would have prosecuted Swainson for income tax evasion.[20]

But John Swainson was never charged with tax evasion.

And, finally, there is Harvey Wish.

Wish was seventy-nine years old and not in the best of health when I asked him to recall the events of thirty-five years earlier.

Assessing the credibility of his statements is not easy. Some are contradicted by other evidence. Some are at least partially confirmed by other evidence. Some were self-serving, while others were modest. And some must be assessed alone.

Naturally, there were questions he could not answer. Too much time had gone by, and he had not thought about these things for a long time; they were not pleasant memories. He had a vague recollection of meeting John Whalen in Windsor, but didn't recall the reason. He remembered that Whalen would not pay the premium on his bail bond, but denied using a bribery story to con Whalen into paying. The FBI transcripts of Wish's conversations with Whalen belie that denial, as did Wish's own attorney in his closing argument to the jury.

But there were some things that Harvey Wish remembered quite well, and they were at least partly corroborated.

He said that the strike force, surprisingly, made no attempt to turn him into a cooperating witness against Swainson. They did not make him any offer. This is consistent with the recollections of the only known surviving members of the prosecution team, FBI Special Agent Ed Diem and Stan Hunterton, an attorney who began his legal career by working for Ozer on the Swainson case. Diem was definite that they did not make Wish an offer before the indictment.[21] Hunterton did not remember one way or the other.[22]

I asked Wish why his attorney called no witnesses. He said he didn't know. During the trial he and Murray Chodak "sort of split . . . and I had nothing to do with him. I didn't trust him. I couldn't get another attorney at the time." Wish said that their split was caused by Chodak's friendliness with the prosecutor, Robert Ozer, that Chodak and Ozer had hung out together at night, even as the trial was going on.

Stan Hunterton confirmed that "Ozer was close to Chodak. . . . Indeed, it was his relationship with Chodak that got him into trouble." This is a reference to Ozer's hiring Chodak as his divorce attorney the year after the trial, which was cited by unnamed sources within the Justice Department as one reason why Ozer was fired from the strike force.[23]

I asked Wish about his relationship with Swainson.

Wish said that he and John Swainson "were just friends. We talked a lot, about a lot of things. I can't remember ever giving him any presents. I may have delivered stuff for him . . . I might have picked up a lot of things for him. I didn't pay for anything for him."[24]

After the trial, "I could see that he was scared to be with me, so I said good-bye. After that I only saw him at banquets and events. He was scared to death of me, and I was not going to push." Their friendship was over.

Late in life, Wish was not particularly positive toward John Swainson; perhaps partly because of the sudden end to their friendship. He felt that "Swainson was not a good guy" because of his involvement with women. He recalled that Swainson had asked him to serve as a "beard," accompanying Swainson and a woman with whom Swainson wanted to have lunch. Wish resented it.

It would therefore seem that Harvey Wish would have no particular reason to exonerate John Swainson's reputation.[25] Yet when asked the direct question—"Did you bribe him?"—he answered without hesitation, "Absolutely not. I did not pay John Swainson any money. . . . There was no bribe. . . . He and I probably did discuss Whalen's case, but I sure as hell didn't ask him to do anything."

CHAPTER NINETEEN

Governor, Convicted and Died

BEFORE THE TRIAL THERE HAD BEEN A FEW CALLS FOR JOHN SWAINSON TO RESIGN from the Supreme Court. But he had satisfied most of the mainstream press and legal community by remaining as a justice but stepping aside from all court business temporarily, pending the outcome of the trial. After all, he was presumed innocent.

But now he had been convicted of three felony counts, and Michigan Compiled Laws, section 938 provided that a person convicted of a felony could not hold public office.

After the guilty verdict, Bruce Leitman, who had joined Swainson's legal team to present his motion for a new trial and, if necessary, his appeal, argued against immediate resignation. Even though the statute prohibited a convicted felon from holding office, Leitman argued that the conviction was not final until all appeals had been exhausted.[1]

Initially, Swainson agreed. Two days after the jury found him guilty, and obviously still reeling from shock, he delivered a letter to Chief Justice T. Giles Kavanagh:

Because of the misuse of a Grand Jury, I have been publicly humiliated and financially ruined. My career of public service has been threatened, but I have no doubt of my eventual vindication, because I am innocent.

I have been found guilty of failing to remember a specific event totally unrelated to the inquiry of the Grand Jury, and two telephone conversations that occurred two and one half years prior to my appearance before the Grand Jury. I have not been convicted of bribery or found to be in any way involved in a conspiracy to bribe.

The integrity of the Supreme Court remains unsullied and the reputation of its members unchallenged.

The members and staff of the Supreme Court, my family, my friends and thousands of unknown persons stood with me throughout this ordeal, and I owe each and every one an eternal debt of gratitude.

I request that the Court retain my salary in escrow during the post-trial proceedings, and I look forward to again assuming the position to which I was elected.[2]

In other words, he had no intention of resigning.

But public opinion leaders swiftly announced a different view, and it was practically unanimous.

The president of the State Bar of Michigan was George Bushnell Jr. Bushnell, the son of a Michigan Supreme Court justice, was a partner in the major Detroit law firm Miller Canfield, and would go on to serve as president of the American Bar Association. Witty and sophisticated, a self-described "liberal curmudgeon," Bushnell was an outspoken advocate for the poor and minorities, as well as legalization of marijuana. Robert Ozer's conduct had become a source of increasingly serious concern to Bushnell.

Yet when Swainson was convicted, Bushnell did not hesitate to call for his resignation, pointing out that the verdict "cannot help but reflect on the integrity of the entire judicial system."[3]

Detroit's two major dailies, the News and Free Press, quickly published editorials calling upon Swainson to resign immediately. The Free Press had supported his candidacies for statewide office.

After seeing the public reaction, Swainson's well-developed sense of public opinion told him his initial impulse to stay was wrong. And his sense of honor agreed.

Swainson telephoned Michigan governor William Milliken, who was at his family home in Traverse City on the northwestern tip of the Lower Peninsula. Swainson asked if he could come and see Milliken the next day. Milliken, who admired Swainson, surmised his purpose, and agreed to see him.

On Friday, November 7 Swainson flew to Traverse City in a chartered plane. He arrived at Milliken's family home a little before noon. Milliken ushered Swainson into his study. Milliken later recalled, "In this very solemn moment, he formally submitted his resignation. . . . He felt it was the appropriate thing to do to come in person. He mentioned that he had talked with Alice before making the trip."[4]

Then John Swainson went home to Manchester. That night he and Alice attended the local high school football game. It was Dad's Night, and daughter Kristina's last game as a cheerleader. Swainson walked to the center of the field with the other fathers of graduating seniors.[5]

The trial had cost Swainson in excess of $50,000, and the appeals promised to exhaust his resources. He was, for the present, without an income, save for approximately $10,000 a year in veteran's disability pension for his World War II injury. But he still had loyal friends, and they came together to help.

On December 16, a committee of prominent Democrats and union leaders hosted a fund-raising dinner at the United Auto Workers Local 652 Hall in Lansing. Between 175 and 250 people paid $10 apiece for drinks and a spaghetti dinner donated by Council 32 of the American Federation of State, County and Municipal employees. The *Detroit News* reported that "a beaming Swainson—accompanied by his wife, Alice and daughter Tina, 17—heard four standing ovations as he thanked his friends for their support."[6]

The proceeds from the dinner went into a Swainson Defense Fund, overseen by a committee chaired by David Sparrow. Committee members included Jane Hart, wife of U.S. Senator Phil Hart of Michigan, former Detroit mayor Jerome P. Cavanagh, former Supreme Court justice Thomas Brennan, Michigan AFL-CIO president William Marshall, and Zolton Ferency.

On the morning of January 26, 1976, the U.S. District Court in Detroit reconvened for sentencing. As was customary, Judge Rubin had received a presentence report from the federal probation office.

The judge asked if Swainson's attorney wished to be heard, and Kohl stepped to the podium. He said, "I represent a man who has overcome odds that would have destroyed many of us. I am sure it would have destroyed me."

Kohl then narrated a brief biography of his client, including his years as a Wayne County circuit judge who "was never once reversed on appeal."[7]

It is to me a personal tragedy that my client . . . would not follow the advice that I gave him. My advice to my client was that he not testify before the Grand Jury and that he take the Fifth Amendment.[8] It is a personal tragedy to me that I was not more emphatic, more forceful . . .

I ask simply that he . . . be given justice as Your Honor sees fit to sentence him. I can ask no more. I would be demeaning the courts and my client if I should ask for anything else, and I thank you."

With that, Kohl returned to the defense table and sat down. The judge turned to Swainson and asked, "Mr. Swainson, do you wish to be heard?"

Swainson rose and said,

I do, Your Honor. I am sure that you know that a judge is always in . . . an almost impossible position to respond to any criticism of . . . his official conduct. And since I chose to remain as a member of the Michigan Supreme Court during the pendency of this matter, I refrained from any comment.

. . . It is true, as Mr. Kohl said, that I did not heed his advice regarding my appearance before the grand jury. Today I would do the same thing. I think it is incumbent on a public official, particularly a Supreme Court Justice, to appear before a grand jury and to respond and testify to any areas of inquiry that they may have.

I sincerely regret that you have the unhappy duty of imposing sentence on a person that has held high office. I have had in my life other things happen which I thought were insurmountable, but I think that has given me the strength to withstand that which you in your heart and mind feel you must do in my case. Thank you.

The judge turned and addressed the prosecution table: "Mr. Ozer, does the United State Attorney wish to be heard in this matter?" Ozer declined.

Now it was time to pass sentence upon John Swainson. Standing "erect and still" and frequently glancing at the floor,[9] Swainson listened attentively as the judge delivered his sentence.

"In considering this matter in great detail since November 2, 1975, I have taken into account this Defendant's education and background, his military service and his sacrifices, and his long service to the citizens of Michigan," said Judge Rubin. "I am conscious of the severe and continuing punishment that has already been imposed."

His presence this day in this Court is punishment, but I am equally conscious that he stands convicted of the offense of perjury. It is not difficult to impede or frustrate a grand jury. . . . Without truth under oath a grand jury must fail.

Accordingly, it is the judgment of this Court . . . that John B. Swainson be, and he is hereby committed to the custody of the Attorney General of the United States . . . for imprisonment for a year and a day. . . .

It is further provided that the Defendant John B. Swainson be confined in a minimum security institution for a period of sixty days and that the execution of the remainder of [the] year and a day sentence be and it hereby is suspended and that the Defendant John B. Swainson be thereupon on unsupervised probation for the balance of such period.

It is the further determination of the Court and the Court does so recommend that the Defendant John B. Swainson be confined in the Community Treatment Center, Detroit, Michigan.

Finally, the judge announced that he would continue Swainson's bond pending the defendant's decision on whether to appeal. (Swainson was free on a personal recognizance bond, requiring no money but only his promise to appear at all proceedings as ordered by the court.)

Next it was Harvey Wish's turn to be sentenced. His attorney, Murray Chodak, addressed the judge for less than a minute. Wish himself declined to speak at all.

Judge Rubin sentenced Wish to two years. Then, as he had with Swainson, he suspended most of the incarceration. The final sentence was six months in a minimum security institution, and probation for the remaining eighteen months. However, in contrast to Swainson's case, the judge did not recommend a place of confinement, leaving it to the U.S. Bureau of Prisons to decide where Wish would spend his six months.[10]

Swainson walked over to the spectator gallery, where Alice stood, waiting for him. He kissed her on the lips. Then, they walked out of the courtroom with Kohl. A group of reporters awaited them. Swainson paused to speak to them. He said, "I've been destroyed. My reputation has been smeared. This has been horrendous for my family and great punishment for me. I am very sad."[11]

There was never any doubt that Swainson would appeal his conviction. As a former appellate judge, he was well aware that he had nothing to lose by appealing.

A convicted defendant does not appeal the jury's verdict. Formally, the jury decides only issues of fact, and a jury's decision on a fact issue is, in and of itself, unappealable. What *is* appealable is any decision made by the *judge.* If the appellate court concludes that any of the judge's rulings were (1) in error, and (2) denied the defendant a fair trial, the appellate court will reverse the conviction and usually—as we have seen—send the case back for a new trial.

For the appeal Swainson and Kohl turned to a specialist. At age thirty-five, Bruce T. Leitman was a veteran appeals attorney, having served as the appellate litigator for the Oakland County Prosecutor's Office. Leitman remembered, "They were out of money and I was asked to help and I made the commitment. And I did it all the way through the application for certiorari to the U.S. Supreme Court."

Several legal issues gave Swainson hope that his conviction could be reversed.

As we have seen, the judge had allowed the jury to hear tapes of Harvey Wish discussing the alleged bribery with John Whalen, and even though the jury ultimately found Swainson not guilty of bribery, the recorded statements of Wish might well have contributed to their finding Swainson guilty of perjury. Yet Swainson's attorney never had the opportunity to put Wish under oath and cross-examine him, seemingly a denial of Swainson's Sixth Amendment right to confront the witnesses against him. Wish declined to testify, and Swainson could not call him as a witness because Wish was also on trial, and thus could not be compelled to testify; this would have violated Wish's Fifth Amendment rights.

The judge had ruled that there was independent evidence that Swainson and Wish were co-conspirators, and this triggered the so-called co-conspirator exception to the right to cross-examine. Leitman believed that the "independent evidence" of conspiracy to bribe cited by the judge was very shaky. Essentially, it amounted to no more than Swainson and Wish being acquainted, Wish possibly giving Swainson gifts, and the Michigan Supreme Court reversing Whalen's conviction.

The second major issue arose from a seeming conflict between two federal statutes. The first statute made perjury during any federal proceeding a federal crime.[12] The second statute specifically made perjury *before a grand jury* a federal crime, but it contained an exception: a witness who testified falsely could return to the grand jury and admit the falsity of his or her initial testimony, and this would bar a prosecution for perjury, unless it was already "manifest that such falsity has been or will be exposed."[13]

As we have seen, after testifying that he had no recall of the events Ozer was raising, Swainson had returned to the grand jury room for a second appearance, at which he acknowledged that the events had, in fact, happened. It is clear that he was motivated to make this second appearance by the second statute's promise of immunity. However, Ozer then had chosen to charge Swainson with violating the first, general perjury statute, which contained no immunity exception.

Leitman submitted his brief to the U.S. Sixth Circuit Court of Appeals. In December 1976 he traveled to Cincinnati and presented his oral argument to a three-judge panel.

It took the U.S. Court of Appeals less than two months to reach a decision. In *United State vs. Swainson* (548 F.2d 657, CA6, 1977), The panel unanimously affirmed the conviction. They ruled that Judge Rubin's decision to apply the co-conspirator exception to the right of confrontation had been justified, and rejected Swainson's argument that the 1970 perjury statute gave him immunity, ruling that "[Swainson's] changed testimony came after he had heard transcripts of the testimony of two eyewitnesses to a previous transaction which he had categorically denied in his earlier testimony." Thus, "it had become 'manifest that such falsity' had been exposed."

The Court of Appeals decision dashed Swainson's hopes for reversal. Although Leitman could (and would) still seek review by the U.S. Supreme Court, chances of that Court accepting the case were extremely remote. Swainson, still free on bond until all appeals were exhausted, decided to go ahead and serve his sentence.

Kohl quietly contacted the U.S. Probation Office and arranged for Swainson to turn himself in in February. The office did not notify the press or the U.S. attorney. Swainson wanted to complete his sentence without publicity. He was assigned to the Milner Arms, an older residential hotel in a deteriorating neighborhood near downtown Detroit where the federal government rented several two-man efficiency apartments for use as "halfway house" residences.[14]

Most of the halfway house inmates were federal prisoners transitioning from incarceration to parole. Swainson's roommate was a drug addict,[15] but their contact was limited. During the week each resident had to be out of the building by 8:00 A.M. to look for work. They reported back in at 3:00 P.M. to confer with their caseworkers, then had the rest of the day free until the 11:00 P.M. curfew. Inmates were allowed to go home on weekends.[16]

Swainson served most of his sentence working as an unpaid volunteer for the Legal Aid and Defender Association of Detroit,[17] and visiting friends. Bernard

Klein's apartment was downtown, not far from the Milner Arms. Klein said, "John would come over to my apartment and I would make breakfast and he would then get on the phone and call his cronies. He would complain about the food or the coffee, and I finally told him, 'Any more complaints and I'm going to tell your parole officer that you are not ready to return to society.'"[18]

Swainson could laugh at the remark. Serving his sentence was far from his most serious problem.

Michigan has what is known as an "integrated bar," which means that the State Bar Association not only promotes the interests of the legal profession, but also enjoys a semiofficial status, serving as the regulatory agency for attorneys.

When an attorney is convicted of a crime, the State Bar convenes a grievance panel of three attorneys to examine the case and recommend whether the State Bar should impose its own sanctions. Immediately after Swainson's conviction, such a panel had gathered to begin the process. However, Swainson had assured the panel that he would not practice law until his appeal was decided. In April 1976 the panel decided to adjourn, pending decision of the appeal by the U.S. Sixth Circuit Court of Appeals.

When in February 1977 the Court of Appeals affirmed the conviction, the grievance panel resumed its process. At a hearing in July, Swainson appeared before the panel and told its members that he would continue to refrain from practicing law as long as he was on probation.[19] The chairman of the panel seemed to react favorably to this promise, and Swainson had some reason for optimism that he would be allowed to resume practicing his profession.

His hopes were dashed when the panel released its decision. On October 6, 1977, the panel suspended him for three years. The decision noted that the panel would have suspended him for *five* years if he had not voluntarily refrained from practice since his conviction.

Swainson did not hide his disappointment. He said, "It was my hope that I would at least be allowed the opportunity to pursue a career in law so I could provide my family with the benefits they have a right to expect from my training and long experience in legal matters."[20]

The former governor of Michigan was beginning a descent from the ebullient, optimistic personality he had built over many years to something much darker. Perhaps he best described his emerging view of life in a pre-Christmas interview when he told a reporter, "I'll probably go down in the history of Michigan as an asterisk. An asterisk that says: John Swainson, governor, convicted and died."[21]

CHAPTER TWENTY

The Snitch

WHEN THE MICHIGAN SUPREME COURT REVERSED JOHN WHALEN'S ADRIAN burglary conviction in 1973, the justices remanded the case back to Lenawee County for a new trial. That trial was duly held, and Whalen was convicted again. On May 30, 1974, Lenawee circuit judge Rex Martin conducted the sentencing. Whalen believed it might have helped him if the FBI had sent someone to tell the judge about his cooperation in the Swainson investigation. But the strike force's investigation was still secret in 1974, and its leaders were unwilling to run any risk of exposure. Not only did the FBI decline to speak, they repeatedly told Whalen that he must not reveal his cooperation to anyone, *including his own attorneys,* and Whalen obeyed. No one at the sentencing was aware of Whalen's cooperation in the ongoing investigation.[1]

Judge Martin sentenced Whalen to a minimum of six years and eight months and a maximum of ten years. However, he was allowed to remain free on bond pending his appeal to the Michigan Court of Appeals.

After the Swainson investigation was made public in April 1975, Ozer sought to keep the FBI's promise to Whalen. He asked for a meeting with Lenawee County prosecutor Harvey Koselka and Judge Martin. Ozer brought FBI agent Ed Diem and Whalen's attorney, DeDay LaRene. Ozer recalled that

I outlined really quite comprehensively what Mr. Whalen was doing, how enormously critical the investigation was . . . the sacrifices that I thought John Whalen had made, the danger to his life. . . . I thought I was eloquent, but Judge Martin apparently did not. . . . He spoke at length on the question of whether he could do anything about it because of the question of whether a Michigan Judge could review a sentence unless it were remanded by the appellate court . . . [Finally] he said he would keep thinking about it and after the Swainson trial we could talk about it again.

After the Swainson trial, Ozer called Judge Martin, seeking a second meeting. The Judge told Ozer that he had reviewed the presentence report on Whalen, and had concluded that "no matter how much he cooperated with the federal authorities . . . this was the sentence he should have. I saw no reason to change my mind. In fact, apparently he had committed other crimes while out on bond, so I wouldn't agree to change the sentence."[2] In fact, according to Ozer, the Judge told him he would have *increased* the sentence if he could.[3]

Judge Martin had reasons for his conclusion.

In March 1975—a month after Robert Ozer had arrived in Detroit to take over the Federal Strike Force—John Whalen and two companions were caught with a truckload of stolen clothing valued at $75,000 outside a shopping center in Romulus, a Detroit suburb.

According to the *Detroit News,* "Shortly after his arraignment in the Romulus burglary . . . federal authorities intervened, took him away before he had to post bond, and arranged for his release."[4]

But the Romulus burglary, like the Adrian jewelry store burglary, was a state offense. Therefore, as Whalen now understood, the feds could not promise him immunity or even a sentence reduction. To get those benefits he would have to give something to the local cops.

As it happened, he had something to offer.

Seven months after the Romulus arrest, agents of the Wayne County Organized Crime Task Force fanned out across the metropolitan Detroit area. In a tightly coordinated operation they arrested twelve men alleged to be members of a large fencing organization. According to the *Detroit News,* the arrests were based on evidence supplied by John Whalen and Roger Ribnicki, and "for his cooperation Whalen hopes the police will intercede in the courts in his behalf in a pending burglary case in which he and Ribnicki . . . were arrested on March 10 at a shopping center . . . in Romulus." Jim Mitchell, a Wayne County Task

Force prosecutor, revealed that Whalen and Ribnicki had allowed themselves to be wired with microphones in meetings with the men who were arrested.[5]

In return for his cooperation in furnishing evidence on the fencing ring, Whalen was never charged in the Romulus burglary. The price he paid was the creation of twelve new enemies, and their families and friends.

One day as Konrad Kohl was preparing for the Swainson trial, his secretary buzzed him and announced that a Jimmy Pulvirenti was on the phone. Mr. Pulvirenti claimed to have information about John Whalen. Kohl had never heard of Pulvirenti, but he took the call.

Pulvirenti told Kohl that there was to be a meeting concerning John Whalen at the Leaky Tap Saloon on Six Mile Road in Detroit, and it might be in Kohl's interest to be there. The meeting was to take place at eleven that morning.

Pulvirenti, thirty-nine, had already served time for five felonies, including armed robbery and prison escape. Kohl did not know these details, but the phone call left him with the strong impression that Pulvirenti was a professional criminal. Kohl's secretary tried to dissuade him from attending the meeting, but he decided to go.

When Kohl arrived at the Leaky Tap, he saw a half dozen men seated at one table. Other than that, the place was empty. Kohl joined the group at the table. He later recalled, "It was a serious meeting, like a board of directors meeting." But these were not directors. "They were all criminals who hated John Whalen."

Kohl prudently bought a round of drinks, then listened as the men got down to business.

"The subject of the meeting was how to get rid of John Whalen: kill him, and if so where? Or, should this be a disappearance, like Hoffa? They decided that a disappearance would be best. I was then asked if it would look bad for Swainson if Whalen disappeared before the trial. I said yes, it would look bad." After some discussion, the board of directors decided to spare John Whalen, for now.

After a few minutes, two well-dressed men walked in and sat down at a nearby table. It was apparent to the men at Kohl's table that these two were not "regulars"; they were obviously FBI agents. So the meeting broke up.[6]

At some point during or shortly after the Swainson trial, Ozer arranged for Whalen, his wife, and his child to be given a new identity and placed in the Federal Witness Protection program.[7] They could not make final arrangements until Whalen's appeals of the Adrian conviction were determined, but they decided to move Whalen, his wife, and child to a motel under the protection of

U.S. marshals. It was not a moment too soon. Three days after Swainson was found guilty of perjury, the Whalens' home in an upper-middle-class neighborhood in St. Clair Shores was destroyed by an explosion and fire. It was, concluded the fire marshal, a professional arson, "a complete job."[8]

John Whalen's testimony in John Swainson's federal trial made no difference in the progress of Whalen's own case. Three weeks after the federal jurors had reached their verdict on Swainson, the Michigan Court of Appeals issued its decision on Whalen's appeal. His conviction was affirmed, and the Court of Appeals judges added a pungent comment:

> This crime occurred March 20, 1969. Over 6½ years later and after two trials resulting in conviction, both of which have been affirmed by this Court, defendant is still free. Enough is enough. Defendant's bond is canceled and he shall commence serving his sentence forthwith.[9]

The Court of Appeals had ordered that Whalen be jailed immediately. As was customary, the prosecutor contacted Whalen's attorney to arrange the defendant's surrender, for no later than December 18. But Whalen, never easy to find in the best of times, now disappeared. When he failed to appear on the agreed date, Lenawee County prosecutor Harvey Koselka secured a bench warrant for Whalen's arrest. Lenawee County sheriff Richard Germond began looking for Whalen.

Apparently Koselka and Sheriff Germond were unaware that Whalen had surfaced three days earlier in Hamtramck, a small city within the city of Detroit. Just after midnight on December 16 Hamtramck police had observed Whalen leaving a jewelry store and getting into a car, which then drove the wrong way down a one-way alley, giving the police legal cause to stop the car. The driver was Roger Ribnicki, Whalen's associate in the Romulus burglary. Upon approaching the vehicle, the police officers saw Whalen holding a gold bracelet studded with ninety-six diamonds, which he declined to explain. They arrested him and Ribnicki.[10]

Somehow—the record is unclear—Whalen arranged to be released *again*, and he dropped from sight once more.

But not for long.

Early in the afternoon of Friday, December 21, a woman was driving alone along Dequindre Road in rural Sterling Heights, north of Detroit, when she noticed an unkempt, bleeding figure walking along the shoulder. As she slowed, he flagged her down. She stopped, and John Whalen got in and asked to be taken to the nearest police station. After some inquiry, the woman found her way to the Utica police station, where she deposited Whalen.

When the desk sergeant realized who had walked in, he informed his chief, Maurice Foltz, who informed the FBI. Two federal marshals sped to the scene.

Whalen told detectives that he had been kidnapped the previous day, and his captors had tortured him. Examination revealed thirty-four cigarette burns on various parts of his body. Whalen said that his captors, after holding him overnight, had driven him to a wooded area. Believing that he was about to be murdered, he bolted, and they had fired shots at him as he ran away. Examination revealed a flesh wound in his left arm and another in his right thigh, both from small-caliber bullets. Whalen said that he had eluded the men in the woods for about an hour before feeling safe enough to emerge and flag down a motorist.[11]

Arrangements were made to get Whalen to St. Joseph Hospital West in Clinton Township northeast of Detroit, under guard by the marshals. All the while Foltz's detectives questioned Whalen, while other detectives walked the woods to see if they could verify his story. The FBI was also investigating it as a possible attempt to obstruct justice. After thorough examination of his wounds and visits to the locations he had described, the Sterling Heights detectives concluded that Whalen's story could not be true.

When they confronted him with their conclusions, he admitted that he had made up part of the incident: his captors had not taken him to the woods and shot him as he escaped. They had held him in a building and tortured him in an attempt to learn what he had told authorities. They shot him as a warning, then let him go. He had arranged for a friend to take him to Sterling Heights so that he could emerge from the woods.[12] Whalen also admitted, apparently for the first time, that he knew his abductors. But he refused to say who they were. He offered to take a polygraph test to confirm that he was now telling the truth.

Things never got that far. On Christmas Eve two U.S. marshals escorted Whalen out of the hospital. They declined to reveal his destination. When Lenawee County sheriff Germond learned that federal agents had taken Whalen away, he was livid. "They promised to keep me informed and turn him over when he was in condition to do so," said the sheriff, who now entertained "serious questions" about whether Whalen would ever serve his sentence for the Adrian burglary.[13]

The sheriff was prescient. The federal government relocated Whalen to California with a new identity, and never revealed his whereabouts to Michigan authorities.[14]

But Whalen was not satisfied with his ambiguous legal status. He came out of hiding and launched a series of federal habeas corpus suits, arguing that the FBI agents had violated his Sixth Amendment right to the effective assistance of legal counsel when they forbade him from disclosing his cooperation in the Swainson investigation to his own attorneys.

Whalen's suits were opposed at every step by the Michigan attorney general, but Whalen would not give up. Finally, in 1991, a federal judge ordered the attorney general to settle the case.

After fifteen years of litigation (and nineteen years after the Adrian burglary) the parties agreed to let Whalen satisfy his debt to the State of Michigan by serving five years of probation in California.

Pariah

ALL OF HIS ADULT LIFE HE HAD RISEN EARLY AND HEADED OFF TO WORK. AND IT HAD been meaningful work, doing things that would affect the lives of others. Now there was nothing. He was barred from every vocation that he had ever pursued.

He had been the subject of wide admiration. Now he was the subject of scorn.

John Swainson's life from 1976 to 1980 traces two nonparallel courses. The first is his descent into alcohol abuse. The second is his struggle to make a living and—just as important to him—to maintain the personal and political contacts that had sustained his persona as the quintessential "people person" for over two decades.

Many alcohol experts recognize a legitimate distinction between what they call "social drinking" and alcoholism, but there are degrees, shades.

By most accounts Swainson had been a convivial and frequent social drinker his entire career in politics. As a Supreme Court justice, Swainson invited Ronald Carlson to conduct his job interview for the law clerk position over lunch at the Detroit Press Club. Swainson immediately put Carlson at ease, and Carlson enjoyed the interview. He also noticed that Swainson drank two Manhattans, each with a cherry on top.[1]

When Swainson was a Wayne County circuit judge, he kept a bottle of whiskey in his chambers, and occasionally invited his colleagues on the bench in for a social drink at the end of the day.[2]

As Joe Collins put it, "John liked to have a good time, to go to a party. And when he was a judge in Detroit there was a party just about every night of the week. If you're inclined, you can go to a party, a fundraiser, every night of the week. And John went to lots of them."[3]

Every elected official has to raise money to pay for the next campaign, and the time-honored tradition is to sell tickets to a fund-raising reception—"fund-raiser" for short. Many of the tickets are purchased by those who hope to have some influence on the official's decisions—lobbyists in the case of legislators, attorneys and bail bondsmen in the case of judges.

But nearly every politician also attends the fund-raisers of other politicians—often on a complimentary ticket. This is done to show support for the "honoree," and in hopes of receiving reciprocal support later. In addition, the politician-guest has the chance to meet and interact with people who are not yet his or her supporters, but might be won over.

And finally, for a person like Swainson, who enjoyed social occasions and loved being the center of attention (which, as an ex-governor, he assuredly was), it was just plain fun.

But Swainson also had known where to draw the line, perhaps not as narrowly as some, but narrowly enough so that he would always get to the office early the next morning, and put in an effective day's work.

Now, there was no office. The party invitations did not completely disappear, but they diminished, so there was an absence of distraction, more time to think about his situation.

He went to visit friends, and they'd offer a drink. He'd accept, then go to visit another friend, and accept another drink. As he later put it, "If they're having one, I'm having six."[4]

Those who have studied alcohol abuse recognize various levels. The worst is "alcoholism," which is defined as the inability to get through the day without drinking, and physical symptoms of withdrawal. There is no evidence that Swainson reached that level. But he probably was a "problem drinker," which is characterized by the inability to stop once the drinker begins imbibing on a particular occasion.

He needed money. His only income was his veteran's disability pension, which amounted to about $10,000 a year.[5] His accumulated years of state government service qualified him for a decent pension, but he would not be eligible to begin drawing it until he turned sixty-five. When he resigned from the court he was only fifty.

There was one profession he could still practice, and for which he was well qualified: lobbying. He had been liked and respected by his colleagues in the legislature, on both sides of the aisle.

William Milliken, whose term in the State Senate had overlapped Swainson's as governor, found him "always straightforward, always businesslike . . . an honorable and honest man."[6]

Many of his old friends had advanced to powerful positions. Milliken was now in his second term as governor. Coleman Young, a union activist who had represented Detroit in the State Senate from 1964 to 1972, was now mayor of Detroit, a position for which he became eligible by virtue of a Supreme Court decision authored by Swainson. Others had stayed in the legislature, advancing in seniority and assuming the chairs of powerful legislative committees (in that era before term limits, a skillful politician who was satisfied to stay in the legislature could realistically aspire to reelection for life).

In May 1976 Swainson and former Wayne County Commission chairman Robert Fitzpatrick announced formation of a lobbying firm in Lansing.

The city of Detroit had contracted for the services of a multiclient Lansing lobbyist, former state legislator James Karoub. But questions arose as to whether Karoub's representation of Detroit was compromised by conflicts of interest with his other clients, and the city terminated the contract. This created an opening, and Mayor Coleman Young proposed to hire Swainson and Fitzpatrick.

The new contract had to be approved by the city's legislative body, the Detroit Common Council. On September 14, 1976, Swainson appeared before the council, answering questions and receiving a generally favorable response. Councilman Carl Levin said, "This would be an effective team to represent Detroit because of their knowledge of the legislature." However, the council delayed a formal vote on the contract to accommodate Councilman Ernest Browne, who had expressed opposition to hiring Swainson, and was absent because of a death in the family.[7]

This delay afforded opponents the chance to express opposition to the prospect of a convicted felon representing the city. The *Detroit News* weighed in the next day with an editorial, saying, "We still entertain the hope that Council will reject him when it votes on the matter Wednesday. . . . The City doesn't need anyone on its payroll who needs rehabilitation."[8]

A week later, Swainson asked the mayor to withdraw his name from consideration. He had dealt with legislative bodies a long time, and he knew how to count. The votes just weren't there.[9]

Swainson's finances were looking bleak. His daughter remembered, "We cut back on everything, not that I ever felt the pinch growing up. I just remember my mom saying, 'We're not getting any newspapers. We're not getting any magazines. We're going to cut where we can.' So we started living more frugally."[10]

Then his friends took action.

Sometime in the summer of 1977, the phone in the outer office of Henry Ford II's suite rang. Ford was in Spain, so his secretary took the message. When he returned, he surely noticed this particular message. He had never met Frank Kelley. Why would the attorney general of Michigan be calling him? He returned the call, and got right through.

Kelley, who had long admired Henry Ford II, said he wanted to see the chairman on a personal matter. "I'd like to see you, about somebody else. It's got nothing to do with you, nothing to do with government, but it's something you might be interested in." Ford, intrigued, said, "That's fine, Mr. Kelley, I'll see you."[11]

A few days later the attorney general traveled to the Glass House, Ford Motor Company's world headquarters in Dearborn. He was ushered into the chairman's large office.

Kelley said to him,

The story I'm going to tell you is about somebody that I have heard you didn't support in the election—didn't think much of—but he's been my friend for many, many years and he's got all kinds of problems. He was wrongfully accused of something he didn't do. Now he's lost a major . . . [office] and he's depressed and he needs help. I didn't know who to turn to and I thought maybe you, through your foundations or something, might do something to help this person."

He said, "Well, who is it?" I said. "Former governor Swainson."

And Ford said to me, "Well, I'm not against John personally, but I didn't like his policies as governor. I thought he was too much for the unions. But the fact that you would come to me for a friend, with no motive on your own, and want to help somebody who is down and out, out of the goodness of your heart, if I were not to respond favorably to that, then I wouldn't be a very good human being myself. You leave it to me, I'll take care of it. But I don't want anyone to know about it. Understand?"

I said. "OK, Mr. Ford. Case closed."[12]Two weeks later John received from the

Ford Family Trust (not the Ford Foundation) a job as a consultant on the problems of addiction and children, which he had done work in. At a salary of $50,000 a year. . . . And that just raised John up, made him ebullient and took him out of his mood. Nobody ever knew about it until after Ford died."

Swainson's supporters in organized labor made their own gesture. The Michigan AFL hired him as a consultant. This brought him to Michigan State AFL headquarters in Lansing several days a week, where he did research for William Marshall, the Michigan AFL president. After work, Swainson would often join lobbyists and legislators at the bar of the Capitol Park Hotel.[13]

Now, with an income, he could resume something like a political life; he could go to political fund-raisers, be among friends and supporters, the center of friendly attention again.

On Tuesday, November 15, 1977, he drove to Lansing and attended a fund-raiser for State Senator Arthur Cartwright at Alex's, a popular downtown Lansing restaurant and bar. He was in his element, greeting old friends and colleagues, and drinking three martinis. As with most weekday fund-raisers, the party broke up around seven-thirty, but there were stragglers who stayed, congregating at the bar. Among them was John Swainson.

Finally, at ten, he said his good-byes and got into his 1978 Oldsmobile according to his later account.[14] From Lansing the easiest and quickest route to Manchester was to get on the U.S. 127 expressway east of downtown, then take that expressway south 40 miles to its terminus at State Highway 50. From there it was a straight drive east twenty miles on Highway 50, a two-lane road, to Manchester.

The village of Napoleon sat astride Highway 50 about twelve miles west of the farm where John Swainson made his home. At 1:05 A.M. a Michigan State Police trooper driving through the village noticed a car weaving back and forth across the center line. He pulled up behind the car and switched on his overhead "gumball" flasher, and the vehicle pulled over.

The trooper asked the driver for his license, then ordered him out of the car. John Swainson used his arms to pull himself out of the car—as he always did—and then, according to the trooper, he "lurched" as he began to walk. Of course, the trooper was watching for signs of intoxication, and this could have been his interpretation of Swainson beginning his normal walk; after rising from the seated position, Swainson would have to move his body into balance to take the first step.

Regardless, the trooper made a decision. He later reported that Swainson had refused a sobriety test. Swainson said he was never offered a test. In any event, the trooper arrested Swainson for driving under the influence, put him in the back of the patrol car, and took him to the Jackson County Jail.

By all accounts, Swainson acted like a "perfect gentleman," cooperated with all requests, and never asked for special treatment.

At the jail the sheriff's deputies followed standard booking procedure. They issued a set of jail clothing and ordered Swainson to hand over everything in his possession, including the clothes he was wearing, which they then searched for weapons or contraband.

Inside a pocket of his suit jacket they found a "roach"—the butt of a marijuana cigarette.

John Swainson, the former governor of Michigan, spent the night in jail.

The next morning he was formally arraigned on charges of drunk driving and possession of marijuana, then freed on $100 bail bond. The press had learned of his arrest and was waiting outside the courthouse. Swainson did not try to avoid them. He said that he was "mortified" at his situation; "all of a sudden my world is tumbling down."[15]

"I have no idea—none—how it got into my coat pocket. I have never smoked marijuana in my life. I'm a consultant to SHAR House (a drug rehabilitation facility)[16] and was with some SHAR people on Monday. The question is, did someone put contraband in my pocket then?"[17]

Trial on the marijuana charge was scheduled for January, and Swainson retained a local attorney, Edward Schomer. On January 11 Swainson and the attorneys appeared for jury selection, but the judge adjourned the trial after speaking with the attorneys. Jackson County prosecutor Edward Grant told the assembled reporters that the purpose of the adjournment was to allow Swainson to take a lie detector test. If Swainson passed the test, the prosecutor would drop the charge. If not, he would proceed to trial.[18]

When Swainson's attorney learned of Grant's statement, he denied that Swainson ever had agreed to the polygraph test. He then filed a motion to dismiss the charges, contending that Grant's public statement had poisoned the jury pool, making it impossible for Swainson to receive a fair trial, because any prospective jurors who were called for service in a trial would assume that Swainson had taken and failed the polygraph.

The local district court denied the motion to dismiss. Schomer appealed to the Jackson County Circuit Court, which affirmed the district court's decision.

Schomer then appealed to the Michigan Court of Appeals, which declined to accept the case. The Court of Appeals decision could be appealed only to the Michigan Supreme Court.

This posed something of a dilemma for Swainson. When the State Bar Grievance Board had disbarred him, Swainson had made a decision not to appeal, because "members of the Supreme Court are my former colleagues and remain personal friends, any further appeal might place a burden on them. I cannot in good conscience impose that burden on them."[19]

This time, Swainson decided to appeal to the Michigan Supreme Court, even though five of the serving justices were his former colleagues on the Supreme Court, and the other two had served with him on the Wayne County Circuit Court.

"I think they can decide it fairly," Swainson said. It's an unusual case for them to be on, but it is unusual for anyone in my position to be charged with a crime."[20] Neither the prosecutor nor Swainson asked the justices to disqualify themselves.

In August 1978 the justices of the Michigan Supreme Court issued a one-sentence order. They denied leave to hear the case. But this was not the end. Swainson applied to the U.S. Supreme Court for certiorari, which was that Court's equivalent of leave to appeal, and it was extremely rare for the Court to grant leave in a case like Swainson's.

Finally, on October 29, 1979, the U.S. Supreme Court issued its decision, in a two-word order: "Certiorari denied."

Swainson had fought to avoid a trial for nearly two years. Now, with no appeals left, he had to make a decision: either go to trial or enter a plea. He chose the plea.

In January 1980, without notifying the prosecutor, Swainson entered a plea of guilty to driving under the influence of intoxicating liquor, first offense, and a plea of no contest to possession of marijuana (a "no contest" plea allows the court to make a finding of guilt without the defendant making any admission). The sentence was a $250 fine and suspension of Swainson's driver's license. Subsequently, Swainson was granted a restricted driver's license, allowing him to drive a motor vehicle only to and from work.[21]

Why did John Swainson want to avoid a trial so badly that he lodged four successive appeals, then pleaded guilty?

The answer lies in the timing. Swainson said that he left the party at 10:00 P.M. The driving distance from Alex's Restaurant in Lansing to the village of

Napoleon was fifty miles, of which all but eight miles was expressway.[22] A driver averaging 55 mph in light traffic would easily make the trip in less than an hour. Yet Swainson was stopped by the State Police trooper in Napoleon after 1:00 A.M., three hours after he said he left the party.

This leaves two hours unaccounted for.

Of course, Swainson might have pulled over somewhere to "sleep it off" before resuming his drive home. But then he would have had nothing to hide, and would have no reason to avoid a trial.

The more likely scenario is that he went to a private residence somewhere in Lansing, and someone at that residence was smoking marijuana. It could have been a woman. It could have been a legislator or a lobbyist. Whoever it was, Swainson did not want it made public, and the only way to avoid that was to avoid a trial.

With the two misdemeanor charges behind him, Swainson believed it was now time to apply for readmission to the bar. "They were certainly a cloud under which I've lived. I'm thankful they've been disposed of. I'm anxious to get my life started again."[23]

In 1978 Swainson had appeared before the State Bar Grievance Board and argued that the board should give him credit for the nearly two years he had voluntarily refrained from practicing law following his perjury conviction. A majority agreed with Swainson, which made him eligible to apply for reinstatement in November 1980.[24]

He was clearly looking forward to resuming the legal profession and, to all outward appearances, putting past disappointments behind him. But there was one demon that had not let go.

At 12:30 A.M. on Saturday, May 17, 1980, a local police officer saw a car driving erratically through the village of Clinton in Lenawee County, about five miles from the Swainson farm. The officer made a traffic stop and, a few minutes later, John Swainson was once again under arrest for drunk driving. He was also in violation of license restrictions imposed as a result of his previous drunk driving plea, allowing him to drive a car only to and from work.

Swainson was allowed to post a $50 cash bond and go home. This time, he had no public comment, and neither did the Lenawee County prosecutor, Harvey Koselka, who still held that office after having prosecuted John Whalen—twice—for the 1969 Adrian jewelry store burglary.

John Swainson had hit bottom.

A More Difficult Recovery

TWO DAYS AFTER HIS SECOND DRUNK DRIVING ARREST, JOHN SWAINSON CHECKED himself into the alcohol rehabilitation program at the Veterans Administration Hospital in Ann Arbor. To a reporter who tracked him down by telephone he explained, without drama or self-pity, "I've got a problem, I want to cure that problem, I want to save my life. I've been arrested twice in three years for drunk driving. Obviously, I've got a problem and it's alcohol."[1]

The program required six weeks and he had to live at the hospital for the first three weeks.[2]

The VA alcohol program seems largely to have succeeded. After Swainson completed the program, he was not observed drinking hard liquor again, though he would drink small amounts of wine or beer on social occasions.[3] He was never arrested for drunk driving again.

In July he resolved the May 17 incident by pleading guilty to driving under the influence of intoxicating liquor. In return, the prosecutor dropped the charge of violating the terms of a restricted license. District judge James Sheridan sentenced him to three days in jail, and Swainson served the sentence immediately.

In reflecting on his period of exile, Swainson later wrote:

The recovery from my trial in 1975 was much more difficult than the recovery from the loss of my legs in 1944. In 1945 I was young . . . and couldn't wait to get started on my career. The world was warm and accepting of my wounds and, like all who served, I was treated as a hero.

In 1975 . . . I was fifty years of age and had been stripped of my career, . . . humiliated and my license to practice law suspended . . . I was psychologically unable, as a former governor and Supreme Court Justice, to even bring myself to seek ordinary employment . . . I wanted at least to preserve my self-respect, and this too got in my way. I sought refuge in escape, and escape came in a bottle.[4]

In December 1980 the clouds began to lift. The State Bar's Attorney Discipline Board ruled that, having served out his three-year suspension, he was eligible for reinstatement as an attorney. Eugene LaBelle, the State Bar attorney, explained that alcoholism, in and of itself, was not evidence of incompetence to practice and that Swainson's second drunk driving conviction, while relevant, "should not bar readmission unless it is symptomatic of [a] greater problem." A jubilant Swainson said, "I've been called in from the cold."[5]

At age fifty-five, Swainson had no interest in resuming the practice of law as an advocate, but restoration of his license allowed him to offer his services as a mediator and labor arbitrator. As a former judge, still viewed with respect by organized labor, he would find a ready market for these services.

In 1969 the legislature had enacted a statute prohibiting strikes by police and firefighters, and mandating compulsory arbitration of their labor disputes. When a police or firefighter union reached a collective bargaining impasse with the local government employer, the dispute was referred to an arbitration panel composed of one labor representative, one employer representative, and an impartial chairman, to be selected from a list of qualified persons maintained by the Michigan Employment Relations Commission.

Swainson served as impartial chairman on numerous arbitration panels, receiving the $300 per day fee provided by law, plus expenses.

In February 1982 the judges of the Washtenaw County Circuit Court requested that the State Court Administrator's Office (a branch of the Michigan Supreme Court) appoint a temporary visiting judge to preside over a complex medical malpractice suit that threatened to monopolize one of the judges' time for an extended period. The court administrator offered the assignment to Swainson, who happily accepted.[6] But the parties then settled the case.

John and Alice put roots down in Manchester. They had purchased the

167-acre farm in 1964, and they devoted five years of weekends to gutting and renovating the house, using contractors and their own labor. They added a family room, walled with bookcases, a large garage, and an apartment above the garage, which John used as his home office. They expanded the second floor master bedroom and lined it with bookcases as well.

They wrapped a porch around the front and one side of the exterior. Alice supervised the planting of twenty-eight crabapple trees along the drive from the road to the house, and kept them carefully pruned. The result was an appearance at once comfortable and elegant, a vision out of Currier and Ives.

Swainson named the farm "The Hustings," adopted from a common journalistic synonym for campaigning, as in "He spent the afternoon on the hustings."

Swainson loved the idea of living on a real working farm, of seeing growing crops and grazing livestock. But he had no interest in doing the work of a farmer. Instead, he made arrangements with neighboring farmers to "sharecrop," lending them the use of his fields in return for a portion of the crop, or the income from the crop. The Swainsons acquired a small flock of sheep, primarily to keep the grass low. A neighboring sheep farmer took care of them, probably for a share of the wool and mutton.[7]

The Hustings was well suited to entertaining, and the Swainsons used it liberally to entertain friends and political associates. Thomas Brennan remembered taking his family there in winter to harvest a Christmas tree. In the summer

> they had a picnic . . . and Jim Ryan had his two boys with him out there . . . they were tots, little guys and we played a little backyard soccer game as I recall and John was out there kicking the soccer ball with his artificial legs. I think he was playing goalie. And after we played, I remember John sitting down under a tree and showing the two little boys how he could take his legs off, stumps and so on, and the kids, their eyes were just as big as saucers.

The fields and wood lots were filled with wild game, and Swainson enjoyed inviting friends to hunt or skeet-shoot. He particularly enjoyed initiating novice hunters—in his own manner. Brennan was one of a group of judges invited to a bird hunt.

> I'd never hunted in my life. Didn't own a gun, didn't know what the hell to do with one. We went to this farm where the guy would let the birds loose and the dog would go out and we'd go out and stomp around and the dog would get the

birds up and then we'd shoot at them. We were shooting and the birds would fall down and I don't even know what the hell I'm shooting. And Swainson would say, "Nice shot, Tom, nice shot, you got 'em, you got 'em." Pretty soon I got four or five birds.

Well, then I discovered that the guy who runs the farm charges you so much for each bird that you shot, and I'm paying for all the birds. And I knew damn well, Swainson and those guys were knocking down the birds and they were telling me it was me.[8]

Swainson never forgot that the people of Manchester supported him and his family during his time of trouble.

The Manchester High School football team played a home game on the evening of Swainson's resignation from the Supreme Court following his perjury conviction. It was the last game of the year, and by tradition, each graduating football player and cheerleader was escorted onto the field by a parent. Kristina Swainson was a cheerleader, and a senior. She vividly recalled that night: "Yes, he escorted me onto the field, and everybody clapped. The whole town was behind him. I think he was quite moved by everybody applauding, and supporting him."

Ever after he strove to give back to Manchester.

Howard Parr observed that Swainson "always fit in well here. He was proud to say he was from Manchester. He was always down at the coffee shop in the morning. However, the one thing he did not do was convert many of us [from being Republican]."[9]

It was soon after the start of his exile from the legal profession that Swainson began his active career in the preservation and enhancement of local history, and he started in Manchester.

In 1976 a small group of local women had founded the Manchester Area Historical Society. In 1981 the group began looking for a permanent space to store and display artifacts and documents of Manchester's history. Paar, a Manchester native who had returned after retiring as superintendent of schools in Gibraltar, Michigan, was serving as president of the association. He noticed that Swainson "seemed to need something to do," so he asked the former governor to chair the finance committee, raising funds for the Society's permanent home. The result was everything Parr could have wished, "He went all over the state, raising money to pay for the building, selling memberships; we had members all over the state—even Suttons Bay [in the far north]! We were able to pay for the building quickly."[10]

The Society purchased a former blacksmith shop in downtown Manchester, restoring the forge room to its nineteenth-century appearance as a working smithy. Swainson continued his active work on the Society's behalf, originating an annual calendar and a July 4 raffle as fund-raising projects, and serving a three-year term as president. He also designed the Society's logo, introduced the annual production of a video about Manchester people and businesses, and led the drive to build a gazebo on the village green (dedicated in 1987 with a speech by Swainson's friend, Michigan attorney general Frank Kelley).[11]

After John Swainson's reinstatement to the bar, he and Alice lived alone at the farm. Their oldest son, Steve, had moved to Ann Arbor while still on probation in 1970. After successfully completing his term, he moved out west, first to Colorado and then to Madrid, New Mexico, where he lived among drug culture free spirits in a loosely communal life, getting by on odd jobs. Their younger son, Peter, after graduating from a private school, attended St. Clair Community College, living with John Swainson's parents in Port Huron. In 1970, facing the draft, he enlisted in the navy, and was stationed at a submarine base in Groton, Connecticut. When he mustered out he stayed in the East, and became a born-again Christian.

Both of the Swainson sons drifted away from the family, seldom initiating contact or responding to overtures. Neither of them had a telephone. Alice sent them money from time to time. Neither of them attended her funeral.[12]

Kristina, born nine years after Peter, had grown up on the farm, graduating from the Manchester public schools and earning a degree at Michigan State University. If the demands of public life had robbed John Swainson of time he wished he had spent with his sons, he did his best to make up for it with his daughter.

When she asked him for help with her homework, "He'd take a legal pad and start writing it, and I'd say, 'No no Dad, I just want some ideas.' He was a go-to person."

When she wanted his advice on a decision, "He would say, 'Okay, well, let's weigh this side and that side.' And I would say, 'For God's sake, just tell me yes or no!'"

But by 1980 Kristina was grown up, and she moved to California to be close to her high school sweetheart—by then her fiancé—Louis Way. They married in 1982 and remained in California.

Swainson's mother, Edna, had passed away in 1979. Swainson's father, Carl, lived alone in Port Huron.

On August 25, 1983, Swainson traveled to Port Huron to visit his widowed father and spend the night. At 2:00 A.M. he was awakened by abdominal pains. Unable to get downstairs where his father was sleeping, he managed to telephone his brother Tom, who lived two blocks away. Tom drove Swainson to the Port Huron Hospital. Swainson thought he had a bad case of food poisoning and asked the staff to pump his stomach. But the physician on duty examined Swainson and suspected something much more serious. He summoned a medevac helicopter team. At 7:00 A.M. they flew the fifty-eight-year-old ex-governor to Ann Arbor's Veterans Administration Hospital.

There a team of surgeons found an aneurysm—a bulging out of a major artery—on the verge of bursting, which would have been fatal. They performed eight hours of surgery to repair the artery. Swainson remained in intensive care five days.[13]

He recovered fully, and by December was back to work, accepting a new arbitration between the city of Novi and its police union.

In November 1984, nine years after his resignation, the justices of the Michigan Supreme Court invited him and Alice back to the Capitol, for the formal presentation of his portrait, a tradition for all retired justices.

Swainson's old colleague T. G. Kavanagh, who had written the opinion reversing John Whalen's conviction, was still on the court, and Mennen Williams was now chief justice. Williams presided, and the speakers included State Bar of Michigan president Dennis Archer, Swainson's loyal friend David Sparrow, and Frank Kelley, who had been appointed attorney general by Swainson, and had been reelected to the job every four years ever since.[14] Former colleagues John Fitzgerald and Thomas Brennan were in attendance.

After the scheduled speakers were finished, Mennen Williams asked if anyone else wished to share a reminiscence. Bill Saxton, a noted Detroit labor attorney, stood up. He said, "I'll volunteer. I have a story that nobody knows about John Swainson, except John Swainson and me."

Many years ago, when he first went to that Cadillac Square office and could not pay the rent, I was fortunate enough to be associated with a larger office . . . and was involved in a project called the Lake Head Pipeline, which was a multimillion dollar thing going through Michigan. I prevailed upon . . . the late Philip Van Zile . . . to let me hire a young friend of mine, John Swainson, as an assistant.

The two gentlemen from the pipeline company noticed that John walked with a slight limp, but hadn't given it much thought. One night we went to an outdoor boxing match. It was in October, outside at the State Fair grounds, and it had turned very cold. John was really enjoying the fight, and the two fellows from California seated next to us turned to me and said, "Would you like to leave, is your friend cold?" I turned to John, talked it over, and then I turned back to the two contractor/vice presidents and said, "John says when his feet get cold we're going to leave."

In keeping with tradition, the honoree spoke last. He began, "I'm sort of overwhelmed by the number of my friends and supporters who took the time from their daily lives to travel to Lansing and to be with me on this occasion. I want to thank everyone who contributed to this effort."

Swainson complimented the artist who painted his portrait, Dorthea Stockbridge, for capturing the essence of his person. He recalled that when he had been a member of the Supreme Court a portrait of one of the court's first members, Epaphroditus Ransom, had hung on the wall of his office. "Quite often I would sit and contemplate his very stern visage as I wrestled with a particular matter before the Court . . . but I didn't really know much about him."

After leaving the court, Swainson had become a student of Michigan history, and he had searched out Ransom's life story. He had found that after serving on the court Ransom had been elected governor, winning a majority in every county in the 1847 election.

But during Governor Ransom's term, a national issue arose over the Wilmot Proviso, which would have prohibited the introduction of slavery in the territories which the United States had acquired from Mexico. Senator Lewis Cass of Michigan joined with Illinois's Stephen Douglas in opposing the Wilmot Proviso, arguing instead for "popular sovereignty," in which the inhabitants of the territory would decide whether to accept or prohibit slavery within its borders. Ransom strongly disagreed with Cass; he publicly opposed popular sovereignty and supported the Wilmot Proviso. As a result, the Democratic Party denied him renomination and he served only one term as governor.

Ransom did not abandon his political career. He was elected to the Michigan legislature from his Kalamazoo home in 1853. But he lost his fortune through investments in a plank road company that failed. He had to sell his Kalamazoo homestead in the midst of a real estate depression. He ended his career as a minor federal official in Kansas, where he died in 1859.

Swainson did not have to spell out the parallels between Epaphroditus Ransom's career and his own. All those present understood that each had failed of reelection to the state's highest office because he had done what he believed to be the right thing, and each had persevered.

Swainson concluded:

> I relate these few events . . . to emphasize that all of the portraits collected here
> bring with them much human experience that lies behind the robes. My life,
> too, goes on, and I'm happy to say that nine years after my resignation from
> the Supreme Court, Alice and I are enjoying our farm homestead in beautiful
> Washtenaw County. And further, and much more important, we are enjoying our
> middle years together, and have finally found the time to do those things that
> we put aside earlier. I will let history, of which I have become quite fond, be the
> judge of my public career, and I'm honored to have my portrait placed with the
> Michigan Supreme Court. Thank you.[15]

Swainson's enthusiasm for history would become the foundation for the
final stage of his public rehabilitation. In 1982 Michigan voters had elected
forty-year-old Democratic congressman James Blanchard governor. Blanchard
was the first Democrat to hold the office since Swainson.

Frank Kelley, who was entering his third decade as Michigan's attorney
general, had served as a political mentor to Blanchard. He went to see the young
governor. Blanchard remembered:

> Frank said—and I believed him—that he [Swainson] had been very unfairly
> treated, . . . that he had been a victim of gross injustice and had his reputation
> smeared and that he had a great interest in history and that if I could appoint
> him to the Michigan Historical Commission, it would mean a great deal to John
> Swainson. And it would be a way of acknowledging and helping rehabilitate
> him. He felt that Swainson deserved that and that I was in a position to do that
> for him. And I remember thinking that I ought to do it.
>
> I remember some people around me saying that they were worried, that
> it would make me look bad or condoning a crook, but I did not see Swainson
> as that. And I had always felt that he probably got railroaded. . . . But I didn't
> really know. All I knew was that sufficient time had passed and. . . . if it would
> be important to him, it was something I ought to do. And I ought not to worry
> about what people were going to say about what he had or had not done and
> what was quite possibly a technical conviction years before.[16]

In 1985 Governor Blanchard appointed John Swainson to the Michigan Historical
Commission.

The legislature had created the commission in 1913 to receive and preserve the records and artifacts of an existing private historical society. In 1917 the legislature expanded the commission's charter, making it the official keeper of the state's archives, and mandating that the commission collect historical materials and display them in a Michigan historical museum, as well as assist and encourage local historical societies.[17]

Swainson accepted his appointment with enthusiasm. He visited the Historical Commission's Lansing offices every Tuesday morning, and poured his energy and intellect into the work, using his lobbying and budgeting skills to work with legislative leaders in securing adequate funding. When the state built a new State Library and Museum, he took the lead in creating a foundation to raise funds for the creation and continuing upkeep of the historical exhibits.

At a session on archaeology, he volunteered to chair the discussion on excavating an outhouse. He appeared wearing a surgeon's mask and rubber gloves.[18]

His friend and former secretary, Margaret Halava, saw what a difference the appointment made: "Some of his best times were . . . when he served on the Michigan Historical Commission. He loved that. He just loved that."

Jerry Roe, a history buff who had been the chief executive of the Michigan Republican Party, was a member of the commission. He welcomed Swainson and found him "very levelheaded, and he added the prestige of having been governor. He was a very good lobbyist for the commission."

"We all got along fine. We never made our commission partisan. And when we were lobbying for money, for the museum or whatever, we would of course go talk to legislators. And here's John Swainson and Jerry Roe."

In fact, Swainson proved so effective that the other members elected him as president of the commission. And Blanchard's Republican successor as governor, John Engler, reappointed Swainson to the commission.

Roe said, "Normally, we rotated the presidency, but when we got Swainson, because he had been governor, we just kept him on as president. . . . And I said to Swainson, 'I've been on the commission twenty years I've only been president once or twice. You get on there, and we make you the eternal president.'"[19]

In the fall of 1987 John and Alice flew to California to visit Kristina and Louis and to get to know their grandson, Andrew, born the year before. Swainson also planned to visit his old friend from Percy Jones Hospital, "Tak" Goto, who had made a career in social services in Los Angeles.

The day before he was to visit Tak, Swainson suffered a cardiac irregularity. He was taken to a local hospital, and physicians performed an angioplasty to restore blood flow to his heart. Instead of Swainson visiting Tak, Tak came to visit him.

But there was a problem. Hospital policy prohibited non-family members from visiting heart patients. Louis Way witnessed the nurses' attempt to bar Tak. "He was a forceful fellow. He went marching in there and they said, 'Family only,' and he said, 'That's my brother.' Which in a way, he was." In the end Tak prevailed, and the two legless veterans reminisced, enjoying each other's company.

As he was leaving, Tak took Louis and Kristina aside, and said, "I don't know what you guys are doing, but you better take care of him, because he doesn't have long. None of us make it past seventy." Tak was sixty-five. Like Swainson, he was a history buff. A month later he traveled to Washington, D.C., to attend the opening of the Japanese-American Museum. There he suffered a sudden cardiac arrest and died. Saddened almost beyond words, Swainson wrote to Tak's widow, June: "He made me proud of having served this country with a person of his fortitude. Please tell your children and grandchildren, over and over again of his goodness and how he touched the lives of all who were privileged to know him."[20]

Swainson was now sixty-two, and he had suffered two serious circulatory episodes within four years. Louis and Kristina decided to move back to Manchester, where Louis's family had lived for three generations. In 1988 they built a house on the outskirts of the village, a few minutes' drive from The Hustings.

John Swainson now commenced what was assuredly the most contented period of his life. The ambitions and struggles of his early years had dissipated. The unchosen idleness and disgrace of his middle years were behind him. He had meaningful work in his arbitrations and the Historical Commission. He was a respected contributor to his local community. Best of all, his grandchildren were nearby (Louis and Kristina's son was joined by a baby sister, Allyson, in 1990).

On weekday mornings he would drive into town and pick up the newspapers. Then he would hit the local donut shop, where he would sit at a table with a rotating group of local men from all walks of life. Dave Little, a banker who served two terms as mayor of Manchester, was a regular participant. "What did we talk about? We'd talk about golf, we'd talk about the news, we'd talk about women. The gamut. Nothing too serious. A lot of camaraderie and a lot of joking. We were all friends."[21]

After discussing the day's news for an hour or so, Swainson would buy a bag of donuts or cookies and drive over to the Ways' house. He would let himself in, pass out his goodies to the grandchildren, then watch them while Kristina went out on errands. She thought it was a good match: "We always joked with him, we didn't know how much he was watching them or they were watching him, because he would just spread out his newspaper and then give them a donut."

In the afternoons he would work on arbitration cases in his office over the garage at the farm. He still traveled to political events, and he still accepted speaking invitations all over the state. One week each summer he would go up north to join old friends Frank Kelley, David Sparrow, Herb Sillman, Jerry Rowin, and longtime Democratic fund-raiser Stuart Hertzberg for a "stag" at a summer cottage. There, Sparrow reflected, they "solved all the world's problems. Sometimes it took us until 4:00 or 5:00 A.M. But it never stuck, because we had to go back the next year to do it all over again."[22]

John Swainson, like many men of his generation, did not take particularly good care of himself. For much of his adult life he drank heavily and smoked. He partied hard. His eating habits were so indiscriminate that his family referred to him as "the human garbage disposal." His daughter Kristina remembered him eating "head cheese sandwiches, tongue, just awful combinations. . . . He really did not watch what he ate. Even after his heart problems. He would come back from the doctor and we would ask what the cardiologist said, and he'd say, 'He said I could eat anything. He said I could put salt on anything. I can have my bacon and eggs every morning.' Now, whether the cardiologist really said that . . ."

Swainson was not always totally candid with his doctors, either. On one occasion he went for a regular checkup. He neglected to mention to the doctor that he had recently acquired a new, lighter pair of legs, made of titanium. He told Louis Way, "The doctor looked at me and said, 'John, you're looking pretty good. Did you lose some weight? You're down like twenty pounds.' I said, 'Well, yeah!' I didn't tell him about my legs."[23]

One morning in October 1993, Swainson awoke and could not remember how to attach his legs. Alice called the Way residence, and Louis drove to the farm. Swainson was slurring his words. Louis insisted on taking him to the nearest major hospital, in Chelsea, over Swainson's protests that it was unnecessary.

But it *was* necessary. John Swainson had suffered a stroke. The prompt diagnosis and treatment he received at Chelsea probably saved him from severe paralysis, and possibly from death. He had to enter a program of therapy before he regained full physical function.

However, he could not recover two things that were of great importance to him. He had to give up driving, and thus much of his independence. And he lost the ability to speak his thoughts clearly.

His old friend David Sparrow visited him in the hospital. Swainson's speech problem "was bothering him and he didn't want people to see him. His legs were one thing, but to not be able to articulate what he wanted to say, that bothered him more than losing his legs."

Kristina felt that he had always been "probably the smartest person I knew, and he just was not as sharp, and it frustrated him so much. He wanted to get it back. He would say, 'I know what I want to say, I just can't articulate it.'"

After going through therapy he resumed as much of his routine as he could, going to the coffee shop in the morning and taking donuts to his grandchildren (a Manchester friend, Don Boutell, picked him up and dropped him off), but he had to turn down speaking engagements that he had always accepted, and it was harder for him to write letters now. He called Sparrow and told him that he would be unable to make it to their annual "stag" up north, something he had always looked forward to.[24]

Alice began pushing him, gently, to sell the farm. He wouldn't hear of it. "You're going to have to take me out feet first," he said.

On May 12, 1994, he wrote Norma Ketchum Yow, who had worked for him in the 1960s: "At present I am the president of the Michigan Historical Commission . . . I enjoy this very much. I suffered a major stroke in October 1993, and am still recovering from that experience, which I do not recommend to anyone. Alice and I are enjoying our grandchildren, and they live only 2½ miles away."[25]

The crabapple trees that lined the driveway bloomed once a year, for three days in May. They were in full flower on Friday morning, May 13, 1994. From the kitchen table you could see the whole line of them, and so John Swainson sat at the kitchen table, hand-writing a letter of regrets to a group that had invited him to speak. He put a stamp on the envelope and looked out at the fruit trees, covered with pink blossoms. He said, "It just doesn't get any better than this. You know, I never want to move." He clutched at his chest, then collapsed in his chair. His heart had stopped.

Alice called for an ambulance, then called the Ways. They both arrived within minutes. The emergency medical technicians worked to revive him as the ambulance sped to the hospital, but they could not. John Swainson was gone. He had lived sixty-eight years.

On the following Tuesday the people of Manchester put up American flags along Main Street, and 350 mourners gathered on the lawn of Emanuel Church of Christ. They included former governors George Romney and James Blanchard, as well as incumbent governor John Engler.

In his eulogy, David Sparrow reminisced about their long friendship, and told the mourners, "I read in a recent church publication a quote from the *London Sunday Express:* 'Most people wish to serve God—but only in an advisory capacity.' This was not John Swainson. He was a true servant and contributor, and willing to accept the sacrifice that that entails."

Sandra Clark, director of the Michigan Bureau of History, who had worked closely with Swainson in his role as president of the Michigan Historical Commission, spoke of his attitude toward the history he loved: "History's highest value was, for him, its ability to build community pride, to give individuals a sense of time and place, to inspire. He pushed us to collect the stories of everyday people using video recordings. And his final authority for any controversy over what should be on a [historic] marker . . . was what the local community or the boys in the donut shop would want."

Gayle Main, the daughter of John Swainson's sister Carroll, remembered, "As he often told Alice, 'You can never say that your life was dull with me.' With him we met people from every walk of life. He included us and shared his spotlight. We met the President, danced at the Inaugural Ball, and vacationed on Mackinac Island. We also watched a cross burning on his front lawn and shared in his sorrows."[26]

Finally, Michigan attorney general Frank Kelley stepped to the podium. Kelley recalled the day, over four decades ago, when he had first met his friend: "I thought . . . that I was a sophisticated, experienced young man, ready to face the future. Then, when the social hour began and John Swainson talked with me, I realized that I was a mere novice in life—for John had already, at the age of twenty-five, survived more adversity than most men face in a lifetime."

After recalling the ups and downs, the hardships his friend had faced and overcome, Kelley concluded, "It was never to be easy for John Swainson. I sometimes thought God continuously put John to special tests, and God never found him wanting."[27]

The mourners made their way to their cars and formed into a funeral cortège, which wound its way past the American flags lining Main Street, out to the pretty green Oak Grove Cemetery on the edge of the village. There, in the bright sunshine, an American Legion honor guard stood at present arms as the casket, draped with an American flag, was borne to the grave site. The flag was removed and presented to the family, in keeping with military tradition. Then they laid John Swainson to rest.

Reflections

Donald McKim, in editing *The Cambridge Companion to John Calvin*, commented:

> The biographer . . . would accomplish only half his task if he were content to offer a value-free chronological treatment, for we are dealing with . . . a person whose life is inseparable from his effect on history. . . . It would be inadequate to present such persons without any evaluation, all the more since they themselves saw the meaning of their existence in the battle for social values.

Much of John Swainson's life was dedicated to the battle for social values, albeit in the context of the political and judicial arenas. Some evaluation of his achievements, his failures, and his character is therefore appropriate.

Why did John Swainson fail to accomplish his major goals as governor of Michigan?

In 1960 he won election against great odds, and this victory may well have caused him to underestimate the even greater odds against accomplishing his goals for that office.

As governor, Swainson made his share of mistakes. In 1961 he waffled back and forth on the sales tax extension and the Milk Bill, which made him look indecisive and immature, and hurt his standing with legislators of his own party.

He knew that the Republican bill reversing the Ford-Canton court decision on unemployment compensation was a ticking time bomb, yet he seems to have avoided taking any action until he had no choice. He could have at least threatened a veto to try to negotiate a compromise; instead, he kept silent and allowed business leaders to believe there was a chance he would sign the bill. When he vetoed it, many of them felt betrayed.

These errors of judgment weakened his support among Democratic legislators, which he could ill afford to lose.

The major plank in his personal platform was total fiscal reform, implicitly including an income tax. Yet the same electorate that chose him also authorized an increase in the sales tax, implicitly rejecting an income tax. Legislators of both parties read these election results, which only added to their extant fears of voting for new taxes.

Yet with his window of opportunity limited to two years, and both houses of the legislature controlled by the opposing party, he still came excruciatingly close to getting the tax reform he sought. For a moment it had a majority in both houses. Then it slipped away.

Although he did not succeed, it was a magnificent effort.

Consider that Swainson's successor as governor, George Romney, called a special session of the legislature in 1963 for the purpose of taking up an individual and corporate income tax. In the Senate, which his party controlled twenty-three to eleven, Romney couldn't even get the tax bills out of committee.

It was not until 1967, after four and a half years in office, and ensconced in a four-year term under the new constitution, that Romney finally got the income tax enacted.

In a sense, John Swainson was ahead of his time, and many of his policies have become part of the fabric of Michigan: a modern tax structure based on ability to pay, a decent level of state services to the mentally ill, equal opportunity for jobs and housing.

We might conclude that Swainson ran for governor too soon, that he should have waited. But it is a truism in politics that when the opportunity for high office comes, you have to go for it, because it may never come again. What if he had waited? Jim Hare might have been elected, probably with Swainson as his lieutenant governor. Then, Swainson would have had to wait for Hare to leave the office before he could seek it, and he would have been stuck with Hare's record to defend.

Everyone who knew John Swainson agreed that he was sharply intelligent, articulate and a diligent student of government. Yet there was one quality, indispensable for a governor, that he lacked: the ability to shape public opinion. Many of his public statements seem strangely tone-deaf, wooden. When he spoke to the people about policy issues, he tended to use the same language he used in a meeting with other experts, a kind of bureaucratic patois. He didn't talk down to the people, but neither did he use the kind of clear language that would win them over.

When Franklin Roosevelt needed the American people's support for the Lend-Lease program of sending war materials to Britain, he said, "Suppose my neighbor's home catches fire, and I have a length of garden hose 400 or 500 feet away. If he can take my garden hose and connect it up with his hydrant, I may help him to put out his fire. Now, what do I do? I don't say to him before that operation, 'Neighbor, my garden hose cost me $15; you have to pay me $15 for it.' . . . I don't want $15—I want my garden hose back after the fire is over."[1] This homely analogy was later given much credit for moving public opinion to favor the Lend-Lease bill, allowing its approval by Congress.

When John Kennedy needed to prepare the American people for sacrifices, he said, "Ask not what your country can do for you; ask what you can do for your country."

But when Swainson needed the people's support for fiscal reform, he said, "Michigan needs tax revision—revision that is fair, equitable and adequate to meet state and local revenue needs. We must modify our interrelated state and local tax structures, basing such modification on business and individual abilities to pay."[2]

One of the most baffling aspects of John Swainson's public personality was the coexistence of a benign objectivity with a bitter partisanship.

In his parting message ("exaugural") to the legislature that had denied him nearly everything he had proposed, he said, "Partisanship is not responsible for what some have called the stalemate in Michigan. People are people . . . We can only assume that those of you who opposed fiscal reform did in fact represent your constituencies. It was your sincerely held opinion that your constituents did not want . . . the fiscal reform program as it was constituted in 1962."

Since the chief executive is elected directly by the majority of voters, we are faced with a system in which stalemate is part of the structure. A governor, in keeping faith with the voters, must attempt to accomplish what he has pledged while seeking election—as must the legislators. Consequently, a governor elected by a majority and a Legislature elected by a minority are born, so to speak, to conflict.[3]

But when the Republicans frustrated his purposes, he lashed out in harsh, partisan terms " . . . local taxpayers have been robbed of millions of dollars in tax relief by the Republicans' stubborn refusal to act on the highway and ADC bills."[4] This may have played well with his fellow Democratic activists, but he did not seem to consider how these statements sounded to the independents who were growing into the decisive bloc in the Michigan electorate. And, of course, the media nearly always emphasize controversy.

And yet, in spite of these errors, John Swainson's dedication, hard work, and sparkling personality might well have pulled him through to reelection as governor, if not for a classic political trap, not of his making, that unfolded with the inevitability of a Greek tragedy. This was the Bowman Bill, outlawing Detroit's imposition of a city income tax on nonresidents who worked in the city. Once the legislature enacted this measure, Swainson was put in the impossible position of having to alienate one major part of his constituency (suburban workers) if he signed it, or another major part (Detroiters) if he vetoed it.

• • •

Was the federal prosecution of John Swainson politically inspired, a product of the Nixon administration's fear that he would run for the U.S. Senate? Many of Swainson's surviving friends believe that it was.

However, there is a good deal of circumstantial evidence against it.

First, as we have seen, the FBI's investigation of Swainson and Harvey Wish originated locally, from John Whalen's 1972 claims to Detroit FBI special agents. Both Whalen and the agents testified to this origin.

Whalen testified that he had first contacted the FBI about a possible bribe to a Supreme Court justice in June 1972.[5] At that time there had been no public discussion of a possible Swainson run for the U.S. Senate. In fact, Swainson had already flatly rejected suggestions that he consider a run against Republican incumbent Robert Griffin, who was up for reelection in 1972. The first public speculation that Swainson might consider a run for Phil Hart's seat—if Hart retired—was in a *Lansing State Journal* column by Don Hoenshell, in late September 1972, three months *after* the investigation commenced.[6] And at that time the election was still four years away.

Second, and most significant, as we have seen, the investigation floundered until February 1975, when the Justice Department sent Robert Ozer to run the Detroit Strike Force. Sending Ozer was the one instance in which the Swainson investigation was influenced, albeit indirectly, by officials in Washington. However, those officials were not Nixon appointees. Nixon had resigned in 1974, to be replaced by Gerald R. Ford. And the U.S. attorney general was no longer a Nixon appointee, but a Ford appointee—Edward Levi. Levi was probably one of the least partisan attorneys general of the twentieth century. He was a former president of the University of Chicago, and had served on two presidential task forces appointed by Democrat Lyndon B. Johnson. The idea that Levi would be a party to a politically motivated criminal prosecution beggars the imagination.

In any event, if the prosecution was politically inspired, it failed of its purpose. Phil Hart did retire, and in the 1976 Michigan election for the U.S. Senate, Democrat Donald Riegle Jr. was elected. Riegle held the seat for the next eighteen years.

• • •

Would Swainson have run for the U.S. Senate in 1976? There is no question that he put the word out that he was considering it, but this exploratory suggestion is far from conclusive. Experienced politicians who have not made up their minds often float trial balloons, designed not so much to test the waters as to prevent major potential supporters from committing to someone else prematurely.

His daughter believed that he was leaning towards a run. His friend David Sparrow said that no final decision had been reached. "[In 1975] I was getting letters and phone calls from all over the state and wanting to know when he was going to announce and what could they do to work for him and there was real strong support for that and the only question in John's mind was physically. It was a state-wide campaign. That was hard on his legs."

Jerry Roe had the definite impression of a decision: "No question in my mind that he had made the decision to go for it. He wanted that and he felt he could get it. In fact, he was excited about the prospect of running' . . . He told me, 'Jerry, I think I can get the money. I've got the name, and I've got the support of the Democratic Party, and I'm going to run.'"

On the other hand, Frank Kelley was sure that no final decision had been made: "His enemies had the plan more developed than he did. He was flirting with the idea."

Swainson's Supreme Court law clerk Thomas Carlson continued to see Swainson after the conviction and resignation. He recalled that Swainson "in hindsight . . . told me that he had pretty much decided he wasn't going to do it, and they really didn't need to go after him with this false indictment to keep him from being able to run for the Senate."

In the end, the question is unresolvable.

• • •

Assuming he was physically up to it and decided to make the race, could Swainson have been elected to the U.S. Senate in 1976?

In the 1976 U.S. Senate Democratic primary, Riegle, of Flint, beat Richard Austin, James O'Hara, and Richard Ellsman. Riegle then trounced Republican U.S. congressman Marvin Esch of Ann Arbor in the general election. Riegle was a former Republican who had changed parties, but he had excellent relations with organized labor, which was still a powerful force within the Democratic Party. O'Hara, a congressman from the Detroit area, was also close to labor. However, neither Riegle nor O'Hara had the statewide election experience and name recognition of Swainson, nor did either of them have as strong a relationship with union leadership as Swainson.

Riegle was a formidable and well-organized campaigner. If both he and Swainson had entered the primary, it would have been a close contest between them. If Riegle had stayed out, then Swainson would have been the heavy favorite to win the primary. If Swainson had won the primary, he undoubtedly would have gone on to beat the relatively unknown and colorless Esch in the general election.

If he had run, and if he had won, John Swainson likely would have been very successful in the U.S. Senate. He always did well as a member of a collegial body. In the Michigan State Senate he was elected minority leader after only two years. On the Michigan Supreme Court, he held the affection and respect of all of his colleagues.

• • •

Finally, what lay behind the rumors of corruption?

As we have seen, in the early 1960s an FBI wiretap picked up an organized crime figure bragging that Swainson was willing to be of service.

The wiretap story is long forgotten, yet its ripples have never entirely dissipated. Even today, vague rumors persist among Lansing veterans that Swainson was somehow corrupt. But when they are asked for particulars, none are forthcoming.

In the course of interviewing people and researching this book, I was able to find only one specific allegation.

Vincent Piersante said that when Swainson was on the Supreme Court, he came to the office on a Saturday, when other justices were away, and asked a secretary to poll the other justices by phone to see if they had any objection to granting bond to Max Stern, a Detroit gambler and organized crime figure who had been sentenced to a year in jail for refusing to testify before a grand jury. None of the justices objected, and Stern was granted bond pending appeal of his conviction. Piersante's view was that "Swainson was interfering with the processing of a case to a grand jury for personal reasons."[7]

But Corbin Davis, the clerk of the Michigan Supreme Court, reviewed the court's records and reached a very different conclusion. Davis, who has worked at the court since before Swainson's time, found that Stern's attorney filed an emergency motion for bond on December 21, 1971, and the Court granted the bond December 24.

"Because Stern's papers were filed as an emergency, they would have been assigned to a [Supreme Court] commissioner that day . . . It was not then and is not now unusual for orders to be entered without conference consideration [i.e., without being considered at a regularly scheduled in-person meeting of the justices]. If the order recommended by the commissioner is approved, there is no appearance at conference."

Moreover, the justices subsequently did consider the matter at an in-person conference, and ratified their December 24 decision. Their formal note reads "Moved by Adams, supported by T. G. Kavanagh to enter order recommended by commissioner."[8]

It therefore appears that Stern's bond was not due to any unilateral action by Swainson. A commissioner reviewed the emergency petition and recommended granting the bond, and—acting under its standard procedure—the court approved the order without meeting, ratifying its action later at a regularly scheduled conference.

There is no question that the emergency was genuine; Stern was gravely ill and died within three months, according to Piersante.

It is, of course, impossible to prove a negative. However, one instance of an attempt at corruption has come to light, and its outcome may be illustrative.

Sometime in the late 1950s, when Swainson was running for lieutenant governor, an imprisoned businessman who had bragged that he had Swainson "in his pocket" sent an intermediary to meet with Swainson's law partner, Alan

Zemmol. The intermediary said the businessman would pay Swainson $50,000 to secure him early release from prison. This was a huge sum at the time.

The offer was flatly rejected without further discussion.[9]

People do not, generally, act in contradiction to their fundamental character. Virtually everyone who knew John Swainson commented on two aspects of his character: he would befriend and help anyone who asked, and he was no dissembler; he did not try to hide or cover up even the most embarrassing personal facts—not his stumps, not his son's drug addiction, not even his extramarital affairs. Although he never flaunted them or humiliated his wife in Manchester, he did not hide them from people in Lansing.

The idea that he would accept money in return for using his office to help criminals, and then cover it up, does not fit. What does fit is something much more subtle.

In Swainson's correspondence files one finds many letters from those caught in the criminal justice system (or from their family members). Most of them were young and poor. Swainson looked thoroughly into each case. Where he could help, he did. Where he could not, he explained why. He did not expect anything in return, except gratitude. One can easily imagine an organized crime member (or his emissary) approaching Swainson with a sad story, and Swainson promising to look into it, and actually looking into it, and helping if he could. Then, the gangster, being a gangster, would brag to his colleagues that John Swainson was in his pocket. And the police, being the police, would hear about this and consider it their duty to investigate.

●　●　●

Of all the qualities that went to make up John Swainson's character, by far the most unusual was a persistent guilelessness, ranging at times to what can only be called naïveté.

He was, without question, the most approachable person to hold the office of governor in modern times. He would talk to anyone—not just a brief greeting, but long, substantive conversation.

As his law partner Alan Zemmol put it:

He never judged people. Which was a terrible mistake on his part. He was totally nonjudgmental. Everybody was, you know, decent, as far as he was concerned. Even when, to any other person you would say watch your step . . . He would meet somebody and we'd have a discussion, and I would sense that the guy was on the make. And John would say, "No, he seems like a nice enough guy." He was very naive and not circumspect. That is both a good quality and a very dangerous quality in anybody that's in politics. . . . He may have been—if you want to use a term that is harsh but not altogether inaccurate—he was foolish in his judgments of other people. He really was. He didn't really judge other people. He was not cautious and he did not recognize that if you are a public figure holding public office, some nasty people are going to . . . attempt to latch on to you.

Swainson's close friend David Sparrow saw exactly the same thing: "There was nobody that he wouldn't be a friend of, regardless of his station in life. . . . He'd meet [someone] at a party and he'd say give me a call. They would call and he'd respond. Never turn anybody down . . . If they wanted to say John Swainson is my friend, he wasn't going to say, 'No, I'm not your friend.'"

This quality persisted in the face of experience. In the course of a decade in the judicial system, Swainson presided over or reviewed scores of criminal prosecutions. He knew as well as anyone—and better than most—how the criminal justice system worked. Yet when he himself was faced with the might of the federal prosecutor, he purposely chose a lawyer with no criminal experience, because he didn't want people to think he had something to hide.

Few have been as worldly and yet as ingenuous as John Swainson.

Few have paid a higher price.

Afterword

AFTER JOHN DIED ALICE SWAINSON SOLD THE HUSTINGS, IN SEVERAL PARCELS, AND built an airy, light-filled house across the Raisin River, adjacent to the Ways' home. Her house was filled with art objects that she had created and collected over the years. She played with her grandchildren and kept in touch with the art world for eleven more years, passing away in 2005.

The family provided a grouping of John's political and military mementos to the Manchester Historical Society, which used them to create a Swainson Memorial Room at the building housing the old blacksmith shop, which was now its headquarters. As time went on, visitors became increasingly rare and in 2005 the Society closed the Swainson Memorial Room.

The Swainsons' son Stephen continued to live in Madrid, New Mexico, until his death in 2005. As of this writing Peter still lives in the East, and Louis and Kristina still live in Manchester.

Carl Swainson, widowed in 1979, outlived his oldest son, passing away in 1997 at age ninety-three.

After Joe Collins was defeated for reelection as chair of the Michigan Democratic Party, he returned to the insurance business, where he helped to found two companies. He passed away in 2008.

Zolton Ferency won the Democratic nomination for governor in 1966, losing the general election to George Romney. He ultimately left the Democratic Party, partly over the Vietnam War. He became an independent activist for liberal causes and founded his own party, the Human Rights Party, running for various offices, and was elected to the East Lansing City Council. He died in 1993.

Mennen Williams continued as chief justice of the Michigan Supreme Court until his retirement at the end of 1986. He passed away in 1988.

James Blanchard served two four-year terms as governor of Michigan, and was upset by John Engler in his 1990 bid for a third term. He went on to serve as U.S. ambassador to Canada in the Bill Clinton administration.

Neil Staebler served one term as Michigan's congressman at large, lost the 1964 gubernatorial election to George Romney, and was appointed to the Federal Election Commission, serving from 1975 to 1978. He died in 2000 at ninety-five.

In 1970 Gus Scholle ran for U.S. representative in the heavily Republican Eighteenth District, losing to the Republican incumbent. He was awarded an honorary doctor of laws degree by Michigan State University in 1971 and died in 1972.

Frank Kelley eventually acquired the sobriquet "The Eternal General of Michigan," beginning in 1961 as the youngest-ever occupant of that office and finishing at the end of 1998 as the oldest.

After leaving government service in 1979 Robert Ozer practiced law in Colorado, passing away in 2005.

Percy Jones Hospital continued to serve wounded veterans through the Korean War, then closed in 1953. Its buildings were converted for use as regional offices by various federal agencies. On May 31, 2003, a ceremony was held and the name of the complex was officially changed to the Hart-Dole-Inouye Federal Center, in recognition of three wounded World War II veterans who had been treated at Percy Jones and gone on to serve in the United States Senate: Philip Hart, Bob Dole, and Daniel Inouye.

In 1996 the Michigan Historical Commission established an annual honor, to be given each year to a state, county, or municipal employee who has gone above and beyond the duties of his or her job in contributing to the preservation of Michigan history. It still is presented each year. It is called the John B. Swainson Award.

ACKNOWLEDGMENTS

MARTHA BATES, ACQUISITIONS EDITOR AT MICHIGAN STATE UNIVERSITY PRESS, served as my editor. She made numerous suggestions for improving the structure and flow of the book, while listening patiently to my arguments.

Barbara Bean, reference librarian at the Michigan State University College of Law, gave generously of her time in finding superseded Michigan Canons of Judicial Ethics.

The Bentley Historical Library, University of Michigan, Ann Arbor, is the repository for the papers of many prominent Michiganians, including John Swainson. It is a small jewel where I spent many hours. The library's staff enforces and follows the highest professional standards, and treated me with the greatest courtesy.

Lou Ann Bluntschley, Lenawee County clerk and Irv Shaw, Lenawee County prosecuting attorney, located and generously afforded me access to long-forgotten boxes of records that enabled me to piece together much of the true story of John Whalen.

Sue Carter, professor of journalism at Michigan State University, and leader of an extraordinary all-woman polar expedition described in her book *Ordinary Women*, provided invaluable advice and support.

Linda Dack, U.S. District Court, Western District Michigan court clerk, and members of the U.S. Marshal Service, treated me with the greatest courtesy and helpfulness as I returned again and again, poring over the 2,000 pages of transcripts of *U.S. v. Swainson and Wish.*

David Dempsey, lifelong environmental activist and successful author, was this book's greatest supporter from the beginning; indeed, without his constant encouragement and helpful ideas, there might have been no book. He kindly reviewed all chapters and tightened them up, while making tactful suggestions that greatly improved the writing.

Robert Fenton, author, attorney, and movie producer, first suggested years ago that I had some talent for writing, and that maybe I should do more of it when I had time.

Dr. Bruce Getzan, now dean of economic development of the College of the Canyons in Santa Clarita, California, generously shared his research notes and his memories from six interviews of John Swainson conducted in 1988, when he was contemplating writing a full biography.

My wife Patricia Glazer was the first person to read each chapter. A lover of good literature (indeed, one of the most literate people I know), she shares my love of history and provided invaluable counsel throughout this project.

Robert Ianni, Michigan assistant attorney general, and John Mulvaney, special agent, Criminal Division, kindly provided me access to long-forgotten files of the Attorney General's Organized Crime Unit.

At the Michigan Room of the St. Clair County Library in Port Huron, Barbara King found the Port Huron High School yearbooks from the 1940s and laid them out for my inspection.

Thomas Kulick and Mike Leffler, Michigan assistant attorneys general, gave generously of their memories of long-ago trials.

The staff of the Library of Michigan work diligently, under conditions of fiscal uncertainty, to organize and preserve our state's documentary archives. I spent even more hours there than at the Bentley.

Hugh McDiarmid, former chief of the *Detroit Free Press* Capitol Bureau (retired), relentlessly urged me to do this book, which he himself had considered writing.

Hon. David McKeague, judge of the U.S. Sixth Circuit Court of Appeals, kindly interceded with the U.S. judicial system to get me meaningful access to the 2,000-page transcript of *U.S. v. Swainson and Wish,* without which this would have been a far different book.

David Murley, president of the Michigan Political History Society, used his amazing breadth of knowledge of Michigan political history to review many chapters, pointing out errors and omissions and making this a more accurate book, and probably a much fairer book.

The Michigan Political History Society is a group devoted to encouraging and assisting the study of Michigan's political history. The Society generously provided me with two grants that helped offset the costs of travel and research.

Lori Robison, the first editor of my writing career (at the *Lansing State Journal*), reviewed several chapters and helped me puzzle out questions of structure.

Tom Scott, editor and publisher of *Dome,* an award-winning online magazine devoted to Michigan state politics and policy (web address: domemagazine. com), taught me the difference between legal writing and readable writing, and then published the products of this education, including my first article on John Swainson.

When I retired from the bench, a reporter came to my office and interviewed me for over an hour. I delivered to him the distilled wisdom of fifteen years of judicial experience and eagerly awaited the lengthy article I anticipated was coming. To my disappointment, he used only one quote, and it wasn't the quote I would have chosen. But now I see that he wrote the best story he could make out of the material. In researching this book, I interviewed forty-five people, many for much more than an hour. Some of them may be similarly disappointed. I thank them and hope for their understanding. They were the following:

- Victor Adamo, John Swainson's second law clerk at the Supreme Court
- Hon. James J. Blanchard, governor of Michigan 1983–90, who appointed John Swainson to the Michigan Historical Commission
- James Blount (by e-mail), law school classmate of John Swainson
- Hon. Thomas E. Brennan, John Swainson's colleague on both the Wayne County Circuit Court and the Michigan Supreme Court, and the only survivor of those justices serving on the Supreme Court in 1972
- Ronald Carlson, John Swainson's third law clerk at the Supreme Court, who served at the time of the federal indictment and trial
- Tom Cleary, deputy state treasurer before and during the Swainson administration
- John "Joe" Collins, manager of John Swainson's successful 1960 campaign for Governor, later chairman of the Michigan Democratic Party

- Lattie Coor, graduate student who went to work for John Swainson in the Governor's Office, later president of Arizona State University
- Corbin Davis, clerk of the Michigan Supreme Court, and its institutional memory
- Anthony Derezinski, Democratic state senator, 1975–78
- Edmund Diem, FBI agent who placed John Swainson under arrest, handled John Whalen, and testified at the trial
- Gene Farber, John Swainson's first law clerk at the Michigan Supreme Court
- Charles Goldfarb, prominent Detroit bail bond agent, indicted along with Swainson and Wish in 1975 (charges were later dismissed)
- Hon. Edward Grant, who retired as Jackson County, Michigan circuit judge in 2008, was Jackson County prosecutor at the time of John Swainson's 1977 arrest for drunk driving and possession of marijuana
- Margaret Halava, personal secretary to John Swainson as governor
- Kathleen Davidson Hunter, assistant Michigan attorney general, Habeas Corpus Division (retired), who represented the state in contesting Whalen's later petitions to avoid imprisonment
- Stan Hunterton (by e-mail), junior member of the prosecution team in *U.S. v. Swainson,* later a highly respected attorney in Las Vegas
- Hon. Frank J. Kelley, the person who brought John Swainson into the Democratic Party and whom Swainson later appointed to fill the vacant office of Michigan attorney general, who went on to serve thirty-seven years as Michigan's elected attorney general
- Bernard Klein, retired former political science professor, city of Detroit comptroller, Democratic Party activist, and John Swainson's friend
- Conrad Kohl, John Swainson's defense attorney in the federal trial
- Hon. Harvey Koselka, Lenawee County prosecutor during John Whalen's first trial for the Adrian burglary, subsequently circuit judge for Lenawee County
- N. C. Deday LaRene (by e-mail), noted Michigan criminal defense attorney, who represented John Whalen in the 1970s
- Michael Leffler, Michigan Assistant Attorney General, who litigated some of John Whalen's post-conviction cases.
- Bruce Leitman, John Swainson's appellate attorney after the federal trial
- Hon. Lawrence Lindemer, colleague of John Swainson on the Michigan Supreme Court
- David Little, former mayor of the village of Manchester

- Seymour Markowitz, attorney who ran against John Swainson for Wayne County Circuit Court in 1965
- Hugh McDiarmid, chief of the *Detroit Free Press* Capitol Bureau (retired)
- Hon. William G. Milliken, governor of Michigan, 1969–82
- Meri Lou Murray, member and chair, Washtenaw County Board of Commissioners, 1972–96, and friend of John Swainson
- Howard Paar, long active in the Manchester Historical Society, serving three terms as its president
- Vincent Piersante, chief of detectives, Detroit Police Department, 1965–68, later chief of the Michigan Attorney General's Organized Crime Unit
- Frank Ragen, John Whalen's attorney for the last several years of his battle to avoid imprisonment for the Adrian burglary
- James Ramey, longtime UAW local and regional officer in Michigan
- Jerry Roe, former member of Michigan Historical Commission, Michigan Republican Party executive, friend of John Swainson
- Kelly Rossman-McKinney, who worked with John Swainson on the Michigan Sesquicentennial
- Vickey and Leo Seide, political supporters and personal friends of John and Alice Swainson.
- Paul Seldenright, longtime Michigan AFL official
- David Sparrow, attorney, John Swainson's best friend
- Christina and Louis Way, John Swainson's daughter and son-in-law
- Harvey Wish, John Swainson's co-defendant in the 1975 federal bribery-conspiracy trial, who never publicly commented on the case until this interview
- Carroll Whitehead, John Swainson's sister
- Allen Zemmol, John Swainson's law partner and friend

I was inspired by the following persons:

- The professors who taught me history: Alfred Kelly, Margaret Stern, Goldwyn Smith, Milton Kovinsky, and Finley Hooper. And most of all by one professor who, quite rightly, would not allow me to take his class: my uncle Sidney Glazer, who studied, taught, and wrote about the history of Michigan for forty-five years at Wayne State University
- Joe Fink and Harriet Rotter, two wonderful public school teachers who showed me the joys of the life of the mind

- Maury Dean, my pal since we were eleven, who showed me that with perseverance and hard work you can write a book and get it published, and then thanked *me* in his acknowledgments

Finally, I have greatly appreciated the warm support and encouragement of Meredith Sharp, Stephen Sharp, and Ed Glazer.

Naturally, any errors and all opinions in this book are mine alone.

THE 1960 ELECTION: THE NUMBERS

HOW COULD THE PRE-ELECTION POLLS HAVE BEEN SO WRONG? NO DRAMATIC EVENT occurred between the last poll and the election. And even if all the 2.3 percent of voters the pollsters reported as not planning to vote had changed their minds and voted for Bagwell, Swainson still would have won by a comfortable margin. But he won by a hair. What happened?

The answer is turnout. The pollsters had weighted their samples based on past elections. In presidential election years, Michigan turnout as a percentage of voting-age population had typically been in the high 60s. In the 1960 election it exploded to nearly 73 percent—a figure not seen before or since.

In 1960 election polling was, if not in its infancy, at best entering its adolescence. Two of the leading pollsters of that era (Elmo Roper and Mervin Field) recognized that correctly predicting turnout was critical:

> This procedure depends in part upon an accurate estimate of the voting ratio, or proportion of the adult population who can be expected to vote. We obtain this by projecting from past relationships observed between answers to the series of voter participation questions and actual turnout in previous elections.[1]

The challenge of predicting turnout still bedevils pollsters. In 2004 Sara Robinson, writing in the *Society for Industrial and Applied Mathematics News,* observed:

> Just about all pollsters will try to predict which of their respondents will vote. This, too, is an art: People often aren't honest about their intentions, and the intention to vote doesn't always translate into a vote. When registered voters are asked whether they intend to vote, "something like 98% will say 'yes,'" . . . and after the election about 78% will say that they voted. In fact, typical voter turnouts are under 60%. "Likely voter" models involve a lot of guesswork.[2]

In 1960 the Democratic/labor machine turned out the same large group of voters as it had before. For twelve years that had been enough. But this time it barely sufficed. A huge group of new voters, not identified in advance by either party organization, swamped the base Democratic vote. They were not partisans. That was one reason both parties failed to identify them ahead of time. As an example, we can view the vote for state auditor general as a proxy for each party's base vote. Bagwell received nearly 85,000 more votes than the Republican candidate for state auditor general, while Swainson received 10,500 fewer votes than the Democratic candidate.

These new, nonparty voters were drawn to the polls by the dramatic presidential race, not the state parties' appeals. For many of them, the vote for governor probably was an afterthought. Perhaps Neil Staebler was more right than even he knew when he advised John Swainson to avoid stands on issues and associate himself with John Kennedy; Kennedy won Michigan with 50.85 percent of the vote. Swainson won with 50.48 percent.[3]

THE 1962 ELECTION: THE NUMBERS

THE AVERAGE VOTE OF ROMNEY'S FIVE REPUBLICAN RUNNING MATES (ALL OF whom lost) in Wayne, Oakland, and Macomb Counties was 487,278. Romney's vote in the tricounty area was 602,857 a difference of 115,579. As John Dempsey saw it, Romney's margin in the tricounty metropolitan area clearly was provided by ticket-splitters: "Romney, in the three-County area received 23.7 percent more votes than his companions on the state ticket, and most of the 115,579 voters who gave him his margin here chose to cast their ballots for Democrats for all other races."[1]

Dr. Dempsey's ticket-splitter statistics are persuasive. But George Romney also benefited from trends that would have aided any Republican candidate for governor in 1962.

In the 1950s many political observers concluded that Michigan's voting population had changed from its historical Republican identity to one that was predominantly Democratic. This was true, but not the whole truth. The major change was the emergence of a Democratic/labor organization that could identify potential Democratic voters and then get them to turn out to vote.

Such an organization works most efficiently where large numbers of the target population live in relatively compact geographical areas—in other words, cities. The Republican voters were still present in Michigan, but they were more dispersed than the Democratic voters, predominant in smaller cities and rural areas. Geographically, the Republicans dominated, winning sixty of Michigan's eighty-three counties in 1960. If the gubernatorial election were decided by an electoral college with one elector per county, the Republicans would never lose. It is much more difficult and expensive to identify and turn out voters residing in far-flung, low-density areas.

But by the late 1950s the Republican state leadership was beginning to identify an expanding group of potential Republican voters living in relatively compact areas—the suburbs. This growth was particularly strong in the state's fastest-growing suburban area, Oakland County, just north of Detroit. Evidence of Oakland County's growing vote emerges clearly in an examination of that county's vote as a percentage of the total statewide vote for governor:

> 1956 . . . . .8.25%
> 1958 . . . . 8.40%
> 1960 . . . . . . .10.69%
> 1962 . . . . .9.32%

During that same period, the Republican share of the Oakland County vote for governor also increased steadily:

> 1956 . . . . 50.51%
> 1958 . . . . 51.75%
> 1960 . . . . 55.67%
> 1962 . . . . . . .60.24%

This suburban political phenomenon was not limited to Oakland County. Although Wayne County entirely contains the city of Detroit, it also contains numerous suburbs. Unlike Oakland, Wayne County's vote as a percentage of the statewide vote for governor grew very little:

> 1956 . . . . 37.34%
> 1958 . . . . 35.30%
> 1960 . . . . 35.42%
> 1962 . . . . 35.58%

However, just as in Oakland County, the Republican gubernatorial vote in Wayne County increased during this period :

1956 . . . . 33.28%
1958 . . . . 32.99%
1960 . . . . 35.75%
1962 . . . . 39.10%

In contrast, if we examine the combined vote in the eight counties with the lowest voting populations (i.e., the most rural, dispersed populations), we do not see the steady increase in Republican gubernatorial vote that occurred in the suburbs.[2] Instead, the Republican portion was essentially stagnant until 1962, when it took a big jump:

1956 . . . . 53.50%
1958 . . . . 54.15%
1960 . . . . 54.16%
1962 . . . . 59.68%

THE GRAND JURY IN HISTORY

THE GRAND JURY MAY BE THE OLDEST CONTINUING GOVERNMENTAL INSTITUTION in the English-speaking world. Its roots are traceable to the Assize of Clarendon in 1166, in which "King Henry II established a system of local informers (twelve men from every hundred or four men from every vill to tell him who was suspected of 'murder, robbery, larceny, or harbouring criminals.'"[1] The king established this system in order to advance his power, displacing local barons, and he received any fines or forfeitures that resulted.

The system "required the twelve men to report all suspects and fined them if they failed to indict any suspect or even if they failed to indict an acceptable number of suspects."[2]

Two centuries later, during the reign of Edward III, power began to shift; "the twelve men were superseded by twenty-four knights chosen by the county sheriff, who had authority for beginning a prosecution. The knights were called 'le grande inquest.'"[3]

In an era that predated what we know as due process, the power to formally accuse was near tantamount to the power to convict. Therefore, the barons and clergy pushed to make the grand jury independent of the Crown. The grand jury, which had begun as an instrument of the king's power, became "a useful buffer between the state and the individual, infusing an effective community voice into the early judicial process. By the time the Magna Carta was adopted [in 1215], the opportunity to have a grand jury decide whether criminal charges should be brought was considered important enough to be included as a guaranteed right."[4]

The beginnings of our modern system can be traced to the eighteenth century. By 1765 the great commentator and scholar William Blackstone could write:

> An indictment is a written accusation of one or more persons of a crime or misdemeanor, preferred to, and presented upon oath by, a grand jury. To this end the sheriff of every county is bound to return to every session of the peace . . . twenty four good and lawful men of the county. . . .
>
> This grand jury are previously instructed in the articles of their inquiry, by a charge from the judge who presides upon the bench. They then withdraw, to sit and receive indictments, which are preferred to them in the name of the king, but at the suit of any private prosecutor; and they are only to hear evidence on behalf of the prosecution: for the finding of an indictment is only in the nature of an inquiry or accusation, which is afterwards to be tried and determined; and the grand jury are only to inquire upon their oaths, whether there be sufficient cause to call upon the party to answer it.
>
> So tender is the law of England of the lives of the subjects, that no man can be convicted at the suit of the king of any capital offense, unless by the unanimous voice of twenty four of his equals and neighbors: that is, by twelve at least of the grand jury, in the first place, assenting to the accusation; and afterwards, by the whole petit jury. [5]

Although Blackstone's language is archaic to the modern reader, the basic structure he describes would be recognizable to a contemporary American lawyer: the government calls twenty-three local citizens to sit as a grand jury, a judge instructs them on the law they are to follow, and the prosecutor then presents evidence to them. If they find there is probable cause to believe the accused has committed the crime ("whether there be sufficient cause to call upon the party to answer it"), they issue their indictment. The accused is then tried before a jury of twelve local citizens, still known formally as the "petit jury."

The reason for the similarity is that the grand jury was imported into the American colonies well before the Revolution, and its role as a bulwark against the Crown's powers assumed a new significance:

Indeed, the actions of grand juries figured prominently in the beginnings of the Revolution. In 1765, a Boston grand jury refused to indict Colonists who had led riots against the Stamp Act. Four years later, as tensions intensified, a Boston grand jury indicted some British soldiers located within the city boundaries for alleged crimes against the colonists, but refused to treat certain colonists who had been charged by the British authorities for inciting desertion in a like manner. A Philadelphia grand jury condemned the use of the tea tax to compensate the British officials, encouraged a rejection of all British goods, and called for organization with other colonies to demand redress of grievances.[6]

By the time of Independence, the role of the grand jury in resisting the tyranny of George III had became so widely regarded that the Founding Fathers wrote it into the Bill of Rights. The Fifth Amendment, which most people associate with the right against self-incrimination, actually begins: "No person shall be held to answer for a capital, or otherwise infamous crime, unless on a presentment or indictment of a Grand Jury."

But 150 years later, though the language of the Fifth Amendment stood exactly as ratified in 1791, the federal grand jury's mighty role as protector of individual rights was dead. This transformation was caused by many factors, including amendments to the Federal Rules of Criminal Procedure, the changing views of Americans about their roles as citizens, and the rise of career federal prosecutors. But whatever the causes, today virtually all commentators agree that the federal grand jury has become little more than a tool of the prosecutor. The American Bar Association's official "Frequently Asked Questions on the Grand Jury System" is representative:

WHAT IS THE PURPOSE OF THE GRAND JURY?

The primary function of the modern grand jury is to review the evidence presented by the prosecutor and determine whether there is probable cause to return an indictment. . . .

The original purpose of the grand jury was to act as a buffer between the king (and his prosecutors) and the citizens. Critics argue that this safeguarding role has been erased, and the grand jury simply acts as a rubber stamp for the prosecutor.

In the federal system, the courts have ruled that the grand jury has extraordinary investigative powers that have been developed over the years since the 1950s. This wide, sweeping, almost unrestricted power is the cause of much of the criticism. The power is virtually in complete control of the prosecutor, and is pretty much left to his or her good faith.

HOW INDEPENDENT IS THE GRAND JURY?

The grand jury is independent in theory, and although the instructions given to the grand jurors inform them they are to use their judgment, the practical realities of the situation mitigate against it.

The grand jury hears only cases brought to it by the prosecutor. The prosecutor decides which witnesses to call. The prosecutor decides which witnesses will receive immunity. The basic questioning is done by the prosecutor on a theory he or she articulates. The grand jury members are generally permitted to ask questions at the end of a witness's testimony. The prosecutor generally decides if he or she has enough evidence to seek an indictment. Occasionally the grand jurors may be asked whether they would like to hear any additional witnesses, but since their job is only to judge what the prosecutor has produced, they rarely ask to do so.

The prosecutor drafts the charges and reads them to the grand jury. There is no requirement that the grand jury be read any instructions on the law, and such instructions are rarely given.

WHAT PROTECTION DOES A TARGET HAVE AGAINST WITNESSES LYING TO THE GRAND JURY, OR AGAINST THE USE OF UNCONSTITUTIONALLY OBTAINED EVIDENCE?

None. The target's only redress is to challenge the evidence at trial. One of the reasons a witness may assert the Fifth Amendment is that he or she does not know if the prosecutor has presented witnesses who have lied. The witness cannot risk testifying contrary to those witnesses, for fear of being charged with perjury if the prosecutor does not believe his or her testimony.[7]

NOTES

When citing testimony given at the October 1975 federal trial of John Swainson, this book gives the witness name, "TR" (transcript) and then the page; e.g., "Schley, TR 287" means testimony of Ed Schley, page 287. The FBI transcript of its recordings of Whalen's conversations with Harvey Wish were reproduced in the trial transcript. Thus, e.g., "wire, TR 1271" means the recording as transcribed by the FBI and reproduced at page 1271 of the trial transcript.

Testimony given at the April 1980 Lenawee Circuit Court postconviction relief hearing of John Whalen is cited as "PCR," with witness's name and page number; thus, e.g., "Ozer, PCR 230" means testimony of Robert Ozer, found at page 230 of the transcript of the postconviction relief hearing.

■ CHAPTER ONE. GOAD

1. Because of a feared rubber shortage, tires had been rationed and a national 40 mph speed limit put into effect. Gasoline rationing was scheduled to go into effect in November.
2. *Port Huron Times-Herald,* 10/10/42.
3. This account is taken from the *Port Huron Times-Herald* of 10/10/42. It is the historian's good fortune that Port Huron was small enough to have only one major public high school, but large enough to support a daily newspaper, whose coverage of Port Huron High's games was detailed.
4. *Port Huron Times-Herald,* 9/18/42.
5. Letter to JBS from Geoffrey Swainson, University of Michigan, Bentley Historical Library, John B. Swainson Collection, Box 70.

6. Bruce Getzan interview with Swainson.
7. In fact, Carl's formal name was "John Adam Carl Swainson." "Carl" was his "family" name, and is used here to avoid confusion.
8. Connecting Port Huron with Sarnia, Ontario, it opened in 1938.
9. Swainson funeral eulogy of Gale Main, May 17, 1994, copy in author's possession.
10. Author's interview with Carroll Whitehead.
11. 1943 Port Huron High School Yearbook, St. Clair County Library.
12. Author's interview with Carroll Whitehead.
13. Ibid.
14. Letter to his mother from Swainson, Bentley Library, Swainson Collection, Box 1. From this point forward, I refer to John Goad Burley Swainson as "John," and his father as "Carl."
15. Hugh McDiarmid interview with Swainson.
16. Roger Rosentreter, "Making Sacrifices," *Michigan History*, November–December 1991.

■ CHAPTER TWO. AMPUTEE

1. MacCormac, "King George Visits Beachhead Front," *New York Times*, 6/17/44.
2. Rosentreter, "Making Sacrifices."
3. Ninety-fifth Division Institutional Training History, U.S. Army Reserve, http://www.armyreserve.army.mil/arweb.
4. "Bravest of the Brave," *Stars & Stripes*, Paris, 1945.
5. Currivan, "Americans Can See Buildings of Metz," *New York Times*, 11/16/44.
6. Ibid.
7. Hugh M. Cole, *The Lorraine Campaign* (Washington, D.C.: Center of Military History, U.S. Army, 1993).
8. *The German Soldier*, training booklet published by *Infantry Journal* (Washington, D.C., undated [1944]).
9. Bruce D. Getzan, "Michigan's 'Kismet' Governor," *Chronicle: Magazine of the Historical Society of Michigan*, 5–6/88.
10. Rosentreter, "Making Sacrifices."
11. Ibid.
12. Ibid.
13. Though described as an antitank weapon, a teller mine was normally triggered by a pressure of about 300 lbs. An empty jeep weighed about 1,200 lbs., and this particular jeep was laden with supplies, including munitions, plus Sgt. Deanie. Thus, its gross weight easily could have been 2,000 lbs. or more. If one wheel of this jeep passed directly over the teller's detonator, it would have been enough to set off the mine. *The German Soldier.*
14. All quotes from Aunt Terry are from letters in Carroll Whitehead's personal collection, used with permission. Aunt Terry, based on what the officers at the hospital told her, said it was twenty minutes. JBS in McDiarmid interview said it was ten minutes.
15. According to Swainson, who later encountered him in a Tennessee hospital, Sgt. Bruso survived physically but lost his mind.
16. Rosentreter, "Making Sacrifices," *Michigan History*, November–December, 1991.

17. Aunt Terry letter, 1/2/45.

18. Hugh McDiarmid interview with Swainson; I have inferred this from the context.

19. Getzen, "Michigan's 'Kismet' Governor."

20. Hugh McDiarmid interview with Swainson.

21. An 88 was a type of German artillery shell. Swainson subsequently described the incident several times over the years, but never again connected it to shelling by the Germans. It is, of course, possible that they attempted to shell the jeep, but no other mention of it has come to light. In any event, it would require an incredible coincidence for a shell to hit a mine at all, and a near-miracle for it to do so just as a jeep was about to pass over the mine.

22. This statement is not quite accurate, as only one lower limb had been "blown off" and the other was too severely injured to save, so was amputated. But Swainson did not know all of the medical details when he wrote this letter.

23. Carroll Whitehead personal collection, used with permission.

24. Carroll Whitehead personal collection, used with permission.

25. Hugh McDiarmid interview with Swainson.

26. Carrol Whitehead personal collection, used with permission.

27. *Port Huron Herald*, 2/11/45; I have assumed a ten-day Atlantic voyage.

28. U.S. Defense Logistics Information Service website.

29. "Commemorative Guide to the First 100 Years of the Hart-Dole-Inouye Federal Center," Office of Public Affairs, 2003.

30. Rosentreter, "Making Sacrifices."

31. Hugh McDiarmid interview with Swainson.

32. Hugh McDiarmid, "Ex-governor Plays Morale Booster for Little Amputee," *Detroit Free Press*, 7/18/79.

33. All direct quotations from Carroll Whitehead are from the author's interview with her.

34. Hugh McDiarmid, "The Private Life of John Swainson," *Detroit Free Press*, 12/29/85.

35. Hugh McDiarmid interview with Swainson.

36. Author's interview with Allen Zemmol.

37. Swainson letter to Tak's widow, 10/26/87, personal collection of Bruce Getzan.

38. Bentley Library, Swainson Collection, Box 1.

39. Carroll Whitehead personal collection, used with permission.

40. Detroit Free Press, 8/4/60.

41. McDiarmid, "Private Life."

■ CHAPTER THREE. THE BEST-ADJUSTED VETERAN

1. Hugh McDiarmid interview with Swainson.

2. Alvin L. Muilenburg and A. Bennett Wilson Jr., *Manual for Below-Knee Amputees* (Linthicum, Md.: Dankmyer, 1996).

3. Hugh McDiarmid interview with Swainson.

4. Progress Reports, Bentley Library, Swainson Collection, Box 1.

5. Ibid.

6. Ibid.

7. Dowdy, "Immigrant to Governor," *Detroit News*, 1/10/61.

8. Author's interview with Meri Lou Murray.

9. Swainson oral history project interview, October 18–19, 1990, Supreme Court Historical Society.

10. "College Faculty, Classmates, Recall Swainson," *Lansing State Journal*, 1/9/61.

11. Author's interview with James Blount.

12. "College Faculty, Classmates, Recall Swainson," *Lansing State Journal*, 1/9/61.

13. Ibid.

14. *Lansing State Journal*, 6/6/61.

15. Author's interview with Kristina and Louis Way.

16. Author's interview with Frank Kelley.

17. Hoenshell, "Sen. Swainson Bids to be Hart's Successor," *Detroit News*, 2/17/58.

18. *Detroit Free Press*, 8/4/60.

19. Larson, "Sen. Swainson Climbs the Political Ladder," *Lansing State Journal*, 2/5/58.

20. Author's interview with Frank Kelley.

■ CHAPTER FOUR. A PARTY REBORN

1. Thomas J. Noer, *Soapy: A Biography of G. Mennen Williams* (Ann Arbor: University of Michigan Press, 2005), 61.

2. Neil Staebler, *Out of the Smoke-filled Room: A History of Michigan Politics* (Ann Arbor: George Wahr, 1991), 29.

3. Ibid., 11.

4. Noer, *G. Mennen Williams*, 55.

5. Ibid., 61.

6. Roberts, "Gus Scholle's Story Is Labor's Story," *Detroit Free Press*, 9/1/63.

7. Dudley W. Buffa, *Union Power and American Democracy,* vol. 1 (Ann Arbor: University of Michigan Press, 1984), 16.

8. Ibid., 17.

9. *Time*, 9/9/57.

10. Buffa, *Union Power*, 14.

11. Staebler, *Smoke-filled Room*, 32.

12. Buffa, *Union Power*, 15.

13. The Political Graveyard (http://politicalgraveyard.com).

14. Buffa, *Union Power*, 19.

15. Noer, *G. Mennen Williams*, 72.

16. Ibid., 71.

17. *Time*, 11/15/48.

18. Staebler, *Smoke-filled Room*, 33.

19. Noer, *G. Mennen Williams*, 75.

20. Ibid., 81.

21. Buffa, *Union Power*, 27.

22. Ibid., 35.

23. Noer, *G. Mennen Williams*, 85.

24. *Scholle v. Hare*, 360 Mich. 1 (1960), dissenting opinion of Smith, J.

25. Noer, *G. Mennen Williams*, 151.
26. *Detroit News*, 11/3/54.

■ CHAPTER FIVE. LEGISLATOR

1. Hoenshell, "Senate Asked to Continue Debt Management Quiz," *Detroit News*, 2/27/56.
2. *Detroit Free Press*, 3/27/56.
3. "Fight For Scholarship Commission Is Lost," *Detroit News*, 3/30/56.
4. "NAACP Will Honor State FEPC Leaders," *Detroit News*, 4/18/56.
5. Noer, *G. Mennen Williams*, 177.
6. Deatrick, "Stormy Seas Ahead," *Detroit Free Press*, 1/27/57.
7. "Special Applause," *Detroit Times*, 1/8/57.
8. Deatrick, "State Dems in Senate Drop Ryan," *Detroit Free Press*, 1/10/57.
9. Deatrick, "Stormy Seas Ahead," *Detroit Free Press*, 1/27/57.
10. Hoenshell, "State Tax on Income is Drafted," *Detroit News*, 2/10/57.
11. "Tax Profits First, Says Swainson," *Detroit News*, 2/13/57.
12. George, "These Legislators," *Detroit Free Press*, 5/13/57.
13. *Detroit News*, 2/17/57.
14. Green cover scrapbook, undated 1957 clipping, most likely from the *Plymouth Observer*. Bentley Library, Swainson Collection, Box 5.
15. Deatrick, "What's Hart's Political Future?," *Detroit Free Press*, 4/7/57.
16. "Hart's Birthday Wish: Swainson as Successor," *Detroit News*, 12/12/57.
17. White, "Dems Reveal Election Lineup," *Port Huron Times-Herald*, 2/19/58.
18. *Escanaba Daily Press*, 2/18/58.
19. "Swainson is Praised by Williams," *Detroit Times*, 2/18/58.
20. Author's interview with Allen Zemmol.
21. Article by Elmer White for the Michigan Press Association, as printed in the *Cass City Chronicle*, 7/17/58.
22. Noer, *G. Mennen Williams*, 189.
23. Ibid.
24. "Swainson Sits in Boss' Chair but Williams Rules from Afar," *Detroit News*, 9/27/59.
25. Noer, *G. Mennen Williams*, 177.
26. Stetson, *New York Times*, 4/30/59.
27. *Time*, 5/4/59.

■ CHAPTER SIX. THE PRIMARY: A MAJOR UPSET

1. Http://www.senate.michigan.gov/sfa/Publications/Notes/2005Notes/notesmayjun05bb. pdf.
2. *Detroit Free Press*, 3/6/60.
3. Author's interview with Joe Collins.
4. Larson, "Failure to Announce Candidacy Indicates He Has Other Plans," *Lansing State Journal*, 3/4/60.
5. Ibid.
6. See, e.g., Nicholson, "Williams' Decision To Quit Surprises Labor Bosses," *Detroit Free*

Press, 3/4/60.

7. Staebler, *Smoke-filled Room*, 78.

8. Author's interview with Frank Kelley. The Swainson-Scholle meeting was never publicly acknowledged, but both Swainson and Scholle described it to Frank Kelley.

9. Buffa, *Union Power*, 53.

10. In an interview with the author, Joe Collins recalled that "Neil Staebler was my mentor all the way through and I was very close to him. But, for some reason, John got at crosswinds with Neil. Neil was never supportive of him. . . . With respect to the women, John was a bit indiscreet there. No, it didn't disqualify him from public office. But that was the kind of thing Neil would hold against him. Neil was a bit of a puritan."

11. Author's interview with Joe Collins.

12. *Detroit News*, 3/8/60. The poll also showed Mennen Williams *trailing* Bagwell 49.1 percent to 49.6 percent.

13. Courage, "Soapy: No Seventh Term," *Detroit Free Press*, 3/3/60.

14. *Detroit News*, 7/20/60.

15. Buffa, *Union Power*, 54–55.

16. *Ionia Sentinel-Standard*, 5/9/60, as quoted in the "Swainson for Governor newsletter," Bentley Library, Neil Staebler Collection, Box 76.

17. *Petoskey News Review*, 5/9/60, as quoted in the "Swainson for Governor Newsletter," Bentley Library, Staebler Collection, Box 76.

18. News release, Bentley Library, Swainson Collection, Box 1.

19. Muller, "Labor Seeks to Break Pact, Boost Swainson," *Detroit News*, 7/10/60.

20. *Detroit Times*, 7/20/60.

21. Lieutenant governor's schedule for 4/23/60, Bentley Library, Swainson Collection, Box 2.

22. *Detroit Free Press*, date not visible, 1960, Bentley Library, Swainson Collection, Box 5.

23. Author's interview with Allen Zemmol.

24. Buffa, *Union Power*, 55.

25. Official vote tabulation, Bentley Library, Swainson Collection, Box 4.

■ CHAPTER SEVEN. THE GENERAL ELECTION: A SQUEAKER

1. *Time*, 10/24/60.

2. A state university employee was barred from seeking partisan political office. Bagwell had to take a leave of absence, without pay, to make the campaign. In his 1958 campaign for governor, he had gone deeply into debt. As a result, in April 1960 a group of Republican supporters organized a dinner for 1,000 at the Lansing Civic Center to raise $10,000 to pay his family expenses during the 1960 campaign. *Detroit News*, 4/6/60.

3. *Time*, 11/2/59.

4. Quoted in OurCampaigns.com.

5. *Lansing State Journal*, 6/14/60.

6. *Time*, 10/24/60.

7. They were right. When it met, the con-con perpetuated existing State Senate districts with the result that the Michigan Senate continued to be dominated by rural Republicans until

the U.S. Supreme Court decision mandating "one man, one vote" was implemented by order of the Michigan Supreme Court in 1964. See *In re Apportionment of State Legislature,* 373 Mich. 250 (1964).

8. *Time,* 10/24/60.

9. 1960 Campaign Themes, Bentley Library, Staebler Collection, Box 76.

10. John Swainson, John F. Kennedy Library Oral History interview, 1/26/70, 10.

11. Bentley Library, Swainson Collection, Box 1.

12. Chiapetta, "Swainson Leaps Con-con Hurdle," *Detroit Times,* 8/27/60.

13. Author's interview with Joe Collins.

14. Helen W. Berthelot, *Win Some Lose Some* (Detroit: Wayne State University Press, 1995), 232.

15. Swainson, JFK Library Oral History interview, 1/26/70, 7.

16. Ibid., 17–18.

17. Dowdy, "Kennedy Praises Swainson; Bagwell Raps Union Curbs," *Detroit News,* 10/27/60.

18. "Swainson Starts His Campaign," *Detroit Times,* 9/9/60. In the present era of nearly year-around campaigning, it may seem hard to believe that a candidate did not start his official campaign until more than a month after he won the primary, but it is true.

19. Boyd, "Governor Rivals Put in Busy Day Stumping State," *Detroit Free Press,* 9/16/60.

20. Bentley Library, Swainson Collection, Box 1.

21. Ibid.

22. Public expectations change. A century earlier a candidate for high executive office, once nominated, did not openly campaign at all. It was considered unseemly. Abraham Lincoln spent most of the 1860 presidential campaign at home in Springfield, Illinois, making few public statements.

23. Author's interview with Allen Zemmol.

24. Author's interview with Joe Collins.

25. Carlisle, "Bagwell and Swainson Debate on Taxes, Jobs," *Detroit News,* 9/21/60.

26. Robinson, "Candidates List Goals," *Detroit Free Press,* 9/21/60.

27. Author's interview with William G. Milliken.

28. Carlisle, "Bagwell-Swainson Debate Scrappiest of TV Series," *Detroit News,* 10/28/60.

29. Oudersluys, "Swainson Gains, Bagwell Loses In Rural Areas," *Detroit News,* 10/24/60.

30. *Detroit Free Press* interviews of Swainson and Bagwell, 10/16/60 and 10/23/60.

31. *Time,* 10/24/60.

32. Chiapetta, "Swainson, Bagwell Stand Off," *Detroit Times,* 9/21/60.

33. Michigan Legislative Service Bureau, *Michigan Manual, 1997–1998* (Lansing), 930.

34. Carlisle, "Bagwell Concedes to Swainson After Long Hours of Hoping," *Detroit News,* 11/9/60.

35. Berthelot, *Win Some Lose Some,* 235.

36. *Detroit News,* 11/9/60; Berthelot, *Win Some Lose Some,* 235.

37. *Michigan Manual,* 1997–1998, 930.

38. For an analysis of the numbers behind the 1960 election results, see appendix 1.

39. Author's interview with Margaret Halava.

■ CHAPTER EIGHT. GOVERNOR, YEAR ONE: STUMBLES

1. Lattie Coor eventually earned a paid position in Swainson's office, returning to academic life only after Swainson's 1962 defeat. Coor's subsequent career confirmed Swainson's quick judgment about his abilities; Coor served as president of the University of Vermont from 1976 to 1989 and president of Arizona State University from 1990 to 2002. Author's interview with Lattie Coor.

2. *Lansing State Journal*, 10/4/61.

3. In the course of researching the 1960 campaign the author came across a peculiar memo. It was "to John Swainson from Merit Aide." Both its content and style indicated that the writer was an intimate of Swainson's, thoroughly familiar with the people and structure of the campaign. Yet no other memo to or from this person was found, nor was the name "Merit Aide" referenced in any other document. The mystery was solved when the author came across a brief story in the 10/8/60 *Detroit News*. The story revealed that Jordan Popkin, who was a classified civil service employee of Governor Williams—and thus barred from political activities—was listed as research coordinator of the Swainson gubernatorial campaign. Swainson was quoted as saying the listing was a mistake, and Popkin did not have a role in his campaign. The headline over the story was "Swainson Loses Merit Aide."

4. Author's interview with Joe Collins.

5. *Lansing State Journal*, 1/9/61.

6. Author's interview with Vicky Seide.

7. Larson, "Special Session on Sales Tax Is Seen Uncertain," *Lansing State Journal*, 11/10/60.

8. "Special Session Pondered," *Lansing State Journal*, 11/28/60.

9. "Will Urge Cent Sales Levy Hike," *Detroit News*, 11/10/60.

10. "Swainson Mum About Meetings," *Lansing State Journal*, 12/6/60.

11. Rudow, "4-cent Sales Tax Will Start Jan. 1," *Detroit News*, 12/8/60.

12. Courage, "Swainson Changes GOP's Attitude," *Detroit Free Press*, 3/26/61.

13. Robinson, "It's Money Time For The Legislature," *Detroit Free Press*, 4/3/61.

14. Courage, "GOP Austerity Budget Goes To House," *Detroit Free Press*, 4/16/61.

15. Ibid.

16. Ibid.

17. Robinson, "Swainson Lifts Bar On Nuisance Taxes," *Detroit Free Press*, 4/20/61.

18. Rudow, "Indecision Mars Swainson's First 6 Months On The Job," *Detroit News*, 6/18/61.

19. *Detroit Free Press*, 4/23/61.

20. Editorial, "Milk Bill Rises From Its Grave," *Detroit Free Press*, 6/10/61.

21. Rudow, "Indecision Mars Swainson's First 6 months On The Job," *Detroit News*, 6/18/61.

22. Baird, "Veto Reactions Sting," Lansing *State Journal*, 7/9/61.

23. Courage, "Swainson: One Down, One To Go," *Detroit Free Press*, 12/17/61.

24. 355 Mich. 103.

25. In the Ford-Canton decision the Supreme Court was interpreting the language of a Michigan statute. If the legislature disagreed with the Court's interpretation, it was free to amend the statute to clarify its meaning. Like any other statute passed by the legislature, it could not become law without the governor's consent.

26. William Baird, "Veto Reactions Sting," *Lansing State Journal*, 7/9/61.

27. Ibid.

28. Courage, "Swainson: One Down, One To Go," *Detroit Free Press*, 12/17/61.

29. Baird, "Swainson Needs Improved Image," *Lansing State Journal*, 12/31/61.

30. Author's interview with Joe Collins.

31. Sidney Fine, *Expanding the Frontiers of Civil Rights* (Detroit: Wayne State University Press, 2000).

32. Ibid., 98 n. 2.

33. Ibid., 78–80.

34. Ibid., 80–81.

35. Michigan Supreme Court Historical Society interview of Otis Smith conducted by Roger F. Lane, 10/23–25/1990; http://archive.lib.msu.edu/MMM/JA/02/a/JA02a023.html. Smith was subsequently elected to fill the balance of his predecessor's term on the court, but was defeated for re-election by Thomas Brennan in 1966. He went on to a distinguished career as an attorney, serving as vice president and general counsel of General Motors Corporation.

36. Author's interview with Margaret Halava.

37. Hugh McDiarmid, "The Private Life of John Swainson," *Detroit Free Press*, 12/29/85.

38. McDiarmid, Ex-Governor Lost His Legs but Not His Sense of Humor," *Detroit Free Press*, 5/14/94.

39. Author's interview with Margaret Halava.

■ CHAPTER NINE. GOVERNOR, YEAR TWO: ALMOST

1. John T. Dempsey, "Romney for Governor: The 1962 Michigan Election Campaign," 81. Private manuscript written by one of Romney's principal campaign advisors, who went on to a distinguished career as a Michigan public servant. The author is indebted to Dr. Dempsey's son, David Dempsey, for permission to use this invaluable memoir.

2. Ibid., 57.

3. Ibid., 60.

4. Clark Mollenhoff, *George Romney: Mormon in Politics* (New York: Meredith Press, 1968), 168.

5. Courage, "Swainson: One Down, One To Go," *Detroit Free Press*, 12/17/61.

6. "Michigan Taxes Urged," *New York Times*, 1/27/62.

7. *Gongwer News Service*, 1/17/62. This service began printing detailed regular reports of political and governmental actions at the Capitol in January 1962.

8. "Swainson Accuses Legislature of Dawdling," *Detroit News*, 2/3/62.

9. Levitt, "Cavanagh, Swainson Clash on Income Tax," *Detroit News*, 2/23/62.

10. Mollenhoff, *George Romney*, 174.

11. *Port Huron Times Herald*, 2/8/08.

12. Gongwer News Service, 4/5/62.

13. Gongwer News Service, 4/5/62.

14. Stetson, "Michigan Studies Income Tax Plans," *New York Times*, 4/8/62.

15. Gongwer News Service, 4/16/62.

16. "Hails Moderates," *Grand Rapids Press*, 4/26/62.

17. Ibid.

18. Smeekens's campaign slogan was "Smeekens Never Weakens."

19. Gongwer News Service, 4/24/62.

20. Ibid.

21. Dempsey, "*Romney for Governor*," 168.

22. Gongwer News Service, 4/27/62.

23. Gongwer News Service, 5/762.

24. "Poll Indicates Romney Trails," *New York Times*, 5/14/62.

25. Dempsey, "Romney for Governor," 103.

26. Ibid., 119.

27. Ibid., 190–91.

28. Ibid., 186.

29. Ibid., 188.

30. Ibid., 195.

31. *Scholle v. Sec. of State*, 367 Mich. 176.

32. Dempsey, "Romney for Governor," 201.

33. *Detroit News*, 7/21/62.

34. Dempsey, "Romney for Governor," 202.

35. Ibid.

36. Ibid., 301.

37. *New York Times*, 10/8/62.

38. Author's interview with Frank Kelley.

39. Dempsey, "Romney for Governor," 242–44.

40. Ibid., 253.

41. Ibid., 254.

42. Ibid., 255.

43. Shawyer, "Swainson's Jibe Angers Romney," *Detroit Free Press*, 10/18/62.

44. Ibid.

45. Ibid.

46. 1962 Campaign Reports, Louis Harris confidential report, Bentley Library, Swainson Collection, Box 69.

47. Dempsey, "Romney for Governor," 261.

48. Ibid., 264.

49. Ibid., 265–66.

50. Ibid.

51. Ibid., 271.

52. *Detroit Free Press*, 11/7/62.

53. *Ibid.*

54. *Ibid.*

55. *Detroit News*, 11/7/62.

56. Mann, "Smiling Swainson a Man in Defeat," *Detroit Free Press*, 11/8/62.

57. For an analysis of the numbers behind the 1962 election results, see appendix 2.

58. *"Swainson KO Linked to Tax Bill," Lansing State Journal*, 11/7/62.

59. Mann, "Smiling Swainson a Man in Defeat," *Detroit Free Press*, 11/8/62.

■ CHAPTER TEN. YOU KNOW YOU'RE NO LONGER GOVERNOR WHEN . . .

1. Mann, "Smiling Swainson a Man in Defeat," *Detroit Free Press*, 11/8/62.

2. Rudow, "Swainson Steps Out, Tells Feeling of Accomplishment," *Detroit News*, 12/31/62.

3. Author's interview with Frank Kelley.

4. "Swainson Visits JFK at Capital," *Lansing State Journal*, 11/10/62.

5. Popa, "Swainson 'Trick' Dumps Collins, Puts Ferency In," *Detroit News*, 2/3/63.

6. Bentley Library, Swainson Collection, Box 70, correspondence, 1–3/63.

7. *Detroit Free Press*, 11/8/62.

8. Robinson and Shawver, "Inside Story of the State Dem Shakeup," *Detroit Free Press*, 2/10/63.

9. Ibid.

10. Ibid.

11. Tyson, "Hero, Governor, Felon—Fate Baffles John Swainson," *Detroit Free Press*, 12/18/77.

12. Author's interview with Vincent Piersante.

13. Author's interview with Allen Zemmol.

14. Vincent Bugliosi, *Reclaiming History: The Assassination of President John F. Kennedy* (New York: W.W. Norton, 2007), 177n.

15. Buffa, *Union Power*, 58.

16. Ibid., 59.

17. Vestal, "Staebler Rejects Apology," *Flint Journal*, 2/4/63.

18. Except where otherwise noted, this account is taken from the *Detroit News* story of 2/3/63. Allen Zemmol, who was a direct participant, told the author that the *Detroit News* story was accurate.

19. Ibid.

20. *Detroit Free Press*, 2/10/62.

21. "Swainson Proves Political Leadership At Convention," *Flint Journal*, 2/4/63.

22. Buffa, *Union Power*, 60.

23. Ibid.

24. *Flint Journal*, 2/4/63.

25. JBS 2/11/63 letter to Lattie Coor, Bentley Library, Swainson Collection, Box 70, correspondence, 1–3/63.

26. "Swainson Buying Home," *Lansing State Journal*, 10/3/62.

27. JBS 5/8/63 letter to Peter, Bentley Library, Swainson Collection, Box 70, correspondence, 4–6/63.

28. Bentley Library, Swainson Collection, Box 70, correspondence, 4–6/63.

29. Shawver, "Swainson '63:Waiting Game," *Detroit Free Press*, 6/9/63.

30. Ibid.

31. John F. Kennedy Presidential Library, President's Daily Schedule for 5/21/63.

32. John Swainson, John F. Kennedy Library Oral History interview, 1/26/70.

33. Bentley Library, Swainson Collection, Box 70, correspondence, 4–6/63.

34. Bentley Library, Swainson Collection, Box 70, correspondence 1963.

35. UPI story, 9/26/63.

36. Bentley Library, Swainson Collection, Box 70, correspondence, 10–12/63.

37. *Lansing State Journal*, 12/22/63. The congressman-at-large position was the temporary product of the legislature's failure to apportion Michigan's congressional districts in time for the 1962 election, a defect that was remedied in time for the 1964 election.

38. "Gubernatorial Push Is Given Swainson Here," *Lansing State Journal*, 12/24/63.

39. Shawver, "His Decision Due Saturday," *Detroit Free Press*, 12/30/63.

40. *Lansing State Journal*, 12/28/63.

41. Bentley Library, Swainson Collection, Box 70, correspondence 1–5/64.

42. "Manchester Area Farm Bought by Swainsons," *Lansing State Journal*, 6/23/64; the story reports the farm as 65 acres, but Swainson's daughter and her husband both recall it as 167 acres, purchased all at once.

43. Michigan Compiled Laws 211.7b.

44. 6/16/65 letter from attorney Jack Born, Bentley Library, Swainson Collection, Box 70, correspondence 1–5/64.

45. Hoenshell, "Swainson Yearns for Lost Job, May Run in '64," *Detroit News*, 4/14/63.

46. In 1968 the new constitution was amended to once again give the Governor the power to fill judicial vacancies by appointment.

47. News release, Bentley Library, Swainson Collection, Box 70, Misc. 1963–1965.

48. Phil Lee, UPI story, 12/30/64.

49. See *Markowitz v. State Canvassers* (1965), 1 Mich. App. 12.

50. The exact number is determined by the legislature, and it changes from time to time in rough proportion to Wayne County's population.

51. Bentley Library, Swainson Collection, Box 70, correspondence, 1968.

52. Michigan Supreme Court Historical Society, oral history project interview of John Swainson by Roger Lane, 10/18–19/90.

53. Author's interview with Thomas Brennan.

54. Author's interview with Allen Zemmol.

55. Author's interview with David Sparrow.

56. Author's interview with Thomas Brennan.

57. Letter to Lattie Coor, Bentley Library, Swainson Collection, Box 70, correspondence 3/25/69.

58. *Lansing State Journal*, 3/18/70; letter to JBS from Anthony Bellanca, Bentley Library, Swainson Collection, Box 70, correspondence, 4/3/1970.

59. Bentley Library, Swainson Collection, Box 70, correspondence 1968.

■ CHAPTER ELEVEN. THE SUPREME COURT

1. Michigan Supreme Court Historical Society, oral history project interview of John Swainson by Roger Lane, 10/18–19/90.

2. An *incumbent* justice has the privilege of simply declaring that he or she is a candidate for election. This guarantees a spot on the ballot without the need to seek nomination at a political convention. In practice, however, incumbent justices have always sought, and

nearly always received, their party's nomination. The exception was T. Giles Kavanagh. In 1976 the leaders of the Michigan Democratic Party, upset over his opinion in a legislative apportionment case, denied him renomination. As an incumbent he renominated himself. Endorsed by seventeen past presidents of the State Bar and depicted in the press as a martyr, he easily won reelection.

This system's absurdity was exploited in 1972 when Court of Appeals judge Charles Levin sought a Democratic nomination for the Supreme Court, but the convention chose another candidate. Levin had designed a backup plan. He created his own political party (The Non-partisan Judicial Party), convened a state convention of delegates, and had himself nominated, in full compliance with state law. His name thus appeared on the ballot alongside those nominated by the Democratic and Republican parties, with exactly the same labels as those candidates—none. His well-financed campaign resulted in his election to the Supreme Court.

3. *Grand Rapids Press*, 8/22/70.

4. Thomas Brennan, interviewed by Roger Lane, Michigan Supreme Court Historical Society Oral History Project.

5. At the 1994 Annual Luncheon of the Michigan Supreme Court Historical Society Professor John Reed related this story:

> Justice [Theodore] Souris recounts the story of Black's role in the famous 1960 case of *Stoliker v. The Board of State Canvassers*. At issue was whether the Michigan constitution required a different vote for the call of a constitutional convention than it required for a constitutional amendment. Souris had just arrived as a new justice at the beginning of January, when Black handed him a 56-page opinion he had written in the *Stoliker* case and asked whether Souris might join him in the opinion. Souris said, "You must be out of your mind. I was a member of the Board of State Canvassers. How can I participate as a justice?" To which Black replied, "That doesn't matter." But that is not the oddest part of it. The *Stoliker* case hadn't even been argued! It was scheduled for oral argument the next day, and yet, Justice Black's opinion was already written. When the Court sat on the morrow, Justice Souris withdrew, as planned. But at the end of the arguments, Black announced from the bench that he had prepared his opinion in the case, which he had filed with the clerk with sufficient copies for distribution to the press—who, by the way, had been alerted and filled the courtroom. A few days later, Souris, the newest justice, moved to strike Black's opinion on the ground that it was "precipitous." (That particular ground probably wouldn't work in England, where opinions are often delivered instanter.) Justice Talbot Smith ultimately wrote the *Stoliker* opinion. According to the official report, "Souris, J., did not sit" and "Black, J., took no part in the decision of this case." Souris says that he and others have copies of Black's abortive opinion.

6. "Supreme Court Processing of Cases and Administrative Matters," issued by the Michigan Supreme Court.

7. Ibid.

8. Like any institution, the Supreme Court's procedures and customs evolve over time. The descriptions in the present tense refer to the court's procedures as of 2007, as described on the court's website. In general, these customs and procedures were similar in the 1970s. Where they were significantly different, they are specifically described in the narrative.

9. During the Monica Lewinsky scandal, Alice Swainson once said of Bill Clinton, "Who does he think he is? John Swainson?"

10. Bentley Library, Swainson Collection, Box 70.

11. Ibid.

12. Ibid.

13. Author's interview with Gene Farber.

14. Author's interview with Victor Adamo.

15. Author's interview with Ronald Carlson.

16. Author's interview with Victor Adamo.

17. Author's interview with Thomas Brennan.

18. Brennan, TR 1371.

19. Author's interview with Victor Adamo.

20. Author's interview with Ronald Carlson.

21. The criminal cases were: *People v. Blocker,* 393 Mich. 501; *People v. Szczytko,* 390 Mich. 278; *People v. Watkins,* 388 Mich. 717; *People v. White,* 392 Mich. 404; *People v. Howe,* 392 Mich. 670; *People v. Schnef,* 392 Mich. 15; *People v. Townes,* 391 Mich. 578; *People v. White,* 390 Mich. 245; *People v. Turner,* 390 Mich. 7; *People v. Grimmett,* 388 Mich. 590; *People v. Heard,* 388 Mich. 182; *People v. Patskan,* 387 Mich. 701; *People v. Cason,* 387 Mich. 586; *People v. Sinclair,* 387 Mich. 91; *People v. Charles O. Williams,* 386 Mich. 565; *People v. Stevens,* 386 Mich. 579; *People v. Hudson,* 386 Mich. 665; *People v. Rios; People v. Contreras,* 386 Mich. 172; *People v. Ramsey,* 386 Mich. 221; *People v. King,* 385 Mich. 274; *People v. Hampton,* 384 Mich. 669; *People v. Whisenant,* 384 Mich. 693; *People v. Nowicki,* 384 Mich. 482; *People v. Jondreau,* 384 Mich. 539; *People v. Matish,* 384 Mich. 568.

22. *Miranda v. Arizona,* 384 U.S. 436 (1966).

23. The employee cases were: *Hakala v. Burroughs Corporation,* 393 Mich. 153; *Lasher v. Mueller Brass Company,* 392 Mich. 488; *Degeer v. Degeer Farm Equipment Company,* 391 Mich. 96; *Keith v. Chrysler Corporation,* 390 Mich. 458; *Regents of the University of Michigan v. Employment Relations Commission,* 389 Mich. 96; *Detroit Police Officers Association v. City of Detroit,* 385 Mich. 519; *Detroit Police Officers Association v. City of Detroit,* 391 Mich. 44; *Valt v. Woodall Industries, Inc.,* 391 Mich. 678; *Smigel v. Southgate Community School District,* 388 Mich. 531.

24. The personal injury cases were: *Javis v. Board of Education of the School district of Ypsilanti,* 393 Mich. 689; *Hanlon v. The Firestone Tire & Rubber Company,* 391 Mich. 558; *Kieft v. Barr,* 391 Mich. 77; *Schneider v. Linkfield,* 389 Mich. 608; *Smith v. City of Detroit; Swarthout v. Beard,* 388 Mich. 637; *Jones v. Bloom,* 388 Mich. 98; *Sliter v. Cobb,* 388 Mich. 202; *Lisee v. Secretary of State; Howell v. Lazaruk,* 388 Mich. 32; 199; *Thompson v. Peters,* 386 Mich. 532; *Washington v. Jones,* 386 Mich. 466; *Buscaino v. Rhodes,* 385 Mich. 474; *Miller v. Detroit Cab Company,* 392 Mich. 480.

25. See first note in this chapter. Charles Levin's cousin, Sander Levin, was the Democratic nominee for governor in 1970 and 1974, losing narrowly to Governor William Milliken. Sander Levin was subsequently elected to the U.S. House of Representatives from a suburban Detroit district, where he still serves. Sander Levin's younger brother, Carl Levin, was elected to the U.S. Senate in 1978, and continues in office as of this writing. Theodore Levin, the father of Charles, served as a federal judge in Detroit from 1947 to 1970.

26. John Fitzgerald, interviewed by Roger Lane, Michigan Supreme Court Historical Society Oral History Project.

    Fitzgerald thought this meeting took place shortly after T. Matthew Kavanagh's 4/19/75 death, probably in April. Mary Coleman agreed with Fitzgerald that it was shortly after Kavanagh's death that they met and learned of the allegations. In 11/75, T. Giles Kavanagh testified that the FBI had informed him of the allegations around March 20 (TR 239). The most likely scenario would seem to be this: the FBI visited Kavanagh and disclosed the investigation to him in late March, making clear that they wanted to interview the other justices as soon as possible, and leaving to him the manner of notifying his colleagues. After wrestling with this news, Kavanagh decided to disclose the investigation to all the justices at the next administrative conference. On the morning of the conference he asked Swainson into his office, so he could let him know privately what was coming. This would explain both Kavanagh's anguish and Swainson's absence from the announcement at the meeting.

    The first public announcement of the investigation appeared in the newspapers on April 17, two days before T. Matthew Kavanagh's death. Therefore the administrative conference must have occurred before April 17.

■ CHAPTER TWELVE. THE BURGLARY

1. This account of the burglary, chase and arrest is taken from the testimony of the respective witnesses in the 1970 trial *People v. John Whalen*, docket number 8709, Circuit Court for Lenawee County, Michigan.

2. It was never determined how they obtained the pattern for the key.

3. Today there is no such location, as U.S. 223 loses its separate identity when it merges into U.S. 23 well before U.S. 23 reaches the Ohio border. However, there is a road called "Old U.S. 223" which does reach the Ohio border, and this clearly is the road the getaway car took.

4. "Court Upholds Martin Action," *Adrian Daily Telegram*, 8/16/69.

5. "Accused Swainson to Stay on Court," *Detroit News*, 4/17/75.

6. This record was obtained from a confidential source.

7. No record of the parole hearing exists. The Michigan Department of Corrections routinely purges and destroys its files on inmates who have been discharged from custody.

8. Kohn and Sarasohn, "Genius Masterminds County Jail Escape," *Detroit Free Press*, June 27, 1971.

9. Unpublished opinion 923 F. 2d 854 (No. 90-3430 1/25/91).

10. The 4/22/80 Michigan State Police record (rap sheet) on Whalen includes the following:

"In Detroit on 11/22/71 and again on 1/18/72 Whalen was charged with possession of counterfeit U.S. currency. Both charges were dismissed on 8/23/72." This record was also obtained from a confidential source.

11. In 1975 Whalen himself finally confirmed that it was he who gave the FBI and Secret Service information that led to Christopher Glumb's arrest (TR 1091).

12. *Detroit News,* 4/17/75.

13. Koselka, PCR 213–19.

■ **CHAPTER THIRTEEN. THE STRIKE FORCE**

1. Author's interview with Vincent Piersante.

2. When this allegation was later made public, Lesinski adamantly denied it. No charges were filed against Lesinski.

3. Whalen, TR 1084–85.

4. Institute of Continuing Legal Education/State Bar of Michigan database.

5. Whalen, TR 1265.

6. The counterfeiting of U.S. currency is severely punished not merely as an economic crime, but because its consequences, if left unchecked, would include destabilizing the currency.

7. Whalen, PCR 159.

8. Author's interview with Vincent Piersante.

9. Whalen, TR 1088.

10. Schley, PCR 15, 23.

11. Author's interview with Vincent Piersante.

12. Cash: wire, TR 475; money back: wire, TR 474.

13. Wire, TR 548.

14. Whalen TR 1125.

15. Wire, TR 604.

16. Wire, TR 607.

17. T. G. Kavanagh, TR 194.

18. Wire, TR 689–90.

19. Wire, TR 707.

20. T. G. Kavanagh, TR 207.

21. Wire, TR 720.

22. Wire, TR 718.

23. Whalen's own estimate, wire, TR 678.

24. Langford, TR 340–43.

25. Langford, TR 339.

26. Diem, TR 804.

27. All telephone records were entered into evidence by stipulation of the attorneys, TR 1419.

28. Fink also argued that the prosecutor's closing argument violated the rules, but the Supreme Court chose not to address this issue.

29. "Sexual preference" JBS, quoting the record of the Whalen trial, TR 1352.

30. *People v. Whalen,* 390 Mich. 672 (1973), 682.

31. Ibid., 678.

32. Ibid., 683.
33. Ibid., 687.
34. Hallas, "Watergate Stalled Swainson Case," *Detroit News*, 7/6/75.

■ CHAPTER FOURTEEN. THE GRAND JURY

1. "Keep the Heat On!" *Detroit News Sunday Magazine* profile of Robert C. Ozer by Al Stark, 1/76.
2. Ibid.
3. Ibid.
4. Ibid.
5. *Pankratz v. District Court in and for the City and County of Denver*, 199 Colo. 411; 609 P.2d 1101; 1980 Colo.
6. *Colorado Chiropractic Council, et al. v. Porter Memorial Hospital, et al.*, 650 F. Supp. 231; 1986.
7. Because the trial judge gave the jury erroneous instructions, the Colorado Supreme Court remanded the case for a new trial, but its ruling recognizing a tort (i.e., personal injury) claim for unreasonable publicity given to one's private life became—and remains—the law in Colorado.
8. Ozer, PCR 79.
9. Ozer, PCR 80.
10. Ozer, PCR 81.
11. Ozer, PCR 82.
12. Ozer, PCR 84.
13. Ozer, PCR 84.
14. Later, just prior to the opening of Swainson's trial, Whalen balked again. It was probably at this time that Ozer approached the Michigan Department of Corrections and secured their agreement to let Whalen serve any remaining time on his sentence for the Adrian burglary in a distant federal prison under an assumed name, at federal expense. Such agreements were not uncommon in the cases of inmates believed to be in danger. Whalen then agreed to testify and presented no further problems. Ozer, PCR 90.
15. Tyson, Land and Briggs, "Swainson Accused of Taking a Bribe," *Detroit Free Press*, 4/17/75.
16. The *Detroit Free Press* reported that as of April 16 the grand jury had already questioned "two Detroit lawyers and two Detroit bail bondsmen." The two lawyers obviously were Deday Larene and Neil Fink. The bail bondsmen had to be Charles Goldfarb and Harvey Wish, who were targets of the investigation. Tyson, Lane, Briggs, "Swainson Accused of Taking a Bribe," 4/17/75
17. *Ibid.*, *Detroit Free Press*, 4/17/75.
18. For a history of the uses and abuses of grand juries see appendix 3.
19. Author's interview with Konrad Kohl.
20. Author's interview with Ronald Carlson.
21. Nehman and Hallas, "Swainson Faces 2nd Grilling by U.S. Jury," *Detroit News*, 5/20/75.
22. We cannot know everything that transpired in the grand jury room, because the law requires that all grand jury proceedings be secret, and the records sealed. The principal

reasons usually given for secrecy are (1) a grand jury, like a prosecutor, investigates many allegations against persons who turn out to be innocent, and disclosure of an investigation would harm their reputation; (2) disclosure that a person is testifying before a grand jury can place the witness in jeopardy. For example, Michigan state senator Warren Hooper was murdered in 1945 because the fact that he was about to testify before a grand jury investigating corruption was leaked. Bruce A. Rubenstein, and Lawrence E. Ziewacz, *Three Bullets Sealed His Lips* (East Lansing: Michigan State University Press, 1987).

The only reason that we have a substantial portion of John Swainson's testimony is that Ozer and Kohl agreed to its release; see next chapter.

23. Author's interview with Ronald Carlson.

24. Ibid.

25. About two weeks before his grand jury appearance, Swainson had been questioned by an IRS agent. One of the agent's questions was whether Swainson had received a television set from Harvey Wish (TR 1684). This is obviously what prompted the pre-grand jury discussion that Zemmol recalled.

26. Author's interview with Allen Zemmol.

27. Author's interview with Meri Lou Murray.

28. TR 1365.

29. *Detroit News*, 5/21/75. Given Swainson's well-known reluctance to claim the Fifth Amendment's protection, I was dubious about this *Detroit News* story until I read the transcript of a discussion between Ozer, Kohl, and Judge Rubin. The subject was which parts of Swainson's grand jury testimony could be read to a jury (TR 1255–1262). During this discussion Ozer said, "Now, with reference to the May 19, 1975 appearance, do I understand correctly that Mr. Kohl objects only to the assertion of Fifth Amendment privilege at the end?" (TR 1257). Later, the judge said, "Well, I don't mean to speak for you, Mr. Kohl, but it would seem to me past that line is not pertinent. This begins the assertion of the Fifth Amendment" (TR 1260).

The discussion then moved to the reading of Swainson's 5/21/75 appearance. Ozer said, "Now, in this case, Justice Swainson gave one narrative answer. The last paragraph involved a gratuitous assertion of the Fifth Amendment privilege" (TR 1260). Any remaining doubt is removed by the judge's last statement on this subject: "Incidentally, this assertion of the privilege, I hope it was a misprint because the reporter has him saying on the grounds of my answers would tend to incriminate me. I think he meant might incriminate me. Obviously, I am not going to let that be read" (TR 1262).

30. The indictment also charged Swainson and Wish with unlawful use of a telephone to further the alleged conspiracy, but these charges were later dismissed by the federal court and never went before a jury. The grand jury also indicted Charles Goldfarb, a prominent Detroit bail bondsman, on similar charges of conspiracy and perjury, but all charges against him were also dismissed by the court.

■ CHAPTER FIFTEEN. THE TRIAL: PROSECUTION

1. His full name was Thomas Giles Kavanagh, and he was chief justice of the Michigan Supreme Court in 1975 at the time of Swainson's federal trial. However, another justice,

Thomas Matthew Kavanagh, had been chief justice during the period 9–10/72. Therefore, to minimize confusion, they are referred to here respectively as "T. Giles Kavanagh" and "T. Matthew Kavanagh."

2. The Supreme Court justices regularly scheduled several different types of meetings. Opinion conferences were devoted exclusively to discussion of proposed opinions after the justices had received the briefs and heard the oral arguments of attorneys. Administrative conferences were more heterogeneous, encompassing decisions on whether to grant leave to appeal, as well as purely administrative decisions.

3. Kavanagh, TR 245.

4. Kavanagh, TR 245.

5. Kavanagh, TR 249.

6. Kavanagh, TR 250.

7. Williams, TR 1443; and see TR 1450.

8. In 10/72 the seven justices were T. Matthew Kavanaugh (then chief justice), Eugene Black, T. Giles Kavanagh, Thomas E. Brennan, John B. Swainson, G. Mennen Williams, and Paul L. Adams. Black was not participating in decisions on leave to appeal because he had decided to leave the court at the end of the year and would not be available to participate in writing the opinions on any new cases. T. Matthew Kavanagh died before the trial. Paul Adams left the court at the end of 1972 and, for unknown reasons, did not testify at the trial. T. Giles Kavanagh was called as a witness by the prosecution. The others were called by the defense.

9. Thomas E. Brennan testified, "Justice T. G. Kavanagh had written a memorandum and had argued on many occasions about this Whalen case. He felt that . . . the prosecutor down in Lenawee County went way overboard in his cross-examination of witnesses. I can't tell you . . . how many times we might have discussed that case along with others at lunch or some other circumstance, but it did come up on that occasion [the 10/72 administrative conference]" (TR 1385).

10. Swainson, TR 1619.

11. Swainson, TR 1620.

12. Swainson, TR 1621.

13. Whalen, TR 1235–54.

14. Langford, TR 338–40.

15. Langford, TR 344.

16. Schley, TR 951–55.

17. Schley, TR 955–56.

18. Epke, TR 1024–25.

19. Leyden, TR 1048–49.

20. Holloway, TR 1042–44.

21. In *Bourjaily v. United States*, 483 U.S. 171; 107 S. Ct. 2775; 97 L. Ed. 2d 144 (1987) the U.S. Supreme Court gave a brief history of the exception: "The admissibility of co-conspirators' statements was first established in this Court over a century and a half ago in *United States v. Gooding*, 12 Wheat. 460 (1827) (interpreting statements of co-conspirator as *res gestae* and thus admissible against defendant), and the Court has repeatedly reaffirmed

the exception as accepted practice. In fact, two of the most prominent approvals of the rule came in cases that petitioner maintains are still vital today, *Glasser v. United States, 315 U.S. 60 (1942)*, and *United States v. Nixon, 418 U.S. 683 (1974)*. To the extent that these cases have not been superseded by the Federal Rules of Evidence, they demonstrate that the co-conspirator exception to the hearsay rule is steeped in our jurisprudence. In *Delaney v. United States, 263 U.S. 586, 590 (1924)*, the Court rejected the very challenge petitioner brings today, holding that there can be no separate Confrontation Clause challenge to the admission of a co-conspirator's out-of-court statement. In so ruling, the Court relied on established precedent holding such statements competent evidence. We think that these cases demonstrate that co-conspirators' statements, when made in the course and in furtherance of the conspiracy, have a long tradition of being outside the compass of the general hearsay exclusion."

22. Wire, TR 542.
23. TR 1734.
24. Whalen, TR 1084.
25. Whalen, TR 1088.
26. Whalen, TR 1105.
27. Whalen, TR 1111–12.
28. Whalen, TR 1124.
29. Wire, TR 791.
30. Wire, TR 799.
31. Whalen, TR 1125.
32. Whalen, TR 1127.
33. Whalen's understanding was incorrect. In 1975 Michigan law expressly authorized a bondsman to charge a premium of up to 10 percent a year. MCL 750.167b(3); MSA 28.364(2) (3), provided: "It shall be lawful to charge for executing any bond in a criminal case, but no person engaged in the bonding business, either as principal or clerk, agent or representative of another, either direct or indirectly, shall charge, accept or receive any sum of money or property, other than *the regular prevailing fee for bonding,* which *shall not exceed 10% of the face value of the bond for a 12 month period or any part thereof,* from any person for whom he has executed bond, for any other service whatever performed in connection with any indictment, information or charge upon which the person is bailed or held" (emphasis added).
34. Whalen, TR 1171.
35. Whalen, TR 1280.
36. Whalen, TR 1281.
37. Whalen, TR 1282.

■ CHAPTER SIXTEEN. THE TRIAL: DEFENSE

1. TR 1526–27.
2. TR 1528.
3. TR 1533.
4. This was related to the author by a person who was close to Swainson at the time of

the trial. It was not his attorney, but was a person with whom Swainson discussed trial strategy, among other subjects.

5. Williams, TR 1437.
6. Williams, TR 1371.
7. Brennan, TR 1372.
8. Brennan, TR 1388–89.
9. Bolle, TR 1398.
10. Bolle, TR 1413–14.

In calling Bolle, Swainson was making an ex parte communication with the judge, arguably in an attempt to influence the outcome of a case. He then compounded this by accepting a television set from the defendant's father (though he did not solicit it).

Swainson's actions may have shown deplorable judgment, but they did not violate the then-extant Michigan Canons of Judicial Conduct, which the Michigan Supreme Court had adopted in 1947. Bolle, on the other hand, was placed in the unhappy position of violating Canon 17, which provided, "A judge should not permit private interviews, arguments or communications designed to influence his judicial action . . ."

Poor Bolle was placed in an impossible situation, as he must have realized. He could either report the communication to the attorneys in the case, which would be embarrassing to Swainson, or recuse himself from the case, which Swainson might interpret as an act of disrespect. Or he could just proceed with the case as though nothing unusual had happened, which is what he did.

Given the Defendant's youth and lack of a prior record, Bolle's testimony was plausible: that her sentence of probation was what he would have given her if Swainson had never called.

11. Bolle, TR 1401.
12. Auer, TR 1548.
13. Auer, TR 1549.
14. Kalkanian, TR 1564.
15. Dean, TR 1470.
16. Coleman, TR 1475.
17. Coleman, TR 1482.
18. *Detroit Free Press*, 10/31/75.
19. Swainson, TR 1598.
20. Swainson, TR 1599.
21. TR 1518 (emphasis added).
22. Swainson, TR 1610.
23. Swainson, TR 1617.
24. Swainson, TR 1647.
25. Swainson, TR 1648.
26. Swainson, TR 1650.
27. Swainson, TR 1651.
28. Swainson, TR 1660.
29. Swainson, TR 1663.

30. Swainson, TR 1663–66.
31. Swainson, TR 1676.
32. Swainson, TR 1678.
33. Swainson, TR 1679.

■ CHAPTER SEVENTEEN. THE TRIAL: VERDICT

1. TR 1693.
2. TR 1695.
3. TR 1726–27.
4. TR 1727–28.
5. TR 1729.
6. TR 1734.
7. TR 1736.
8. TR 1739.
9. TR 1740.
10. Wire 729.
11. TR 1745.
12. TR 1746.
13. TR 1747.
14. Wire 798.
15. TR 1748–49.
16. TR 1750.
17. TR 1753.
18. TR 1755.
19. TR 1756.
20. TR 1757–58.
21. TR 1759–60.
22. TR 1761–62.
23. TR 1762.
24. TR 1765–66.
25. TR 1767.
26. TR 1769–71.
27. TR 1772.
28. TR 1773.
29. TR 1774.
30. TR 1088.
31. TR 1777.
32. Actually, the Michigan elections for statewide offices were to be held in 1976. Chodak was alluding to the theory that the Nixon administration had brought this prosecution to prevent Swainson from running for the U.S. Senate in 1976. TR 1780–81.
33. TR 1786.
34. TR 1780.
35. TR 1794–95.

36. TR 1881.
37. *Detroit Free Press*, 11/03/75.
38. Ibid.
39. Ibid.

■ CHAPTER EIGHTEEN. THE TRIAL RECONSIDERED

1. Nehman, "Swainson Pledges Not To Practice Law During Probation," *Detroit News*, 7/28/77.
2. Weeks, "The Long Road Back," *Detroit News Sunday Magazine*, 6/28/87.
3. TR 1541–42.
4. Because of witness-scheduling problems, the first two defense witnesses, G. Mennen Williams and William Bolle, were actually allowed to testify before the prosecution officially finished its case, but this would mitigate the time pressures upon the defense only a little.
5. TR 1693.
6. TR 1766.
7. Calculated on the basis of seventy to seventy-five seconds per transcript page, at a normal rate of speech.
8. Author's interview with Meri Lou Murray.
9. Author's interview with Ronald Carlson.
10. The list of potential witnesses was read to the prospective jurors before jury selection, TR 24.
11. Author's interview with Allen Zemmol.
12. If Kavanagh had testified about this incident at Swainson's trial, it would have supported Swainson's testimony that Wish merely assisted Swainson by picking up the wall hanging for him. But Kohl never asked Kavanagh about the incident. By the time of his trial Swainson probably had forgotten that Kavanagh was with him that day.
13. Supreme Court Historical Society Oral Interview by Roger Lane, 11/19/90.
14. Whalen, TR 1088.
15. Mennen Speed Stick deodorant was one of the best-known.
16. Wire, TR 718.
17. T. G. Kavanagh, TR 210–11.
18. TR 1792–93.
19. An early example was Al Capone. The FBI and state authorities never succeeded in convicting him of murder, extortion or violation of the Volstead Act. When he finally went to prison, it was for tax evasion.
20. In fact, Ozer presented a tax evasion case against Harvey Wish to the grand jury, which voted to indict Wish on that charge.
21. Author's interview with Edmund Diem.
22. Stan Hunterton e-mail to author.
23. Ankeny, "Ozer's Ouster Called Clash Of Personalities," *Detroit News*, 7/22/76.
24. All quotes are from the author's interviews with Harvey Wish.
25. In making this denial, Wish was, perhaps, offering the testimony that his attorney had

prevented him from offering at the long-ago trial and, of course, defending his own reputation as well as Swainson's.

■ **CHAPTER NINETEEN. GOVERNOR, CONVICTED AND DIED**

1. Author's interview with Bruce Leitman.
2. Bentley Library, Swainson Collection, Box 70.
3. Editorial, "Swainson Should Quit," *Detroit News*, 11/4/75.
4. Author's interview with William G. Milliken.
5. Cain, Ankeny, Bullard, Lochbiler, "Swainson Quits Supreme Court," *Detroit News*, 11/8/75.
6. Wilcox, "Old Friends Gather To Buoy Swainson," *Detroit News*, 12/17/75.
7. This statement was preposterous. No circuit judge who serves a full six-year term escapes reversal, and Swainson was reversed at least eleven times. Why Kohl said this is a mystery.
8. As we have seen, Swainson did take the Fifth Amendment at his second appearance before the grand jury. Clearly, what Kohl meant in his statement at the sentencing was that he had urged Swainson to use the Fifth Amendment to decline to testify before the grand jury at all.
9. "'Career Ruined,' Swainson To Appeal Sentence," *Lansing State Journal*, 1/27/76.
10. Wish ultimately served his time at a minimum security federal prison in Lexington, Kentucky. He did not appeal his conviction. He was told that "it would take a long time and I probably would not win. So I just did the time and got out and got on with my life."
11. "'Career Ruined,' Swainson To Appeal Sentence," *Lansing State Journal*, 1/27/76
12. 18 U.S.C. § 1621, enacted in 1948.
13. 18 U.S.C. § 1623, enacted in 1970.
14. Hart, "Where Swainson May Serve His Term," *Detroit Free Press*, 1/28/76.
15. Author's interview with Bernard Klein.
16. Hart, "Where Swainson May Serve His Term," *Detroit Free Press*, 1/28/76.
17. Nehman, "Swainson Pledges Not To Practice Law During Probation," *Detroit News*, 7/28/77.
18. Author's interview with Bernard Klein.
19. Nehman, "Swainson Pledges Not To Practice Law During Probation," *Detroit News*, 7/28/77.
20. "Swainson Won't Appeal His 3-year Disbarment, Cites A 'Special Irony,'" *Detroit News*, 10/8/77
21. Tyson, "Hero, Governor, Felon—Fate Baffles John Swainson," *Detroit Free Press*, 12/18/77.

■ **CHAPTER TWENTY. THE SNITCH**

1. Ozer, PCR 91; Whalen, PCR 137.
2. Martin, PCR 186.
3. Ozer, PCR 95.
4. Sincliar, "A Man With Connections," *Detroit News*, 4/17/75.
5. Sinclair, "12 Seized as Huge Fencing Ring Is Smashed," *Detroit News*, 10/29/75.
6. Author's interview with Conrad Kohl. After the Swainson trial, prosecutor Ozer alleged that Kohl had hired Pulvirenti and brought him into the courtroom to intimidate Whalen.

He then offended Kohl—and most of the Michigan bar—by hauling Kohl before a grand jury, for which Ozer subsequently apologized. Kohl's account of how he came to know Pulvirenti, as reported in the press at that time, was somewhat different (and much less colorful) than the account he gave me. When Kohl spoke with me, his memory was hazy about many of the events of the mid-1970s, but not this one. In addition, I found that there really had been a Leaky Tap Saloon, and it really was frequented by criminals. I could think of nothing Kohl had to gain by making this up. I therefore came to the conclusion that Kohl was probably giving me the true story.

7. Ozer, PCR 89–90.
8. "Explosion Rips Through Home of Informant in Swainson Case," *Detroit Free Press*, 11/7/75.
9. *People v Whalen*, 65 Mich. App. 687, issued 11/24/75.
10. Gill, "Whalen, Pal Charged in Hamtramck," *Detroit News*, 12/16/75.
11. Hadden, "Whalen Was Shot Fleeing Killer-Captors, Police Say," *Detroit News*, 12/21/75 and Hadden, "What Did Whalen Tell Torturers?," 12/22/75.
12. Hadden, "Whalen Now Admits Lying—But Claims He Knows Torturers," *Detroit News*, 12/23/75.
13. Bulgier, "Jailing of Whalen in Conviction Doubted," *Detroit News*, 12/28/75.
14. Although the FBI cooperates with state and local police in the overwhelming majority of cases, there have been significant exceptions besides the Whalen case. For example, Christopher Dickey's *Securing the City: Inside America's Best Counterterror Force* (New York: Simon & Schuster, 2009) enumerates the history of FBI resistance to the New York Police Department's establishment of its own antiterrorism intelligence squad following the 9/11 attacks.

■ CHAPTER TWENTY-ONE. PARIAH

1. Author's interview with Ronald Carlson.
2. Author's interview with Thomas Brennan.
3. Author's interview with Joe Collins.
4. Author's interview with Louis Way, John Swainson's son-in-law.
5. Ankeny, "Appeal Will Clear Him, Swainson Says," *Detroit News*, 1/27/76.
6. Author's interview with William G. Milliken.
7. Walker, "Swainson Expects To Get City Lobbyist Job," *Detroit News*, 9/15/76.
8. Editorial, "Council Should Reject Swainson," *Detroit News*, 9/16/76.
9. "Detroit Won't Hire Swainson," *Detroit News*, 9/22/76.
10. Author's interview with Kristina Way.
11. This account of the Ford-Kelley meeting is from the author's interview with Frank Kelley.
12. Kelley did not reveal this incident to anyone until long after the death of Henry Ford II. The meeting was confirmed by Swainson's close friend, David Sparrow, who waited with Swainson at a nearby restaurant while Kelley met with Ford.
13. Author's interview with Paul Seldenright.
14. Gavrilovich, "Swainson Is Jailed Overnight," Swainson, quoted in the *Detroit Free Press*, 11/17/77.
15. *Detroit News*, 9/22/76; *Detroit Free Press*, 11/17/77.

16. Although Ford archivists contacted by the author were unable to find records of the Swainson consulting contract arranged by Henry Ford II, it is likely that the contract involved SHAR House. David Sparrow remembered that the consultancy involved a drug rehabilitation facility on West Grand Boulevard in Detroit, and SHAR House was located on West Grand Boulevard.

17. *Detroit News*, 11/17/77.

18. "Swainson Lie Test Slated," *Lansing State Journal*, 1/12/78.

19. "Swainson Won't Appeal His 3-Year Disbarment, Cites A 'Special Irony,'" *Detroit News*, 10/8/77.

20. Shellenbarger, "Swainson Takes Plea to Ex-colleagues," *Detroit News*, 8/78 (undated clipping, Library of Michigan, Swainson vertical file).

21. The *Lansing State Journal*, 5/20/80, reported that the penalty was a $250 fine and restricted license. However, the prosecutor, Edward Grant, told me that, as he remembered it, Swainson's license was automatically suspended because he had not taken a breathalyzer test at the traffic stop. Grant recalled that Swainson subsequently petitioned the Jackson County Circuit Court for a restricted license, which was granted. The law in effect at the time provided that upon submission of a sworn affidavit from a law enforcement officer to the secretary of state, stating that an arrested motorist had refused a breathalyzer test, the secretary of state could suspend the motorist's license for up to two years, after affording the motorist a hearing.

22. The quickest and most direct route was to enter Interstate 496 a few blocks from the restaurant, then drive east, exiting onto southbound U.S. 127, then take that expressway south to Interstate 94 near Jackson, travel east a few miles on that expressway, then exit onto the continuation of U.S. 127 southbound, exiting that expressway at M-50. From this exit Swainson would have to drive eight miles on a two-lane road to the village of Napoleon.

23. *Detroit Free Press*, 1/21/80.

24. The dissenter was the panel's chair, Benjamin Watson. *Detroit Free Press*, 6/28/78.

■ CHAPTER TWENTY-TWO. A MORE DIFFICULT RECOVERY

1. Cain, "Swainson Enters Hospital For Alcoholism Treatment," *Detroit News*, 5/23/80.

2. Author's interview with Kristina Way.

3. Author's interview with Howard Parr.

4. Quoted in *Stewards of the State: The Governors of Michigan*, by George Weeks (Ann Arbor: Historical Society of Michigan, 1991), 119.

5. *Lansing State Journal*, 12/10/80.

6. "Swainson On 'Bench,'" *Lansing State Journal*, 2/3/82.

7. Author's interview with Kristina and Louis Way.

8. Author's interview with Thomas Brennan.

9. Author's interview with Howard Paar.

10. Ibid.

11. From the dedication page of the 1996 calendar of the Manchester Area Historical Society.

12. Author's interview with Kristina Way.

13. This account is based on the story as narrated by Swainson to his son-in-law, Louis Way,

and on stories in the *Detroit Free Press*, 8/27/83, and the *Lansing State Journal*, 8/28/83.

14. Archer went on to serve on the Supreme Court, followed by two terms as mayor of Detroit.
15. The ceremony is reported verbatim at 419 Mich. clxiii.
16. Author's interview with James Blanchard.
17. Michigan Compiled Laws sec. 399.4.
18. Eulogy of Sandra Clark, director of the Michigan Bureau of History, at John Swainson's funeral in Manchester, May 17, 1994. Copy in author's possession.
19. Author's interview with Jerry Roe.
20. Copies of this letter and the funeral program were graciously furnished by Bruce Getzan.
21. Author's interview with David Little.
22. Eulogy of David Sparrow in Manchester, May 17, 1994. Copy in author's possession.
23. Author's interview with Kristina and Louis Way.
24. Author's interview with David Sparrow.
25. "A Letter She Will Always Cherish," *Lansing State Journal*, 6/7/94.
26. Eulogy of Gayle Main in Manchester, May 17, 1994. Copy in author's possession.
27. Eulogy of Frank Kelley in Manchester, May 17, 1994. Copy in author's possession.

■ CHAPTER TWENTY-THREE. REFLECTIONS

1. News conference, 12/17/40. Franklin D. Roosevelt Presidential Library (docs.fdrlibrary.marist.edu).
2. Inaugural Address, as reported in the *Lansing State Journal*, 1/2/61.
3. Exaugural Message, Bentley Library, Swainson Collection, Box 66.
4. Courage and McCormick, "Swainson Rips GOP," *Detroit Free Press*, 6/10/61.
5. Whalen, TR 1088.
6. Hoenshell, "Will Swainson Replace Hart?" *Lansing State Journal*, 9/26/72.
7. Author's interview with Vincent Piersante.
8. E-mail correspondence to the author from Corbin Davis.
9. Author's interview with Allen Zemmol.

■ APPENDIX 1. THE 1960 ELECTION: THE NUMBERS

1. Elmo Roper, Paul Perry, and Mervin D. Field, "Election Polling Trends, 1960," *American Behavioral Scientist* 4. no. 2 (1960): 3–5.
2. Society for Industrial and Applied Mathematics News, 11/26/2004 (www.siam.org/).
3. All final vote totals are taken from the *Michigan Manual*, as reported by the Secretary of State.

■ APPENDIX 2. THE 1962 ELECTION: THE NUMBERS

1. Dempsey, Romney for Governor, 277.
2. Alcona, Crawford, Kalkaska, Keweenaw, Lake, Luce, Montmorency, and Oscoda.

■ APPENDIX 3. THE GRAND JURY IN HISTORY

1. Mark Kalish, "Behind the Locked Door of an American Grand Jury," *Florida State U. Law Review*, (1996).

2. Ibid.

3. Ibid.

4. Susan W. Brenner, "The Voice of the Community: A Case for Grand Jury Independence," 3 *Virginia Journal of Social Policy & The Law* 67 (Fall, 1995).

5. William Blackstone, "Of the Several Modes of Prosecution," *Commentaries on the Laws of England*, vol. 4: *Of Public Wrongs* (Boston: Beacon Press, 1962).

6. Roger Roots, "If It's Not a Runaway, It's Not a Real Grand Jury," *Creighton Law Review* 33, no. 4 (1999–2000).

7. "Frequently Asked Questions About the Grand Jury System," www.abanet.org/media/faqjury.html.

BIBLIOGRAPHY

Berthelot, Helen W. *Win Some Lose Some.* Detroit: Wayne State University Press, 1995.

Blackstone, William. "Of the Several Modes of Prosecution." *Commentaries on the Laws of England,* vol. 4: *Of Public Wrongs.* Boston: Beacon Press, 1962.

Brenner, Susan W. "The Voice of the Community: A Case for Grand Jury Independence." *Virginia Journal of Social Policy & The Law* 3, no. 67 (Fall 1995).

Buffa, Dudley W. *Union Power and American Democracy,* vol. 1. Ann Arbor: University of Michigan Press, 1984.

Bugliosi, Vincent. *Reclaiming History: The Assassination of President John F. Kennedy.* New York: W.W. Norton

Dempsey, John T. "Romney for Governor: The 1962 Michigan Election Campaign." Private manuscript.

Fine, Sidney. *Expanding the Frontiers of Civil Rights, 1948–1968.* Detroit: Wayne State University Press, 2000.

Getzan, Bruce D. "Michigan's 'Kismet' Governor." *Chronicle* (May–June 1988).

Kalish, Mark. "Behind the Locked Door of an American Grand Jury." *Florida State University* (1996).

Michigan Legislative Service Bureau. *Michigan Manual.* Lansing [published biennually].

Mollenhoff, Clark. *George Romney: Mormon in Politics.* New York: Meredith Press, 1968.

Muilenburg, Alvin L., and A. Bennett Wilson Jr. *Manual for Below-Knee Amputees.* Linthicum, Md.: Dankmyer, 1996.

Noer, Thomas J. *Soapy: A Biography of G. Mennen Williams.* Ann Arbor: University of Michigan Press, 2005.

Roots, Roger. "If It's Not a Runaway, It's Not a Real Grand Jury." *Creighton Law Review* 33, no. 4 (1999–2000).

Roper, Elmo, Paul Perry, and Mervin D. Field. "Election Polling Trends, 1960." *American Behavioral Scientist* no. 3 (1960).

Rosentreter, Roger. "Making Sacrifices." *Michigan History* (November–December 1991).

Rubenstein, Bruce A., and Lawrence E. Ziewacz. *Three Bullets Sealed His Lips.* East Lansing: Michigan State University Press, 1987.

Society for Industrial and Applied Mathematics News, 11/26/2004 (www.siam.org/).

Staebler, Neil. *Out of the Smoke-filled Room: A History of Michigan Politics.* Ann Arbor: George Wahr, 1991.

Stark, Al. "Keep the Heat On!" *Detroit News Sunday Magazine.* Profile of Robert C. Ozer.

Weeks, George. *Stewards of the State: The Governors of Michigan.* Ann Arbor: Historical Society of Michigan, 1991.

■ INTERVIEWS

Victor Adamo (by telephone): 9/26/2006

Hon. James J. Blanchard (by telephone): 8/30/2006

James Blount (by e-mail): 7/27/2007

Hon. Thomas E. Brennan (by telephone): 5/1/2006

Ronald Carlson (by telephone): 9/20/2006

Thomas Cleary: East Lansing, MI, 12/21/2006

John "Joe" Collins: Clark Lake, MI, 3/14/2006

Lattie Coor (by telephone): 7/10/2007

Corbin Davis (by e-mail): 8/15/2005, 8/9/2006

Anthony Derezinski: Lansing, 6/26/2007

Edmund Diem (by telephone): 9/20/2006

Gene Farber (by telephone): 9/8/2006

Bruce Getzan interview with Swainson: 1988 (unpublished notes, reviewed with author during their telephone interview 6/1/2007)

Bruce Getzan (by telephone): 6/1/2007

Charles Goldfarb (by telephone): 9/19/2006

Hon. Edward Grant (by telephone): 8/7/2007

Margaret Halava (by telephone): 4/20/2006

Kathleen Davidson Hunter (by telephone): 5/27/2006

Stan Hunterton (by e-mail): 2/28/2007

Hon. Frank J. Kelley: Lansing, MI, 10/11/2005

Bernard Klein (by telephone): 8/19/2005, 6/18/2007

Conrad Kohl (by telephone): 9/6/2005, 9/7/2005

Hon. Harvey Koselka: Adrian, MI, 6/9/2006

N. C. Deday LaRene (by e-mail): 9/7/2006

Michael Leffler (by telephone): 4/2006

Bruce Leitman (by telephone): 9/2005

Hon. Lawrence Lindemer (by telephone, date not recorded):

David Little (by telephone): 6/26/2007

Seymour Markowitz (by telephone, date not recorded)

Hugh McDiarmid (by telephone): 5/3/2006

Hugh McDiarmid interview with Swainson: 12/12/85 (unpublished notes, copy in author's possession)

Hon. William G. Milliken (by telephone): 8/16/2005

Meri Lou Murray (by telephone): 10/13/2006

Howard Paar (by telephone): 7/5/2007

Vincent Piersante: Lansing, MI, 12/27/2005

Frank Ragen (by telephone): 5/25/2006

James Ramey: Lansing, MI, 10/11/2007

Jerry Roe: Lansing, MI, 6/14/2006

Kelly Rossman-McKinney: Lansing, MI, 4/26/2005

Leo Seide (by telephone): 6/2/2008

Vicky Seide (by telephone): 6/1/2008

Paul Seldenright: Lansing, MI, 6/25/2007

David Sparrow: Harbor Springs, MI, 8/2/2005

Kristina and Louis Way: Manchester, MI, 9/13/2006, 9/11/2007

Harvey Wish (by telephone): 1/14/2007, 1/20/2007

Carroll Whitehead: Okemos, MI, 1/23/2006

Allen Zemmol (by telephone): 9/26/2006, 1/17/2007

INDEX